From Fingers to Finger Bowls

From Fingers to Finger Bowls

A LIVELY HISTORY OF CALIFORNIA COOKING

by Helen Walker Linsenmeyer

WITH THE EDITORIAL
ASSISTANCE OF DORIS LOEWNAU

Originally Commissioned by James S. Copley,
Edited by Richard F. Pourade
and Printed by Copley Books

This edition published by *EZ Nature Books*
P.O. Box 4206 • San Luis Obispo, CA • 93403

OTHER TITLES FROM
EZ Nature Books
(Soft Cover Unless Noted)

Cover illustrations by Nat D. Fast

Food for Thought

As the years recede, more people are interested in what has happened in the past. How can we know where we're going unless we know where we've been? Much has happened since this book was first published in 1972. Our world has shrunk to the point where we are all neighbors.

California has experienced profound changes in its cuisine. Our expanded world enables us to select fruits and vegetables which were once known to us only in books and in restaurants specializing in exotic foods.

These changes accompany the influx of people from Central and South America, Korea, Cambodia, Vietnam and Thailand. Just as these new arrivals contribute their history and customs, their foods enrich our cuisine immeasurably. California is richer for this contribution.

—Helen Walker Linsenmeyer

Contents

About the Illustrations

Before the days of photography, and even long after the appearance of the camera, sketchers and painters helped to preserve the memory of things as they were in the early West—even at the table.

Not the least of these figures was W.H.D. Koerner, who though he came relatively late on the scene, left paintings that only belatedly are taking their place in the art of the West.

This history of cooking in California reproduces some of his finest works now in possession of his daughter, Ruth Koerner Oliver, of Santa Barbara. He worked primarily as an illustrator for articles in such magazines—and in the days of their glory—as the Saturday Evening Post, Collier's, Country Gentleman, Wallace's Farmer, Harper's, Red Book, McClure's, Scribner's, Pictorial Review, and a number of others.

He was born in Germany in 1878, but his family came to America and settled in Iowa in 1880. His paintings breathe life into the story of the triumphs and trials of our pioneers.

The costumes and characteristics of the racially diverse peoples who flocked to California with the discovery of gold were recorded through the efforts of an Englishman who was by profession a stationer and bookseller. His name was James Mason Hutchings. He had left England at the age of fifteen to seek adventures in the United States. He made a small fortune in the gold fields, composed the Miners' Ten Commandments and led the first tourist party into Yosemite Valley. In 1856 he began publishing Hutching's California Magazine. It was profusely illustrated with excellent woodcuts. Later he was to write several books on his adopted state and when he died he was buried in the shadow of the great cliffs he loved in Yosemite Valley.

Sophisticated magazines on the East Coast sent their own artists to California and left enduring and often sensitive sketches of its scenery, its Indians, its missions and padres, its houses and inns, and its early settlers. Among them were Century Magazine and Harper's Weekly.

One of the most entrancing figures of the early days was James Ross Browne who first sought the fragrance of life in whaling ships. After experiences in both the gold and silver fields of California he wandered through Europe, writing of his adventures. Eventually upon returning home he became commissioner of the Indian Service, later explored Baja California and wound up as United States minister to China.

One of his sketches of diners hard at it in San Francisco, along with a woodcut of a Charles Nahl drawing of feasting in Delmonico's in the same city, may not exactly make you yearn for the good old days. But the Palace Hotel in San Francisco in the Victorian Era before the Turn of the Century was something else. That was living!

Richard F. Pourade

Foreword

In the hope and belief there are others who will share my interest in the evolution of what may be termed California cookery, I have spent a happy time poring over early diaries, personal journals, official reports, histories, autobiographies, cookbooks, newspapers and periodicals dealing with California's past. The result is a nostalgic glimpse into the state's kaleidoscopic and exciting record through a collection of historical anecdotes, combined with recipes and cooking methods from Indian days to 1900.

Some of the earlier recipes which have been included are not necessarily intended for today's cooks to puzzle over, but are printed for historical purposes. The curious homemaker who might wish to experiment with some of these heirloom recipes may find they call for ingredients, measurements and directions which require imagination. Foods easily obtainable in days gone by may not be available today. Mixing and cooking methods often were taken for granted and may seem sketchy, in contrast to the detailed instructions we now expect and enjoy. A young lady of yesteryear was taught homemaking and cooking arts from childhood, and often carried her secrets in her head.

Indians and early California settlers often successfully preserved many foods, as indicated particularly on pages 9, 10, 22, 46 and 129. But there were hazards then as now; caution is indicated and readers should be aware that some scattered cases of botulism poisoning have been noted in dried or smoked fish, beef jerky, smoked beef, and in sausage products improperly prepared at home. Old recipes of preserved foods are included for their historical interest, and anyone wishing to undertake such ventures should obtain more detailed instructions.

Cooking prior to the manufacture of modern stoves with regulated oven temperatures was an art, mastered through long, careful, and sometimes frustrating experience. The cook who could turn out delicious stews, tasty vegetables, hearty breads, perfect pies, feathery cakes and other culinary masterpieces with the rather primitive facilities at hand was truly an artist.

By the end of the 19th Century cooking means had progressed from early Indian methods of roasting over an open fire, baking on hot stones and boiling in baskets of hot water to the joy of using a late model cast-iron stove with an oven temperature gauge and a hot water reservoir. The cook no longer found it necessary to test oven heat by sticking her hand inside and counting, or by spreading a spoonful of flour on a pie tin and setting it in the oven until it turned the desired shade of brown. An increasing variety of ingredients and technological advances were reflected in the sophistication of recipes as early as the 1850's.

During the decades which followed the fever-heat of the Gold Rush immigration in 1849, agriculturists experimented with fruits and vegetables from every country on the globe. The *California Farmer,* founded in 1854, and similar magazines, encouraged agricultural efforts by printing favorite and original recipes solicited from farm wives and other residents. Instructions for mixing or cooking often were meager, but printed cookbooks were rather scarce in California at that period and sharing recipes via the pages of such publications obviously appealed to readers.

Prior to 1872 only a few slim volumes of treasured recipes were printed privately for friends. After 1875, cookbooks proliferated.

Manufacturers of cooking appliances joined the rush by distributing household guides which included recipes, points of etiquette, housekeeping hints, and home remedies. Church groups and women's clubs shared their jealously guarded cooking secrets in books compiled for fund-raising projects.

Cup and spoon sizes were not standardized until the 1890's, and a cook learned strictly by trial and error exactly what proportions guaranteed perfect results. The much-envied cook who had accumulated a collection of fool-proof recipes was besieged with requests for her favorites.

The origin of recipes is not always easy to determine, but in this book it has been given whenever possible. This research primarily aims to reflect the blending process which has given California cooking a reputation that is the envy of the rest of the country, and other countries as well. Each of the groups which has formed the state's population—Indians, Spaniards, Mexicans, South Americans, Russians, Frenchmen, Germans, Englishmen, Italians, Irishmen, Scandinavians, Hawaiians, Armenians, Chinese, Japanese as well as American pioneers and others—has added a special flavor and texture to the heady and unique potpourri that today makes up California's cuisine.

Indians Cooking Food

Victorian Tea Hour

To California

Blessed by nature with sunshine,

Skies of Heavenly blue,

A mighty ocean at her doorstep;

Fertile soil, yielding up an abundance

of fruits, flowers and vegetables,

Gold and silver, filling the dreams

of restless westward-bound pioneers.

Like Juno, she leaped full-blown into

the nation's firmament, the thirty-first

state of the Union.

I dedicate this history of her cookery,

a potpourri of many nations,

TO CALIFORNIA.

Helen Walker Linsenmeyer

Chapter I

The Happy Life of the Indians

A kind voice brings joy like the sound of the lark.
—INDIAN PROVERB

A study of the food habits of the Indians who lived in California when the first White settlers arrived is complicated by the fact that there were at least twenty-one distinct linguistic families with no written languages. Consequently most of what we know comes largely from the observations of the Spanish padres and the early White travelers who were recipients of their hospitality. We will never know whether a fair Indian maiden was courted because of her culinary skills or whether a more casual attitude of "done or raw it'll fill the craw" prevailed.

The story of the California Indians is still being written as archaeologists unearth more evidence of their culture, particularly in the southern part of the state. Hopefully, more of the story can be completed before ancient dwelling sites are covered with cement.

In the late 1700's in California there were at least 135,000, and perhaps as many as 200,000, Indians whose ancestors had come to America probably in many historic waves. The twenty-one language groups spoke approximately one hundred and thirty-five different dialects and had an indefinite number of varied cultural practices, all linked, however, by what can be called the Acorn Culture.

None of the California Indian groups was truly nomadic and they all had well-defined territories. The natives of the higher mountains and desert regions were forced by circumstances of weather to move about regularly in search of food, clothing and shelter. The northern and southern groups were relatively sedentary, though those in the more arid south shifted seasonally between the coast and the low foothills. There is very little evidence they developed agriculture.

Though the typical Indian dwelling was a rude shelter of brushwood and grass called a wickiup, homes in the northern part of the state were constructed more substantially of wood. All of the tribes were true conservationists, living in tune with the elements. They were dependent on nature's bounty for food, clothing and shelter, but took only what they needed—wasting nothing. They believed that animals and plants were imbued with the Great Spirit, and they lived at ease with this philosophy.

Our first glimpse of California Indians and how they lived comes from the summary journal of the expedition of Juan Rodríguez Cabrillo, the Portuguese navigator in the service of Spain who is credited with the discovery of California. The Indians of the coast had clear knowledge of other Spanish expeditions roaming in the interior of the United States.

Cabrillo's log records that the coast from San Diego to Point Conception was densely populated and the Indians were dressed in skins of animals and those in the Channel Islands area had boats and indicated they were fishermen.

Sixty years later Spanish ships under the command of Sebastián Vizcaíno visited the ports of California and while at San Diego his journal records the following, in part:

"...a number of Indians appeared with their bows and arrows and although signs of peace were made they did not dare approach, excepting a very old Indian woman who appeared to be more than one hundred and fifty years old and who approached weeping. The general cajoled her and gave her some beads and something to eat. This Indian woman, from extreme age, had wrinkles on her belly which looked like a blacksmith's bellows, and the navel protruded bigger than a gourd. Seeing this kind treatment, the Indians came peaceably and took us to their *rancherias*, where they were gathering their crops and where they made their *paresos* of seeds like flax. They had pots in which they cooked their food....I do not state, lest I

Indians Gathering Acorns   *Indians Gathering Seeds*

be tiresome, how many times the Indians came to our camps with skins of martens and other things . . ."

In the interval between the visits of Cabrillo and Vizcaíno, Sir Francis Drake landed a few miles north of the Golden Gate in 1579, presumably at Drake's Bay, and took possession of the country on behalf of England, naming it New Albion. He found the Indians friendly and traded a bit with them while his ship, the Golden Hind, was being repaired. His hosts undoubtedly introduced him and his crew to native foods and meat, although his account omits such details.

The original Californians had a well-established money system based on shells. However, dried woodpecker scalps with soft red or green feathers were treasured almost as highly, because of their rarity. The lucky Indian who wore a headdress of red or green scalps to a ceremony was the envy of his friends. The tribes living in or near the Sierra Nevada knew of the existence of gold, but it had no value in their society; however, their attitude changed substantially after they realized its significance in the White man's world.

Theodora Kroeber's biography of Ishi, California's last living wild Indian, provides an insight into the life style of the true natives and illustrates techniques such as firemaking with dry wood, arrow making, and other necessary skills of survival in a time when nature governed man.

It is fitting that some of the most spectacularly scenic features in California are known by the names given them by long-departed Indians: Yosemite, Sequoia, Shasta, Malibu, Hetch Hetchy and Tahoe, for example.

A BOUNTIFUL LAND

The varied botanical zones encompassed by the state provided a more diversified diet than that available to most other North American Indians. Wild game was plentiful, and natives living near the ocean and fresh water streams enjoyed the bounty of these waters. However, acorns, the fruit of the oak trees growing on the slopes of the foothills and along streams, provided their staple food item, that of the white oak being regarded as most palatable. Acorns were gathered in the fall, usually by the women, who spread them out in the sun to dry, then stored them in baskets or cribs near their dwellings. The acorn diet was equal to that of today's enriched rolled oats.

The acorn diet was supplemented in part by wild grains, berries and fruits, piñon nuts, edible plants and even insects. These foods were eaten cooked or raw, as taste and custom dictated. Coastal Indians did not grow corn, beans or squash, although their brethren east of the mountains from the Great Lakes to Peru had been cultivating these staples long before the Europeans came to the New World. The Pilgrims would have died if the Indians had not showed them how to plant corn.

The coming of the white man, bringing corn and beans, marked the beginning of the

Interior of Indian Huts

J. R. BARTLETT'S *PERSONAL NARRATIVE OF EXPLORATIONS*

end of California's Acorn Culture. The Indians learned to plant seeds and harvest abundant crops under the tutelage of the padres. Though the Indians were lured to the missions by this new food supply the advent of the Corn Culture brought troubles they could not foresee.

California Indians exercised great ingenuity in hunting and fishing. Disguised with the skin and horns of deer, the skillful hunter could creep close enough to kill his quarry with an arrow or spear and nooses were sometimes strung along deer trails. They did not kill bears or coyotes. Rabbits were trapped by snares, speared with sharp sticks or killed with slings and arrows. Squirrels were shot with arrows and pigeons and grouse were knocked out of trees as they slept at night. Their flesh was pounded flat before being baked. Quail were caught in cleverly woven traps made of open-work basketry and artificial decoys were used to lure ducks and wild geese close enough to be snared in nets or shot with bows and arrows.

Ocean fish were caught with hooks of sturdy shell or bone and stream fishing was done with spears or with nets and weirs. An unusual way of catching fish was by working up a great lather in the water of small streams with the soap-plant root. The lather anesthetized the fish, which were easily plucked out of the water while stunned. Later Spanish and Mexican colonists made good use of the soap-plant to wash clothes—and perhaps they also caught fish.

NATIVE CRAFTS

Basket making was highly developed, the Pomos of Northern California generally being regarded as the most skillful weavers. Baskets often served specialized functions such as for storing food, carrying water, and even cooking. Sizes ranged from large burden baskets designed to carry a bushel or more and used mainly for acorn storage, to cup-size baskets for dipping or eating. Various fibers from native plants were used to fashion baskets, the most common probably being the yucca.

Some of the decorative weaving patterns of baskets were known as quail-plume, earthworm, fish-teeth, eyes, flying geese, and pine cone. A basket almost encircled by a rattlesnake design was used in special ceremonies. It was believed that the basket maker who completely closed her design would become blind, so the women left a break in the pattern called a *dau*. Many of these artistically designed, waterproof baskets have been preserved in museums. Other evidence of the weaver's skill was found in elaborate fur and feather robes which were worn for ceremonial occasions. Some examples of these beautiful robes are in the Southwest Museum in Los Angeles.

A few of the groups used baked clay pots, very well-made and roughly similar to those found in other southwestern states. But cooking and eating utensils were rare and simple and fashioned of stone, shell or wood. Knives of flint or obsidian were necessities. Though woven bowls were used by the southern tribes, Indians in the central part of the state used gourd dippers, as well as platters and bowls of wood. Abalone shells also served as bowls. Small river mussel shells were used as eating spoons, and where they were not at hand, acorn mush was eaten by dipping first and second fingers into the pot, as the Hawaiians eat *poi*. Wooden paddles or sticks were used to stir mush and other foods while cooking.

HOW ACORNS WERE PREPARED

As acorns were needed, they were shelled and pounded into meal in hollowed-out holes in rocks with a large round stone serving as a pestle. To remove the tannic acid the meal was leached with water and sand before cooking.

To cook acorn mush and biscuits, the nuts were first cooked in a deep basket filled with water and set near an open fire. Stones were heated red-hot and plunged into the vessel until the water reached the boiling point. As the stones cooled, they were removed with crude tongs or hooked forks and replaced with hot ones, to keep the mixture cooking until done. Steatite (soapstone) stones were favored because they held heat longer than any others.

Acorn bread, bulbs, mescal, fish, fowl and meat were often baked in an earth oven which was a pit dug in the ground. L.S.M. Curtin describes the fire pit used for roasting camas bulbs in his leaflet "Some Plants Used by the Yuki Indians of Round Valley, Northern California":

"A round pit about two feet deep was dug, and a fire built therein; when it died down, oak leaves were placed on the hot ashes. Next, a layer of straw on which the camas were spread; this was covered with more oak leaves and finally clean straw. Earth was thrown over the whole, and another fire was built on top and kept alive all night."

The Cahuillas, working with what they had available, used essentially the same roasting method, according to R.F. Heizer, author of a book about the California Indians. They roasted mescal by digging "great fire pits or ovens" in the sand and lined them with stones. A fire was built in the pit and kept up until the stones were thoroughly heated. The mescal heads were laid in the hole, covered with grass and earth and left to roast for a day or so. When cooked, they were fibrous, molasses-colored layers, sweet and delicious to the taste and wonderfully nutritious. For foods which took a little shorter cooking time a second open fire was built in the pit on top of the earth oven, a forerunner of today's barbecue pit.

When the acorn crop was sparse, buckeye nuts gathered from horse chestnut trees were eaten. However, a lengthy leaching process was required to render them palatable, and they were not regarded nearly as desirable as acorns.

Wild rye and other small grains were harvested by burning away the straw and thus roasting the grain, which was mixed with acorn meal or other ingredients. Smaller seeds were cooked by shaking them in shallow parching baskets with live coals.

DELICACIES OF THE NATIVES

Mountain and valley quail were plucked, the breasts cut open, and pounded before being dried for later consumption. Birds and fish were roasted whole in hot ashes and skinned after cooking.

Grasshoppers were regarded as savory tidbits then, as they are now in some cocktail circles. The grasshoppers were shooed into a large earthen pit and covered with stones. A fire was built over the stones and after the insects were roasted they were eaten with great gusto.

Octopus tentacles, barnacles, and turtles were especially prized by the Indians along the coast. Certain kinds of seaweed were dried on rocks, made into cakes, and baked in earth ovens.

There were few bees in California in the early Indian days, but wasps were numerous and regarded as tasty delicacies. To find a nest, an Indian would slit a sweet grain on which the wasps fed, and insert inside a tiny white leaf. When a wasp seized it and flew away, an Indian would follow. Finding the nest, he would build a fire to asphyxiate the inhabitants, then devour them as well as the honey. This procedure was observed by Etienne Derbec, the French journalist, whose letters have been edited by Abraham P.

Nasatir and published under the title *A French Journalist in the California Gold Rush: the Letters of Etienne Derbec.*

Chia, a rough leaved plant of the sage family which grew on dry hillsides or in sandy washes, was much valued by the Indians for its nutritional qualities, not only in California but throughout the Southwest. The roasted seeds of this plant, ground and mixed with water, became an easily digested, high-energy food. Jelly-like in consistency, it tastes somewhat like linseed meal, but one tablespoonful was sufficient to sustain an Indian on a forced march of twenty-four hours. Added to water and sweetened, the seeds made a cooling drink, a decided boon to desert Indians. The Mission padres learned about the remarkable qualities of chia from the Indians and used it for medicinal purposes. Experiments with plants in Southern California in the late 1950's confirmed chia's extraordinary food value.

Wild greens were cooked in tightly woven baskets, or steamed in an earth oven by pouring water around the outer edge of the fire. The cooked greens were dried and stored for winter use and when needed, they were soaked in cold water and cooked again, or were eaten dry.

Salt was obtained from the Coachella Valley by Southern California tribes. Those farther away procured it by evaporating water in salt marshes or by beating out the salt from salt grass. It is said that Indian women would not eat salt for fear it would cause their hair to turn gray.

Sugar was obtained from reeds called *tulares*, which grew at the edge of streams and marshes. Reeds were cut when ripe, placed on a flat stone called a *metate*, and crushed. When the debris was removed, crystals somewhat like rock candy, and of fine flavor, remained. Torogui, a coffee-colored bulb, was another source of sugar. These bulbs were baked in earth ovens and crushed to sweeten *atole*, the name used for gruel. Sugar pine sap was still another sugar source.

The versatile juniper had many uses. The seeds were used in cooking or were ground into meal for cakes, and also served as a base for an alcoholic drink. Dried berries were put in rattles for pacifying babies and to add rhythm to dance steps. They also enhanced necklaces made of colored stones and shells. Juniper bark was combined with fur and feathers to fashion blankets which warded off the winter's cold. The stems and roots were compounded into a washing detergent. Juniper sticks, or boughs, were heated and applied to sprains and bruises to reduce swelling.

Tobacco was widely used by the Indians and generally was gathered in the wild, though the plant was cultivated by Indians in central California. It was dried for smoking. A wine was made from willows, and a more potent drink, called *pispibata*, was concocted from shells which had been burned to a powder, wild tobacco juice, and wild cherries, which, with water added, assumed an almost solid consistency. Sometimes maize or fruit of easy fermentation was added. It was reported that an Indian could get drunk on one good swig of this potion and a few samplings threw him into a stupor, but while the coma lasted the drinker was in ecstasy. An observer described this beverage as equal to a mixture of rum, tobacco juice and opium.

Recipes

ACORN MUSH
When the acorn crop was ripe in the Fall, entire Indian villages turned out to gather and store the nuts for their year's supply. As needed acorns were shelled and ground by hand on a

flat stone into a coarse meal or flour, a time-consuming and arduous task. Then the meal was leached of its bitter and poisonous tannic acid by spreading it in a pit of sand by a stream or in a large bowl. Allowing the sand to settle, the woman would scoop off the clean meal. Cooking was done in a basket by adding hot stones to a mixture of meal and water.

Add acorn meal to boiling water. Simmer until mixture thickens, stirring occasionally to prevent lumps.

ACORN BISCUITS

Indians prepared acorn meal in various ways. This is a novel method of making a cold biscuit, Indian style.

Make a mixture of acorn meal and water as for mush but add a larger amount of meal and cook until almost stiff. Pour into small cup-size baskets. Set baskets in water and when quite cold, tilt basket and tap lightly to turn out the jello-like biscuit into water. Let set until quite cold before handling or it will fall apart.

ACORN BREAD

Indians were inventive in flavoring acorn meal with fresh herbs and berries. We may assume families had their special favorites. This recipe is an example of a simple way in which Indians baked bread.

Add enough water to acorn meal to form a thick paste. Mix with fresh clover pulp or dried berries and shape into flat cakes six or seven inches in diameter. Bake on stones heated in ashes of a wood fire or dry on rocks in the sun.

PIÑOLE

A palatable cereal dish was made from wild seeds which were gathered in season and stored until needed. Even today California woods, fields and roadsides offer wild flowers and grains of infinite variety that produce a bounty of seeds. Indians usually ground the seeds before adding them to their favorite acorn mush or making this gruel.

Grind seeds of pepper grass, chia, shepherd's purse, wild cabbage, prince's plume, lace-pod or a variety of other edible wild seeds. Add

water and cook until thick and mushy. This can be served as a hot cereal or baked in flat cakes.

ROASTED PIÑON NUTS

The piñon (or pinyon) pine is a native of the dry Southwest and bears a small cone full of oily flavorful seed nuts. Indians were especially fond of them, but many a California child has grown up with a love for the satisfying taste of these seeds. In early days harvesting was done just before the cones opened in late August or early September. After the cones had dried they were roasted and the seeds jarred loose by a heavy blow from a stone. The seeds, about one-half inch long and a dark chocolate brown in color, were eaten raw or lightly toasted.

Spread shelled piñon nuts on a flat, heated rock. Stir occasionally and within an hour they should be browned and ready to eat.

PIÑON NUT SOUP

Piñon nuts were used to make a thick soup, a favorite Indian method of preparing food.

Mix nuts and meat broth, about one quart of liquid to one pound of nuts. Add chopped onion and dried mint leaves. Cook until nuts are soft, stirring occasionally. Cool and mash to a smooth paste. May be eaten cold, or reheated.

MUSHROOM SOUP

Mushrooms are a commonplace food luxury nowadays, as they are found in the grocery every day. But for the Indians they were a special spring treat and when conditions were right for the appearance of the edible ones, they were gathered and carefully dried.

Grind dried shredded mushrooms until soft and pulpy. Add to a light meat broth and cook until mixture reaches a gruel-like consistency.

BROILED SALMON STEAKS

There was a plentiful supply of salmon in California streams, mostly in the northern part of the state. Indians usually speared salmon or caught them in nets.

Cut steaks about an inch thick. A ten-pound

salmon will produce about fifteen steaks cut crosswise. Or cut inch-thick fillets the length of the fish and press five or six juniper berries into the flesh of each fillet. Grill over glowing coals six inches from heat, allowing five minutes for each side. Can also be cooked on hot stones.

ROAST CLAMS

Coastal Indians often feasted on clams. They were steamed in a basket of water, brought to boiling by the addition of hot stones, or cooked in a fire pit.

Build fire in an earthen pit about two feet deep and cover with a scattered layer of stones, allowing space for fire to continue burning. Arrange clams on the stones and cover with oak leaves or straw. If a large quantity of clams is to be cooked, continue to alternate layers of clams and leaves as desired.

MUSSELS

This is the way California Indians cooked a "bed" of river mussels.

Poke mussels into sand, with only the tips showing, cover them with grass and twigs, and set fire to the covering. When fire has died off rake away and devour the tiny tidbits.

BROILED DRIED FISH
(See cautionary remarks in Foreword)

Fish were abundant and easily available. They were often cooked fresh but also dried for later use. Here is a tasty way to prepare dried fish for a meal.

Coat dried fish with acorn mush. Fasten firmly to forked green sticks and broil over fire. Cook until coating is well browned. Eat the coating along with the fish.

BROILED SEA LION OR SEAL STEAK

Coastal tribes broiled steaks of sea lion or harbor seal by a simple method.

Cut meat into slices which can be handled easily, fasten firmly on sturdy forked green sticks and hold over coals of a wood fire until browned.

JERKY
(See cautionary remarks in Foreword)

Jerky is dried meat which will keep indefinitely; five pounds of fresh lean meat yields about one pound of jerky. California Indians had no monopoly on this method of preserving the meat of deer, elk and other wild game animals. It was a lightweight and sustaining food which could be carried on the trail with ease. Commercially processed jerky can be purchased in California groceries today.

Cut meat into long strips about as thick as a finger. Remove all fat and hang meat strips on string or wire in the sun, allowing space between each piece for air to circulate freely. Leave on the line for several days until strips become hard, dry and black. Be sure to cover them at night to prevent moisture from being absorbed. Jerky may be eaten dry, or soaked in sea water or brine and sprinkled with pepper, marjoram, basil or thyme.

PEMMICAN

Pemmican was one way Indians prepared jerked meat to make it more palatable with with additions of fat, fruits and berries. Each Indian consumed about one ton of pemmican a year.

Pound jerky until soft and shredded. Cut an equal amount of beef suet or other raw animal fat into pieces about an inch square and try out over a low fire. Pour the liquid hot fat over jerky and knead until the consistency of raw hamburger. Add wild currants, chokecherries or other small fruits or berries if desired. Pack in rawhide or other waterproof bag and seal with deer tallow.

STEWED RABBIT

Rabbits were plentiful in the Indians' heyday, and still flourish in California. They were easy prey for skillful Indian hunters.

Skin rabbit and remove innards as well as glands from under the forelegs, which may affect flavor. Cut at joints into serving pieces. Press juniper berries into the flesh of larger pieces, place in a pot and cover with water. Simmer for about an hour, or until tender.

9

GRILLED RIBS
(See cautionary remarks in Foreword)

Besides drying meat in the sun, Indians also constructed racks over a fire to dry or smoke meats and fish. This method is still employed by campers to grill spare ribs of wild game.

Build a support of several rough-trimmed green tree limbs, which have crotches at the top, by fixing them upright in the ground. Press smaller limbs crosswise firmly between the crotches to form a rack. Build a fire under the rack and place rib sections on the rack over the fire. Turn occasionally until both sides are brown and slightly charred.

GRILLED WILD GAME LIVER

Indians regarded liver as an especially succulent treat, and it often was eaten raw or prepared by quick grilling over an open fire when game was first killed.

Slice liver in slabs and lay on rack of green wood, or impale on pointed sticks stuck firmly in the ground in a position to lean over an open fire. Cook until liver is crisp outside and pink inside.

INDIAN POTATOES

Indians relied on many roots, bulbs and tubers of native plants for variety in their diet. They were often eaten raw or added to boiled dishes of fish or game. The roots of large white water lilies had a flavor which resembled that of navy beans.

Dice roots and simmer in water or stock from meat or fish until softened.

FRUITS AND BERRIES

The abundance of fresh fruits and berries, which still grow on California hillsides and flank highways, were gathered by Indians. In summer they picked the common wild raspberry, grape, currant, blackberry, plum and gooseberry, to name only a few. Along the shore was found the delicious beach strawberry.

The distinct and picturesque evergreen shrub, manzanita, yields only a small, bony berry about ½ inch in size. However, native Indians liked its slightly acrid taste and ate

the berries raw or dried them and pounded them into a flour. Clusters of the bright red berries which ripen in late Fall, are still used by California housewives to make jelly.

California holly, named for its thick clusters of scarlet berries, is also known as the toyon berry. The fruit matures in November or December and was always cooked by Indians before being eaten. So too with the laurel, which bears an olive-like seed, and the elderberry which was dried for winter and used in a fruit soup.

JUNIPER TEA

Aromatic leaves of the juniper were used to make a refreshing tea.

Wash twenty young tender sprigs of juniper. Place in a large vessel and add two quarts of water. Bring to a boil, cover and simmer gently for about fifteen minutes. Remove from heat and let steep for ten more minutes. Strain and serve.

JUNIPER BERRY WINE

California juniper trees bear dark reddish berries which were not only eaten as a fresh fruit but were used to make wine. The desert juniper bore blue-black fruit. The brew may not have been as elegant as that described in later recipes, but may have been as satisfying to those who quaffed it.

Mash fresh berries, cover with water and allow the mixture to settle and ferment, perhaps about two weeks. Strain off liquid and store until ready to serve.

MANZANITA CIDER

Berries of this attractive evergreen bush, easily distinguished by its red trunk, prompted Spanish and Mexican colonists to give it the name manzanita, a diminutive of the word for apple, *manzana*. Indians used the berries to make a cider-like drink.

Boil berries until soft. Grind coarsely, then place in a winnowing basket and pour water over them slowly until all of the flavor has been extracted. Strain liquid and serve. This drink will keep for three or four days.

Chapter II

The Padres, Plows and Cattle

Clear ring the silvery Mission bells
Their calls to vesper and to mass;
O'er vineyard slopes, thro' fruited dells,
the long processions pass . . .
—INA COOLBIRTH

When Spain made a belated decision to occupy distant California, Franciscan missionaries were designated to introduce Christianity among the native Indians. Enthusiasm was quickly generated among the padres to "fish for the souls" of the native population in the time-honored pattern of Spain's colonizing efforts. The best-known of these hardy men, Spanish-born Fathers Junípero Serra, Francisco Palóu and Fermín Lasuén, fervently dedicated themselves to the task set for them. Father Serra's achievements in establishing and directing the growth of the first missions earned for him a special place in California's history. He was one of the first boosters in the long roster of those who have sung the praises of the Golden State. Through the years his spirit of optimism has remained a typical California attitude, with good reason.

Arrival of the padres marked the advent of the Corn, or Tortilla, Culture. What in California is often called Spanish food is not really that at all. In Spain, bread made of corn, tortillas, enchiladas and sauces of chili peppers are virtually unknown. The history of the flat corn tortilla—the basic bread of Mexico—is a venerable one, stretching back into antiquity. In Mexico it still is prepared today from the same ingredients and in the same manner as in olden times. Bishop Diego de Landa, sent from Spain to Yucatan in the 16th Century, recorded the same instructions as those used nowadays to make the basic corn dough, called *masa*.

In addition to corn for making tortillas, the padres brought cattle, horses, beans, chilies, dried fruits, brown sugar and chocolate from Mexico. The hospitable Indians in turn offered the padres acorns, piñon nuts and wild cereal seeds. Game and fowl were in the forest and fish in the ocean, for the taking. Wild berries, grapes and greens grew along the inland waterways and the familiar cactus plants provided edible fruit.

However, mission padres and their flocks of Indian neophytes experienced lean years before their labors produced crops and livestock to support them. Indeed, during the first years when missions were being established in the distant land of California, the inhabitants sometimes faced starvation. They still were dependent upon the arrival of supply ships from Mexico, and in 1772 Father Juan Crespí reported that the fathers of the new mission at San Gabriel, in the Los Angeles area, had tightened the cords around their waists, and at San Diego the guards had maintained themselves for a long time with half a pint of corn and twenty ounces of flour a day. At the same time the mission establishments at Carmel near Monterey and at San Antonio, the third mission to be founded, were short of rations. In desperation the padres sent out a hunting party to kill grizzlies in the Valley of the Bears, near San Luis Obispo and named for the great number of bears in the vicinity. The party brought back a "good supply" of salted and jerked bear meat.

One of the first concerns of the padres was to plant essential and traditional crops of beans, corn and wheat, on which subsistence depended. As field crops and vegetables began to flourish in the fertile soil under a beneficent sun, they were augmented with other seeds and cuttings of plants from Mexico, South America, Spain and other warm countries, and some were brought by traders who came around the Horn or via the Sandwich Islands, as the Hawaiian Islands were then called. Most of these plantings thrived, and later provided the nucleus of California produce and fruit which today is consumed around the world.

In all, the Franciscans established twenty-one missions in California, situated for the most part in coastal areas, from the first one at San Diego in the southwestern corner of the state to the northernmost one at Sonoma above San Francisco Bay. This comprised a 650-mile route linked by a foot trail called

El Camino Real, or the Royal or King's Highway. Mission land holdings eventually exceeded hundreds of thousands of choice acres. In the some sixty years of their tenure from 1769 to the 1830's almost 90,000 Indians were baptized. When Mexico began to take over mission lands under a secularization act, missions ruled over 17,000 neophytes, owned 151,000 cattle, 14,500 horses, and more thousands of sheep, goats and hogs. They harvested thousands of bushels of maize, wheat, beans and other crops, as well as grapes, oranges and numerous other fruits and vegetables from orchards and gardens. The success of the missions focused world attention on the wonders of California's agricultural riches.

THE INDIAN NEOPHYTES

The padres were zealous about capturing the souls of the native population, but it was by the promise of a stable food supply that the Indians were lured to become members of the mission communities. Although the land provided a bountiful seasonal supply of food and the natives had learned to lay in reserves for slack periods, they had not bothered to grow their own crops.

To begin to provide food and clothing for a large population, the Indians were first taught simple tasks, each having his own duty to perform. Women and girls were taught cooking, sewing and weaving; men and boys learned to work the soil, planting necessary staples of corn, wheat, beans, pumpkins, squash, and other vegetables. Instruction, however, was hampered by lack of a common language. While the padres applied themselves to learning native dialects, at the same time they taught the neophytes simple prayers in Spanish. It was natural that young people learned the Spanish language most rapidly.

As mission communities grew and prospered, construction of permanent mission buildings was undertaken. Molding bricks from adobe was the first task. In a trough built of boards or dug in the ground, pulverized soil and chaff from grain or grasses as a binder were trod by natives, with sufficient water added to make a stiff mud. The mud was put into simple molds and left to dry in the sun. Meanwhile, timbers for beams and basic construction were hewn. When a building was erected the walls were plastered and decorated with native motifs. Even today at some missions the marks of an adz made by Indian hands can be seen on beams and boards, and surface decorations inspired by Indian imagination are still visible at San Luis Rey, San Juan Capistrano, San Fernando and other missions.

Another important skill learned under the tutelage of the padres was the tanning of hides and leatherwork. Oakbark, the principal tanning agent, was gathered by Indians and carted to the missions. Animal hides were placed in a solution of crushed bark and water for three to six months, and after curing were ready to be converted into a myriad of uses, some of them being for saddles, reins, leather receptacles and shoe soles. Untanned hides were used to cover doors and bed frames, to make buckets, and even to be used as lashings for building beams.

Indian women easily mastered weaving arts, though the methods were primitive. The historian, Hubert Howe Bancroft, related that the wool would be beaten by two sticks to separate the fibers, then it was spun with a stick. Before looms were constructed, the warp was laid out by means of small sticks hammered into the ground. This crude method produced a coarse fiber but it was extremely durable. Indian women also did the laundry, using water from a nearby river or a pool diverted from an open aqueduct which brought water from a river, or a small

reservoir, sometimes as far away as twenty miles.

In return for their labors, the Indians were given three meals a day, including plenty of beef, veal, corn, beans, and other vegetables. At Mission San Gabriel during its most prosperous years, one hundred head of cattle were killed each Saturday for the five hundred Indian inhabitants. They learned to raise their own pumpkins, squash, onions and chilies on garden plots allotted to them.

In the early 1800's a report from San Luis Obispo stated that 2000 cattle were slaughtered during the year to provide meat for the neophytes and that the entire harvest from fields and gardens was consumed. In a similar report from Mission San Buenaventura Father José Señán wrote that "the Indians take no more than one meal a day, inasmuch as when they work they also eat..." In addition to the meals supplied by the mission, Father Señán said the Indians gathered acorns, seeds and herbs as well as wild game to be prepared in their own houses. They used their traditional cooking utensils of metates, clay pots, jars and baskets. Cooking was usually done over an open fire built between three large stones.

Indians were not furnished liquor, coffee or tea, but at some of the missions lemonade was sent out to them in the fields during the morning, as refreshment and as a preventative of illness.

When Mexico took over the mission holdings and private ranchos assumed their vast lands and herds, the Indians were cast adrift to shift for themselves or work as hired laborers on the ranchos.

THE BREAD OF MEXICO
The tortilla, often called the national bread of Mexico, is a generous-sized maize cake, round and quite thin. In early days it was made with corn which was first cleaned and

softened by parboiling. A cupful of prepared corn would be placed in an Indian stone grain grinder, or metate, and ground into medium-fine dough with a stone pestle. It was then patted into a thin round cake about the size of a salad plate and baked on a piece of heated iron.

Tortilla making was an advanced form of folk art among Mexican women, who taught the California mission Indian women how to master the fine skill. The tortilla was often spread with butter, sprinkled with salt and rolled up like a cigarette, making sure the lower end was pinched tightly to prevent butter from dribbling down the arm. Or it was filled with chopped meat, chicken, grated cheese, lettuce, minced onion, beans, chopped olives or a combination of these or other ingredients. Often it was sprinkled liberally with hot chili sauce. Nowadays, tortillas have been adapted to make the popular taco which is fried crisp in hot fat, folded into a trough and filled with shredded beef or chicken, and garnished with lettuce, onion and cheese.

At one stage of the first expedition to California, that of Don Gaspar de Portolá and Father Junípero Serra in 1769, each man was limited to one tortilla for breakfast, two for dinner and two for supper, with a share of such game as the half-starved hunters were able to provide. Father Serra subsisted at times on a daily ration of three tortillas and wine.

Wheat flour was brought to California with the first expeditions but was in small supply and used only sparingly for sauces and gravies. As wheat crops became more abundant, flour tortillas were made for special occasions.

During much of the mission period the grinding of grain was done by hand on the metate, a flat stone, or by mortar and pestle. Probably the first mechanical mill used in California was presented in 1786 to the padres at Carmel by M. de Langle, a Frenchman traveling with the scientific explorer, La Perouse, so that "four women would in one day perform the work of a hundred." The first water-powered grist mill

Mission Indians Making Baskets and Rope

was erected at Mission Santa Cruz in the early 1790's and, according to Bancroft, began to run in the autumn of 1796. There are indications that the British sea captain, George Vancouver, who explored the West Coast in 1792, donated $1000 to help build this mill. The next two grist mills were operated at Mission San Luis Obispo and the fourth in 1806 at Mission San Antonio. By the 1820's there were other mills in operation at San Jose, Santa Inez, San Gabriel and Santa Barbara, all of which fell into ruin by neglect when mission lands were appropriated.

FARE OF MISSIONARY PADRES

The padres were not noted for an elaborate cuisine and often lived very frugally. However they did bring with them traditional Spanish and Mexican recipes, most of them employing substantial ingredients of beans, corn and other grains. The several different kinds of beans used were called *frijoles*. Tomatoes or piquant chilies were favorite seasonings for meat, vegetable and grain dishes. Chocolate was a preferred and almost indispensable beverage.

The padres usually broke their fast with chocolate and toast or biscuit. About 11:00 in the morning they would take a glass of brandy with a piece of cake and cheese. Noon dinner might consist of vermicelli, rice or bread soup, beef or mutton stew, ham with beans, lentils or Spanish peas, and greens. Dessert was usually fresh or dried fruit, sweetmeats and cheese. And wine, of course. Supper, between 7:00 and 8:00 in the evening, might be roast pigeon or other fowl, and chocolate. Extra dishes were prepared when guests were present.

Before adobe ovens were constructed cooking was done over an open wood fire. Later a room in the mission compound was set aside for meal preparation where a beehive-shaped oven occupied one corner.

Heavy iron pots and skillets were the chief cooking vessels. Pots were hung from a crane and the skillets were set on a crude metal stand, which we call a spider. Cooking heat was regulated by swinging the crane closer or farther away from the flame, or by moving the spider. Today these primitive cooking arrangements can be studied in a number of restored missions.

Most missions owned a herd of cows to provide a supply of milk, which was used in cooking and to make cheese and butter. Range beef was quite tough, a fact commented on by certain travelers more accustomed to grain-fed Eastern beef. Beef tongues were hung in the kitchen chimney on iron spikes for smoking. Hams and other meats were cured in the same manner.

Beef hides and tallow were trade items in great demand. Much of it was used for making soap and candles, but the surplus was traded for manufactured articles and delicacies brought in by Yankees from the East Coast and by other trading ships.

MISSION HOSPITALITY

The bell towers of the missions served as lookout towers from which approaching visitors could be sighted. By the time they arrived a welcoming feast would be awaiting them.

In the golden years of the missions, a traveler fared very well indeed as he made his way from mission to mission. He would be fed and lodged in a guest apartment. His horse was cared for and if the animal was travel-weary, the visitor would be provided with a fresh one to be used until such time as he returned to claim his own mount. When ready to depart, all a visitor had to do was inform the padres, who would furnish him with provisions for the road, which might be a chicken or two, a boiled tongue, a loaf of bread, boiled eggs, and a bottle of wine

Mission of Santa Barbara   *Olive Oil Press*   JOHN DAWSON

or brandy. Of course he would have been provided with generous helpings of religion during his stay.

Mission San Gabriel in Los Angeles was noted for its hospitality and was well known to American trappers and adventurous Mountain Men, as recorded by William Wolfskill, John Bidwell, Kit Carson and others. Typical foods on the menu of its prosperous period were *caldo*, a plain broth of meat and vegetables; *la olla*, boiled meat with vegetables; *albondigas*, meat balls in gravy; *guisados*, stews; *asado*, a roast of beef, mutton, game or fowl; fruit and sweetmeats, tea, coffee, cigarritos, and wine. Pork was eaten very sparingly. No meat on Friday—ever.

By the early 1830's San Gabriel Mission had a plentiful supply of oranges, citrons, limes, apples, pears, peaches, pomegranates, figs and grapes, the latter used principally to make wine and brandy. Apples and pears

of good keeping quality were stored on shelves in a deep nest of straw so they would last through the winter. These fruits were shared with the Indian neophytes and foreign travelers.

MISSION GARDENS AND ORCHARDS

One of the first descriptions of a California vegetable garden was written by Father Pedro Font after a visit in 1776 to Mission San Carlos at Carmel, six years after its founding. He mentioned that it had been well laid out by Father Francisco Palóu in a square about a stone's throw from the mission, and was bordered with flowers. Though a means of irrigation had not yet been developed and watering had to be done by hand with a gourd dipper, the crops of cauliflower, lettuce, artichokes, and other vegetables and herbs "were better than any in Mexico." The mission at Carmel also had fields of beans, wheat, barley, chickpeas and lentils.

George Vancouver, the British sea captain, visited missions in the San Francisco area and was greatly impressed with them. The gardens, he wrote, far exceeded anything he had met with before and there was not one species which had not flourished in abundance and produced vegetables and fruits of excellent quality. There were "apples, pears, plums, figs, oranges, grapes, peaches, and pomegranates, together with plantain, banana, coconut, sugar cane, indigo and a great variety of necessary and useful kitchen herbs, plants and roots. All these were flourishing in the greatest health and perfection though separated from the seaside only by two or three fields of corn."

Many common vegetables were grown in mission gardens, but the padres also were careful to nurture a variety of chilies, which had become a favorite seasoning for sauces, especially to make the beef more palatable. Some mild-flavored chilies were used fresh, some with a very hot taste were dried and powdered for seasoning, and some were pickled for use as a relish.

While cooks in eastern states shied away from the tomato, believing it to be poisonous, Indians in northern South America and Central America had found it a savory addition to their meat and vegetable dishes. The padres had become accustomed to its use in their food and brought seeds to California. It has since been considered an important item in California recipes.

Some of the fruit trees planted in mission orchards were olive, quince, apple, pomegranate, plum, peach, pear, orange, citron, lemon, sour lime and fig. An inventory at Mission San Gabriel in 1834 listed a total of 2333 fruit trees in nine orchards. Grape cuttings flourished in spectacular fashion and were the forerunners of today's extensive California vineyards, from which are produced many fine wines.

THE FRUITFUL OLIVE

Olives were grown at most of the missions. Today the rich, meaty black olives still are known as "Mission Olives." Experts have claimed that the mission olive, as well as the grape, is distinct from varieties cultivated

Making Mission Candles   *Millstones for Grinding*   JOHN DAWSON

in Europe. Though the olive trees differed from one mission to another, there is reason to believe this was the result of climatic conditions or location.

Olives were harvested by whipping them off the trees with switches or by shaking them down by striking the tree limbs with a pole. They were gathered from the ground by Indian children and carried to a mill in burden baskets by Indian women. There they were poured into a circular cement-lined well, about fifteen feet in diameter, and crushed by a revolving stone propelled by a blindfolded burro hitched to a wooden crossarm. The reluctant burro was urged on by an Indian armed with a rawhide whiplash. When the olives were properly crushed, other Indians scooped up the pulp from the well, stuffed it into sacks or bags of strong hempen net and placed it in the press.

The olive press was operated by two or more Indians by means of a bar inserted through a hole in the socket-fitting of a screw. Under pressure, oil and juice ran out the spout extending from the floor board into a tub set below. Oil was skimmed from the juice, then poured into glass jars and bottles for storage. Oil was used in sanctuary lamps, in cooking, as a medicine, and to lubricate machinery. The juice was mixed with water and poured into pits around trees to rid the soil of fleas, mice and moles, and to destroy bedbugs.

Olives for pickling were gathered by hand and only the choicest ones were used. They were steeped in lye water obtained from leached ashes, then washed and bottled in salt water with perhaps a little fennel or other herb or spice added. Sometimes they were kept in a tub or rawhide bag with fresh water for fifteen days, the water being changed every other day, then stored away in a salt water solution for future use. Lacking wooden barrels, the Indians made stiff rawhide bags called *zurrones*, by sewing an animal hide down the side and across the bottom. Into a five-gallon zurrone four gallons of ripe black olives would be placed, with four cups of pure rock salt poured over the contents.

WINE MAKING

The making of wine was an important industry at the missions. Reports indicate that San Gabriel produced the best wine of all the missions, and that San Antonio and San Fernando followed close behind. Two kinds of red wine were made, one being dry and very good for the table, the other sweet. Two kinds of white wine also were produced, one from pure grapes without fermentation, including skins of the pressed grapes, the other of the same juice fermented with a quantity of grape brandy. Both were delicious dessert wines. The wine from pure grape juice was reserved for the altar; the other was for ordinary use. Brandy, called *aguardiente*, also was made from apples and pears, as well as the grape.

Antonio de Herrera, an early 17th Century Spanish historian, admonished that persons who pull the grapes from the vine must be "clean persons, as cleanliness is one of the essentials of good wine making." He said also that the one who treads out the juice must be a young man of good strength, having well-washed legs. Bancroft described the wine-making process at the missions as follows:

"Suitable ground was selected and a platform was placed thereon. This was covered with clean hides and grapes piled upon it. Some well-washed Indians wearing only a zapeta (loin-cloth), the hair carefully tied up and the hands covered with cloth to wipe away the sweat, each having a stick to steady himself withal, with the help of a rope strung overhead, were put to treading out the grape

19

juice which was caught in leather bags. These were emptied into large wooden tubs, where the liquid was kept two or three months, under cover of the grape skins, to ferment. Such as did not flow off was put into wooden presses and the juice into copper jars, and covered with a kind of hat. Through two or three inserted tubes heat was conveyed to the mess to induce evaporation. These jars served as a still for brandy. For white wine the first juice only was taken and stored."

There are still some wine presses which can be viewed in restored missions, and there also is a wine cellar at Mission San Fernando.

CANDLE AND SOAP MAKING

Many candles were needed to light dark mission hallways and illuminate the altars for ceremonies on feast days. Kidney tallow was saved for candle making. The tallow was rendered, strained and stored away in hide bags in cool underground rooms and the making of candles usually began when autumn brought cool weather. A number of wicks were hung from a wheel or a support of cross sticks above a vat or cauldron of warmed tallow. The wicks were lowered repeatedly into the tallow and then raised for cooling, until the candles had reached the desired size.

Molds also were used in candle making. Wicks would be run through holes in the bottom of the molds and tied in knots to keep the tallow from running out. The molds were cooled in a vessel of water and then the knots at the bottom were cut to release the candles.

To make soap, scrap fat from cattle, hogs, goats and other animals was rendered, strained and stored until needed. Wood ashes were leached in large kettles or tall masonry tanks and the liquid, containing sodium and potassium carbonates, was added in a "sufficient amount" to the melted fat, then boiled until thick. After cooling, the soft soap which floated on top of the water was skimmed off and poured into molds to set. When solidified, it was cut into bars which were stored on shelves and turned occasionally, and when thoroughly dried or "cured," they were ready for use.

Recipes

TORTILLAS

Readers who wish to create tortillas from "scratch" may follow the accompanying directions, substituting a food grinder or blender for the metate, using the finest cutting blade. Fresh-ground moist masa also may be purchased today in many Mexican stores. The dry flour, ready to be mixed with water, is available in supermarkets. Even frozen tortillas in different sizes can be found in groceries, ready for use in a variety of ways. This recipe tells how tortillas were made in mission days.

Step 1, Nixtamal: Shell enough dry corn to equal two quarts. Pour into a galvanized vessel containing a gallon of water mixed with ¼ cup of unslaked lime. Stir until effervescence stops. Cook corn over slow heat without boiling for about an hour until the hulls can be rubbed from the kernels easily. Remove vessel from the fire and allow to stand overnight. Remove all hulls and wash corn in several changes of water, then drain well.
Step 2, Masa: Grind nixtamal into coarse meal, called masa, by pouring one cup at a time onto a metate, the grinding slab, and crushing it into a medium-fine dough with a stone pestle, sprinkling a little water on the mixture from time to time. When it is formed into a dough it is ready to be shaped into tortillas. The skilled tortilla maker picks up a lump of masa about the size of a walnut, pats it deftly between the hands until it is a perfectly round, smooth disc, roughly ⅛ inch thick and 6 to 7 inches in diameter. The disc is slapped onto a very hot, slightly greased griddle or baking sheet, to bake until it is blistered and slightly browned on both sides.

PIÑOLE

Breakfast cereal at the missions was made from corn, barley, wheat and other grains. Indians were accustomed to eating a similar dish made of parched and ground wild seeds.

Toast and grind nixtamal or other grains. Serve cold with sugar and milk or cream. For variety flavor with cinnamon or serve with fresh fruit.

ATOLE

Atole was a hot cereal or gruel provided for the morning and evening meal at the missions for the Indian neophytes. The basic ingredient was corn.

1 cup masa
2 cups cold water
½ teaspoon salt
3 cups boiling water

Blend masa with the cold water, stirring until lumps disappear. Add salt. Pour slowly into boiling water, stirring vigorously so no lumps will form. Cook over low heat for about an hour, stirring occasionally. Serve with cream and sugar, adding fruit if desired.

SOUP CRACKERS

Crackers were made with whole wheat flour for special occasions. They were a tasty and nutritious accompaniment to soup or stew and could be stored in tin cracker bins for later use.

4 cups flour
2 tablespoons sugar
1 teaspoon salt
1 tablespoon suet or lard

Sift together flour, sugar and salt; cut in shortening. Add water to make a stiff dough (½ to ¾ cup). Turn out on well-floured bread board or other smooth flat surface and pat or roll out until ⅛ inch thick. Trim into 12 by 12 inch squares; bake on cookie sheet in a slow oven (250 degrees) until dry and pale golden. Score and break into squares.

MEAT BALL SOUP
Sopa de Albondigas

Ingredients for this distinctive method of preparing beef included corn meal, enhanced with chilies, onion and tomatoes, fresh from the garden. This soup might have been the first course of the meal served John Bidwell, William Wolfskill, Kit Carson and party when they arrived at San Gabriel Mission in 1841.

1 pound ground cooked beef
½ pound corn meal (2 cups)
1 egg
1 tablespoon suet or lard, melted
1 tablespoon flour
Salt and pepper
2 onions
4 green chilies
2 cloves garlic
4 ripe tomatoes, peeled

Mix meat with corn meal, egg, salt and pepper. Chop fine 1 onion, 2 green chilies, 1 clove garlic and 2 tomatoes, or grind all together in meat grinder, and blend with meat-meal mixture. Set aside. Chop remaining onion, 2 chilies, tomatoes and garlic clove. Melt fat in deep saucepan, add flour and stir over low flame until golden brown. Add onion-tomato-chili mixture and fry 3 minutes. Add 2 quarts of water and boil 3 minutes. Roll meat mixture into balls the size of pigeon eggs, about ½ inch in diameter, and drop one at a time into sauce pan. Simmer 15 minutes and serve.

PORK STEW
Pozole

A gruel or thick soup of corn meal with the addition of meat and vegetables usually was served to the mission Indians as the noon meal. The dish, called *pozole*, still is popular in Mexico and California and sometimes is made only with pig's head and corn meal, with seasonings of garlic, onion, or chili. This recipe includes the season's offering of mission vegetables and olives.

1 cup plus 2 tablespoons yellow corn meal
4 cups boiling water
¼ cup olive oil
1 cup cubed pork or veal
1 medium onion, minced
1 small garlic clove, minced
2 cups cooked tomatoes (optional)
2 cups whole kernel corn (optional)

1 cup cooked peas, or beans
1 cup ripe pitted black olives
1 teaspoon chili powder

Cook corn meal in boiling water until thick.
Set aside. Heat olive oil in heavy skillet. Add
meat to oil and cook until brown. Add onion
and garlic and cook for about 30 minutes over
low heat. Season to taste. Add tomatoes, corn,
and peas or beans and heat through. Combine
with mush, olives and chili powder. Reheat
and serve.

SMOKED TONGUE
(See cautionary remarks in Foreword)
Lengua Ahumada
Beef tongues to be smoked were hung in the
chimneys of the mission kitchens.

1 smoked tongue
Salt and pepper
1 sliced onion
½ teaspoon chili powder

Cover tongue with cold water and soak for
12 hours. Remove and place in a large iron
kettle, cover with cold water and add salt,
pepper, onion and chili powder. Simmer until
tender, about 3 hours. Leave in stock until
cool enough to handle. Skin tongue and
remove hard portions and small bones at the
roots. Slice and serve with horseradish sauce
or chill and serve cold.

BOILED BEEF
Carne
Wine and herbs may be added to this dish
although the rich flavor of the meat is often
better left alone.

6 pounds lean roast of rump or chuck beef
Salt and pepper

Season meat well with salt and pepper and
place in iron kettle on top of stove. Add cold
water to barely cover meat; place lid on kettle
and simmer until tender, about 3 to 3½
hours.

BEEF STEW
Carne Guisada
Beef cattle were rather tough and chewy in
mission days and needed long cooking. Stewing was a favorite way of preparing the meat.

4 pounds cubed lean beef
Salt and pepper
2 stalks celery, cut in 4-inch pieces
4 turnips, peeled and cut in half
4 carrots, peeled and cut in half
3 onions, sliced
3 cups cooked garbanzo beans
2 dried pico chilies

Place meat in large iron kettle and cover with
cold water. Bring to a rolling boil. Remove
from fire and skim. Add seasonings and
simmer for 2 hours, or until tender. Add vegetables and cook 1 hour longer.

ROAST BEEF
Carne Asada
Here is a recipe for roasting beef on top of
the stove in little water.

6 pounds rump or lean chuck
4 tablespoons melted suet
Salt and pepper
1 cup water
1 medium-sized onion, sliced

Brown meat in suet in an iron kettle on top
of stove. Season well with salt and pepper.
Add cup of water and onion, cover kettle and
cook slowly about 3½ hours, or until tender.

ROAST BEAR
Mission padres were not too fond of bear meat,
but before mission cattle became numerous
they learned to take advantage of the available
bear population.

8 pound hunk of bear meat
3 or 4 onions, sliced
Olive oil
1 clove garlic
Salt
¼ cup melted butter
Pinch of oregano
1 small hot red chili

Marinate bear meat overnight in water into
which onions have been sliced. When ready
to cook, remove meat from marinade, wipe
dry and rub as much olive oil into it as it
will absorb. Cut a gash in the center of the
roast and insert garlic clove, then rub entire
surface with salt. Place in roasting pan and
bake uncovered 4 to 5 hours. Baste frequently

with drippings during cooking. Just before removing from oven, pour melted butter over roast, basting well. Remove meat to platter. Add oregano and chili pepper to the juices in the pan, cook for 5 minutes, and pour over meat.

BEAR TONGUE

Fresh bear tongue became popular with the Indians in mission days. This is a simple recipe for preparing it.

Cover tongue with cold water, add salt and bring to a boil, skimming off scum. Simmer until tongue is tender. Let cool in liquid until it can be handled. Skin with a sharp knife or fingers and remove small bones at the base. Serve hot or cold.

RABBIT FRICASSEE

Quail, pheasants and squirrels were cooked in this same manner, using a smaller quantity of herbs and adjusting cooking time.

Rabbit, skinned and cleaned
Salt and pepper
Flour
¼ cup olive oil
1 quart of water
¼ teaspoon cayenne pepper
¼ teaspoon allspice
¼ teaspoon cloves
Herb bouquet of 2 leaves of sweet marjoram, 1 leaf of oregano, 1 leaf of mace and 2 sprigs of parsley
2 tablespoons of flour
1 tablespoon vinegar or lemon juice

Disjoint rabbit and soak in salted water about 2 hours. Remove from water, drain well and season with salt and pepper. Dust with flour and brown in olive oil in a heavy iron skillet. Add quart of water, cayenne pepper, allspice, cloves and herb bouquet. Cover and simmer until tender. Drain off liquid and thicken with 2 tablespoons of flour and add vinegar or lemon juice. Pour gravy over meat and simmer 5 minutes longer. Serve with gravy.

WILD DUCK

Wild fowl was often prepared for the padres'

table. To absorb the strong "gamey" flavor of duck the bird was stuffed with fruit or vegetables during cooking.

Stuff duck with an apple, celery or carrot and parboil for about 20 minutes. Lift from liquid, place in roasting pan and bake for about 45 minutes. Remove fruit or vegetables before serving.

PAELLA

This very old Spanish dish found its way to California via Mexico. It was varied to suit ingredients at hand but usually included rice, chicken and sea food. We present a slightly modernized version.

1 cup olive oil
2 cups raw rice
12 small chorizo sausages
¾ cup diced cooked ham
1 chopped onion
2 cooked chicken breasts, diced
½ pound lobster meat, sliced
6 shrimps, shelled and deveined
12 clams, shelled and well washed
½ cup peas, cooked
1 sweet pepper, diced
12 green olives, pitted
1 quart chicken stock
Salt and pepper to taste

Heat olive oil in heavy skillet. Add rice, sausage, ham and onion; stir over low heat until rice is well coated with oil. Add chicken, lobster, shrimps, clams, peas, sweet pepper, olives, chicken stock, and salt and pepper. Bring to a boil and remove from fire. Cover skillet and heat in moderate oven (350°) for about a half hour, or until rice has absorbed liquid.

BEANS AND WHEAT GRUEL

Beans perhaps were not as important a staple in mission days as in the later Mexican period. However, this recipe could be an early forerunner of the popular Mexican way of preparing mashed beans, known as *frijoles refritos*. Here the beans are cooked to a mushy consistency and wheat also is included.

2 cups pink beans
2 cups hulled wheat
½ cup suet, lard or drippings

4 quarts water
Salt

Wash beans, picking over carefully and discarding imperfect ones. Place in a large heavy kettle, add water and cook for an hour. Wash wheat and add to beans. Cook mixture for an hour longer. Drain, saving water. Heat fat in heavy skillet, add beans, wheat and salt; simmer until beans have absorbed all the fat. Pour in reserved liquid in which beans and wheat were cooked, cover, and simmer until thick and mushy.

GARBANZO BEANS

Garbanzo beans, also known as chick peas, often were added to stews but could be prepared as a dish in themselves. Today they can be purchased ready cooked in cans, but this recipe describes how to do them from scratch.

2 cups dried garbanzo beans
2 tablespoons fat
1 onion, chopped
1 teaspoon salt
¼ teaspoon pepper

Wash beans well, discarding imperfect ones. Cover with water and soak overnight. To cook, add sufficient water to cover beans, and a pinch of salt; simmer until tender. Heat fat in heavy skillet, add onion, salt and pepper and stir well. Add beans and simmer for 20 minutes or so.

BOILED ONIONS IN CREAM

An appealing recipe for small white onions is as popular today as it was in mission days.

16 small white onions
Cold water
2 tablespoons heavy cream
Salt and pepper

Trim and skin onions. Place in saucepan, cover with cold water and let stand for 30 minutes. Pour off cold water, cover with boiling water and cook for 15 minutes. Drain, replace with fresh boiling water and cook until tender. Drain, add cream, season with salt and pepper and reheat for 5 minutes before serving.

FRESH CORN PUDDING

In old cookbooks there are numerous references to puddings which are not desserts. This recipe is for a baked fresh corn dish.

18 ears sweet corn
¼ cup sugar
¼ teaspoon salt
3 eggs, well beaten
2 cups milk

Cut corn from cob, scraping cob well. Add sugar, salt and eggs. Stir in milk very slowly. Pour into buttered baking dish and bake for 1½ to 2 hours in a slow oven (300°). The pudding is done when a knife inserted in center comes out clean.

CHILIES

Chilies grown most frequently in mission gardens were:

Ancho: *broad, dark red, usually dried before use.*
Chipotle: *golden or dark brown, sun-dried and powdered for use.*
Huero: *small, yellow, hot, usually pickled and served as a relish.*
Pico: *long, bright red, used either fresh or dried.*
Piquin: *tiny, oval, red, used for seasoning.*
Poblano: *long, green, mild-flavored, used fresh, toasted, or dried and powdered.*
Serrano: *small, green, very hot.*

CHILI VINEGAR

This hot vinegar was favored by diners who wished to add more "zing" to their food. A similar decoction, called "pepper sauce" graced my grandmother's table back East.

4 dozen fresh huero chilies
2 cups white wine vinegar

Wash and drain chilies. Boil vinegar for 2 minutes and set aside until cold. Place chilies in bottles, pour vinegar over them and cork tightly. Should ripen for 3 or 4 days before use; yields about 1 pint.

CHILI PULP

Prepared chili pulp was kept on hand ready to add to various dishes or to combine with other ingredients as basting for roasted meats.

Place sun-dried red chilies in a shallow pan and heat in hot oven for about 15 minutes, stirring once or twice. Remove from oven, rinse thoroughly, and remove stems and seeds. Toss into a kettle, cover with boiling water, cover pan tightly and simmer for 2 hours. Drain well and rub through a sieve. Store in covered container until used.

HOT CHILI SAUCE

Chili sauce, whether hot or mild, was a happy way to enliven bland cereal tastes of corn or bean dishes, to serve with meat, or dip into with tortillas. This recipe calls for hot chili pulp and a slight thickening of flour.

*¼ cup lard or drippings
1 medium onion, chopped fine
1 clove garlic, minced
1 tablespoon flour
¼ teaspoon oregano
½ teaspoon salt
½ cup water
2 cups red chili pulp*

Heat fat in heavy skillet, add onions and garlic and cook slowly until limp and golden, stirring occasionally. Stir in flour and remaining ingredients. Simmer for 20 minutes.

INDIAN PUDDING

In the Eastern United States where corn had been cultivated for centuries, this corn meal pudding was a traditional dessert. It remained for mission padres to bring it to California. The missionaries liked to serve it with a brandy sauce. This recipe calls for the pudding to be placed in a cloth bag and steamed in water, similar to the method used by the English to make plum pudding.

*1 quart milk
4 cups yellow corn meal
½ cup beef suet, chopped fine
1 teaspoon salt
3 eggs, separated
¼ cup sugar*

Scald milk and stir in meal and suet. Continue stirring until smooth. Add salt and cool slightly. Add egg yolks and sugar which have

been beaten together. Blend thoroughly. Whip egg whites until stiff but not dry and fold into batter. Dip a cloth bag in hot water, sprinkle flour on both sides and fill half full with pudding mixture. Tie bag at top, allowing space for pudding to swell during cooking. Boil in a kettle of hot water for 10 minutes, reduce heat and simmer 5 hours. Serve warm with brandy sauce.

Brandy Sauce:
*1 cup sugar
1 tablespoon cornstarch or arrowroot
¼ teaspoon salt
1 tablespoon butter
1 cup boiling water
¼ cup brandy*

Mix together sugar, cornstarch, salt and butter. Pour boiling water over the mixture and stir until butter is melted. Cook over medium heat until sauce looks clear, about 8 to 10 minutes. Remove from heat, add brandy, and serve over warm pudding.

BAKED APPLES

During warm months mission inhabitants enjoyed fresh fruit for dessert. During the winter various fruits which had been stored or dried were used, baked apples being a favorite.

*8 apples
Butter
1 cup sugar
1 cup water
Nutmeg or cinnamon*
Core apples and peel about an inch of skin from around tops. Set in a baking dish and place a small dab of butter in each center. Boil sugar and water to a light syrup stage, add spice and pour this into apple centers. Bake in moderate oven (350 °) until soft, about 45 minutes. Remove from baking dish and place in individual serving dishes, spooning syrup over each apple. May be served hot or cold, with cream if desired.

FIG CONSERVE
Conserva de Higo

Figs were grown by most of the missions, and padres shared their fruit with Mexican colonists who were not fortunate enough to have their own orchards.

1 pound fresh figs
2 quarts water
2 tablespoons unslaked lime

Mix lime and water and stir frequently for 30 minutes, then allow to settle. Use only clear lime water. Select firm, half-ripe figs. Wash well, drain, prick with fork and drop into lime solution. Let stand overnight. The following day drain figs well and wash in clear water to remove all taste of lime. While figs are draining dry, prepare syrup by mixing 1 pound of sugar, 1 quart of water and 1 lime or lemon. Simmer for 10 minutes. Drop figs gently into syrup and cook for 1 hour over low heat. Remove from fire and let stand until quite cold. Return to fire and cook until figs are perfectly transparent and tender.

MOLASSES COOKIES

Most of the molasses used by the padres in mission recipes came by trading ships from the West Indies around the Horn, as did many other treats and delicacies.

1 cup suet or lard
1 cup sugar
1 cup molasses
1 tablespoon vinegar
1 teaspoon each ginger, cinnamon and salt
2 eggs
1 teaspoon baking soda
1 tablespoon hot water
6 cups flour, sifted

Combine shortening, sugar, molasses, vinegar, ginger, cinnamon and salt in a saucepan and heat to boiling point. Remove from fire and set aside to cool. Beat eggs well and add to cooled molasses mixture. Dissolve soda in 1 tablespoon hot water and add; blend well. Add flour, about a cup at a time and beat until smooth. Divide into three portions for easier handling. Roll out 1/8 inch thick on well-floured board and cut out with cookie cutter. Bake on greased cookie sheet for 12 minutes.

DATE COOKIES

There is evidence that mission padres were successful in cultivating dates but scanty records indicate that the crops were meager. However dates were prized for their nutritious

qualities and delicious flavor and were undoubtedly purchased from traders.

2/3 cup lard or butter
1 cup sugar
2 eggs, beaten
2 cups flour, sifted
1/4 teaspoon salt
1/2 teaspoon ground cloves
1/2 teaspoon cinnamon
1 teaspoon baking soda
1/4 cup hot water
1 cup chopped nuts
2 cups chopped dates

Cream shortening and sugar until fluffy. Add eggs and beat well. Sift together the flour, salt, cloves and cinnamon and add gradually to creamed ingredients. Dissolve soda in 1/4 cup hot water and beat into batter. Sprinkle nut meats and dates lightly with flour and add to batter. Mix well. Drop from spoon onto a greased cookie sheet and bake for 10 minutes in a moderate oven (350°).

CHOCOLATE

Mission padres and Latin Americans preferred chocolate to coffee, not only for its sustaining nutrients but because it was more easily obtainable. Mexican chocolate is slightly more bitter than the popular American kind of today. When the chocolate was heated and ready to serve it was whipped with a *molinillo*, an elaborately carved wooden whip made especially for this purpose. Today these whips can be purchased in Mexican hardware stores.

6 teaspoons grated chocolate
6 teaspoons sugar
1 cup boiling water
3 cups scalded milk
2 eggs, well beaten
1 teaspoon vanilla
Dash cinnamon
Dash nutmeg

Mix chocolate with sugar and stir in a cup of scalding hot water to dissolve it; cook mixture for 5 minutes. Blend in scalded milk and heat over a slow fire. When very hot, add well-beaten eggs, vanilla, cinnamon and nutmeg. Beat chocolate until frothy with a molinillo.

Chapter III

The Days of the Great Ranchos

Welcome was here with bright and lingering glow
Of happy care-free days of Mexico.
All doors were open, every table spread,
And ever, everywhere a waiting bed.
—MEXICAN BALLAD

The cross-bearing Franciscan padres were accompanied by soldiers whose duties were to handle the practical aspects of the Christian conquest. They guarded the mission establishments, warded off colonizing attempts by other European nations, and established permanent homes.

At first there was little reward for their loyalty and separation from their homeland in Mexico. By 1790, only a handful of land grants had gone to soldiers and settlers. But even then they had not suffered the privations the Pilgrims had endured on the East Coast, as in the early times they had been rather generously provided for by the Spanish government. When colonial Mexico won its independence from Spain in the 1820's, and a short decade later the missions were secularized and their vast lands appropriated, more than a thousand descendants of the first colonists received grants of some of the richest areas of California.

They set up little fiefdoms, hired Indian laborers who had been trained at the missions, and lived in a manner never known before or since in California. Mission gardens and orchards provided plants and seedlings. The first cattle which had been brought from Mexico had multiplied by the thousands and grazed from Baja California to the San Francisco Bay area, providing the mainstay of California's economy. The cattle population during the mission period rose to about 200,000 head; at the height of the rancho era there may have been as many as a million cattle roaming in a thousand valleys and hills. However there was no cross-breeding to improve the quality of beef for the discriminating palate.

In the early years of mission dominance, furs of sea otters had been traded for the products of New England brought to the coast by Boston ships which sold the furs in China. In later years of the ranchos, hides and tallow became the chief medium of exchange. A dried steer hide was called a "California banknote" or a "leather dollar." Hides and tallow were traded to both American and English traders for clothing, household furnishings, building materials, and processed food items not available locally.

Cattle roundups were held at every mission and rancho during the summer months of July, August, and September. Cattle were branded as required by the Mexican decree of 1770, and butchered for meat or trading purposes. Indians did the butchering. The best meat was cut in strips and dried or "jerked" for local consumption; part of the fat was reserved for making soap but most of it was rendered into tallow for trade. The Indians usually smoked the cattle tongues, and the remainder of the animal was left for the coyotes.

The rodeo offered an excuse for a grand fiesta, and all of the families of neighboring ranchos gathered to join in the feasting, drinking and dancing. Entertainment was provided by the *vaqueros* who delighted in displaying their horsemanship and skill with the lariat, called a *reata*. The cowboy of Western legend grew out of the Spanish-Mexican roundups and the rodeo itself has continued to entertain Americans down through the years, even in Madison Square Garden.

The low, one-story adobe dwellings of the Californios were quite lacking in the sumptuous aspects of Anglo-Saxon country houses on the East Coast. The kitchen usually was a separate hut, dominated by a huge fireplace and an adobe oven. Stoves were not generally in use until Americans came in large numbers and had them shipped around the Horn. Simple, traditional cooking satisfied the appetites of the early colonists. The great variety of fruits and vegetables taken for granted today was unthought of; however, the beef, frijoles and tortillas were shared freely with all who

Washing Day on a Ranch

Woman Rolling Corn

came along.

The hospitality of the Californio is legendary. It was said that a traveler could journey from San Diego to San Francisco without paying for food or lodging. Saddle horses were furnished as a matter of course at each stop. Better-class Spanish gentlemen often left a small handful of coins under a cloth on the guest's dresser, so that a traveler in want was free to take an amount sufficient for his immediate needs. This custom was discontinued after the coming of the Americans.

The days of the Dons came into full flower during the brief thirty-year Mexican period. But the inability of Mexico to exert full control over the distant territory eventually led to political disorder, with one faction struggling against another, usually the north against the south, for power and prestige. The indifference to fiscal management and the steady influx of energetic, enterprising Americans also contributed to the gradual demise of "Spanish Arcadia." Land-hungry emigrants, having learned of the incredibly rich agricultural possibilities, poured over the Sierra in increasing numbers, settling in the lush central valleys and planting crops for profit. Faulty titles granted by Spain and Mexico were challenged in American courts and the breakup of the huge ranchos inevitably ensued after California joined the Union.

The Corn Culture gave way to the Wheat Culture of the United States, but California's Spanish heritage has been perpetuated in names of cities, streets and freeways, in architecture, life style, attitudes and food.

FOOD OF EARLY COLONISTS

The two hundred and forty colonists who came from Mexico to California in 1775 with the Anza expedition to establish the presidio of San Francisco were supplied with goods and everything needed from "ribbons to shoelaces" for the long and hazardous journey. Food supplies included one hundred head of cattle, one for each day, thirty loads of flour for tortillas, sixty bushels of piñole (cereal), sixty bushels of kidney beans, six

A California Working Cart

El Baile, or the Dance   W.H.D. KOERNER (1878-1938)

By Carreta to the Fiesta   W.H.D. KOERNER (1878-1938)

The Governor's Equipage

cases of ordinary chocolate, sugar, soap, and three barrels of *aguardiente* to be used at the discretion of the comandante for medicinal purposes and other necessities.

Special luxury items reserved for the commander, Juan Bautiste de Anza, and the chaplain Father Pedro Font, were hams, pork sausage, biscuits, fine chocolate, cheese, olive oil, vinegar, pepper, saffron, cloves and cinnamon.

For some time after their arrival in California early colonists continued to receive essential items by supply ship, such as oil, wine, meat, lard, sugar, figs, raisins, salt, red pepper, garlic, flour, rice, chickpeas, cheese, bran, beans, chocolate, and even live cattle and poultry.

After permanent housing was arranged most of the cooking was done on braseros over the hot coals in a huge fireplace, the oven being used for special-occasion roasts and fancy dishes. Tortillas were cooked on an iron sheet which was placed over the open fire. A few pieces of pottery, ironware or copper, and a handmill for grinding the daily supply of corn flour comprised the inventory of cooking and eating utensils. Later on, cranes were installed to accommodate an iron pot over the fire. One-dish meals generally were the order of the day.

Love of feasting and banquets came naturally to these people of Latin heritage. While the poorer colonists enjoyed simple fiestas and fandangos, the wealthier military had occasions of pomp and ceremony. In 1806 when the Russian Nicolai Rezánof came calling at San Francisco to purchase grain and fresh fruits and vegetables for his scurvy-plagued fur hunters in Alaska, the Spanish comandante, Don José Arguello, entertained him with an elaborate feast which included chicken meat ball soup, tongue salad and toasted red chili sauce, roast fowl drenched with red chili sauce, young chickens stewed with rice and served with tomato and green chili relish, leafy green salad, tamales and enchiladas, beans, tortillas and sourdough bread, red and white wines, turnovers, buns, shortbreads, fruit delicacies, candied pumpkin, and boiled custard garnished with angelica.

Spanish officials were loath to violate government regulations forbidding commerce with foreign nations, though there was a small leeway in terms of desperate need. However, after a number of unsuccessful days of polite political negotiation, Nicolai had to seal the deal with a proposal of marriage to the captain's lovely daughter, Doña Concepción, and we hope, as Bancroft presumed, with true integrity of heart. Rezánof was never to return to claim the charming senorita as his bride because he died on his way to St. Petersburg. But his visit to San Francisco spurred a later attempt of the Russians to claim a part of the California coast.

At another festival which followed the inauguration in 1816 of the last Spanish governor of California, Don Pablo Vicente Solá, guests were served a lunch consisting of domestic and game birds, cordials and wines, fresh and preserved fruits from the southern establishments, olives from San Diego, oranges and pomegranates from San Gabriel, figs and preserved dates from Baja California, wines of the San Fernando Mission, and from San Gabriel Mission bread and cakes of wheat flour, which was famous for its good quality. The table was garnished with roses and other flowers.

Cost of a ball in the early decades of the 19th Century, such as the governor's Monterey ball was $19 for two dozen bottles of wine, $13.50 for a dozen and one-half bottles of beer, $13 for thirty pies, $12 for cake, $4 for a box of raisins, $1.50 for cheese, $13.50 for nine bottles of brandy, $25 for music, $9 for nine pounds of candles, $2.50 for five pounds of coffee, $3 for six pounds of sugar, $4 for servants. This was a total of $120.

THE FLOWERING OF FORT ROSS

Though the romance of Baron Rezánof and the Spanish senorita, Doña Concepción, did not come to a fruitful ending, the idea of Russian occupation of a California base had been born. In 1812 a Russian colony of ninety-five Russians and eighty Aleuts was planted at Bodega Bay in an area north of the Spanish holdings at San Francisco. Spanish Californians referred to it as Puerto de los Rusos; Americans called it Fort Ross. Yankee traders who stopped by occasionally

with sugar, molasses, salt and other goods from Boston were welcomed, and they in turn were certain of a profitable exchange of furs to be peddled in China.

With the help of Indian laborers, fruit orchards and field crops were planted to provide fresh produce for the Russians' Alaskan fur base at Sitka. Seed also was obtained from the Spaniards and the colonists planted barley, rye, buckwheat, maize, wheat, hemp, flax, beets, potatoes, cabbages, radishes, turnips, lettuce, beans, peas, melons, pumpkins, garlic and tobacco in the fertile soil.

One American trader who visited the settlement reported that he saw radishes weighing from one to twenty-eight pounds and "thicker than a stout man's thigh, good, not spongy; cucumbers weighing fifty pounds each, and gourds of sixty-five pounds." Possibly long months at sea made him prone to exaggerate, but his accounts of pumpkins weighing as much as fifty pounds and potatoes yielding "one to two hundredfold" were borne out by reports from other astonished visitors. Another trader commented on the thriving orchard trees of apple, pear, peach, cherry and quince, as well as the vineyard.

There were few wives at Fort Ross at any time during the Russian occupation. In the early years, cooking was done chiefly by Indian women and it is unfortunate that no recipes have been preserved to show how they adapted cooking methods to Russian tastes. We can assume that menus included characteristic Russian fare of thick, hearty soups, sour cream, cucumbers, smoked fish, black bread and highly spiced, richly flavored tea.

Princess Hêlene, wife of the last governor of the fort and possibly the first lady to arrive directly from Europe, certainly saw to it that the amenities of polite society were observed and entertained well when the opportunity arose, according to meager records available.

Under Mexican Rule, Days of the Dons   W.H.D. KOERNER (1878-1938)

The American Explorer–Fremont at Monterey   W.H.D. KOERNER (1878-1938)

Mountain Men in Old California   W.H.D. KOERNER (1878-1938)

Rights to the Land—Pioneers Vs. the Dons   W.H.D. KOERNER (1878-1938)

35

Old Russian Building at Fort Ross

History does not reveal whether the governor was able to include caviar on the menu when entertaining honored visitors. This appetizer, the roe of the noble sturgeon, always has been closely associated with the lavish cuisine of Russia's upper classes.

During the thirty years of its existence the quiet colony expanded to eight hundred souls. As time went on the supply of the fur-bearing sea otter dwindled, and there was increasing political contention with the Mexican government. When President James Monroe issued his famous proclamation that the Western Hemisphere no longer was to be open for European colonization, the Russians became discouraged and the fort was deemed an economic failure. An eager buyer of the fort, land, tools, machinery and fortifications was Captain John Sutter, a Swiss-American who had gained permission from the Mexican governor to establish a trading post in the Sacramento Valley.

When it came time for Princess Hêlene to depart for her native land she tearfully requested Sutter to care for her little rose garden. A few descendants of the old Russian colony live in or near Fort Ross today, and the Russian River perpetuates the memory of the brief colonizing effort. The restored fort and its satellites, the commander's house, chapel, blockhouse and stockade are popular tourist attractions. Had Baron Rezánof lived and returned to claim the Spanish senorita as his bride, California meals today might enjoy a richer blending of the hearty cuisine of Russia.

LIFE ON THE GREAT RANCHOS

When mission holdings fell into the hands of the rancheros in the 1830's, some of the descendants of early Spanish colonists became wealthy land owners. The ranchero would eat a light breakfast of cereal, called *piñole*, with sugar and milk, a tortilla or bread

36

with butter, and chocolate. He would then ride out on his rounds with his *vaqueros*, or cowboys. On his return around 9:00 o'clock in the morning he would sit down to a repast which might consist of chili-flavored pork sausage and rosy beans (*chorizo y frijoles*), tortillas with sweet curd cheese (*asadera*), or perhaps tortilla rolls filled with meat and fresh red chili sauce (*burritos de carne con chile*), refried beans (*frijoles refritos*), and red wine or coffee (*vino tinto o café*).

The work of the harness maker, wine maker, weaver, and other workers near the hacienda would be inspected next. At noon, work would cease and after a brief Ave Maria the midday meal would be served. This might include boiled pot (*puchero*), pigweed salad (*ensalada de verdolagas*), tortillas or sourdough bread, and red wine or coffee.

A siesta followed the noon meal. After this rest period, the afternoon collation was served. On a hot summer day it might consist only of tea or coffee for the ladies, and a small glass of liquor for the men. On festive occasions a more elaborate collation might

be offered, consisting of pumpkin turnovers, either fresh or dried fruits, chocolate, shortbread, buns, boiled chocolate sauce, candied pumpkin, fresh curd cheese, ripe black olives, and California angelica wine.

La cena, or supper, was served at night. This might be cooked greens, beef, frijoles, tortillas, fresh curd cheese, glazed fig pulp, red wine and coffee. Almost all meat dishes were highly seasoned with peppers and garlic. Tomatoes and onions were essential ingredients of meat and vegetable dishes.

During Lent, the first meal was not eaten until noon and the evening meal would not be served until 8:00 o'clock in the evening. Both of these meals usually consisted of fish; *colache*, a Mexican version of succotash made with minced green squash, corn and tomatoes; cooked greens and beans. No coffee or tea was served during this period of fasting and abstinence.

If guests were present at an hacienda, dinner might include soup with rice, vermicelli, noodles, or small dumplings of wheat flour; meat stew, frijoles, tortillas, small meat

Bull and Bear Fight

The Reata, or Lariat for Roping Cattle   W.H.D. KOERNER (1878-1938)

The Homesteaders–When Life Was Renewed   W.H.D. KOERNER (1878-1938)

turnovers, candied pumpkin, and a conserve.

Several of the homes of the Dons have been restored and interested visitors may view the kitchens. Those in the Los Angeles area are Casa de Adobe near the Southwest Museum, the Pico House nearby, and La Casa de Ranchos Los Cerritos in Long Beach, presently in use by the Bixby Branch of the Long Beach Public Library. In San Diego the best known is the Estudillo house.

Poorer Californios who were not great land owners lived almost entirely on beef, red beans and tortillas. Beef was frequently cut in slices or strips and roasted before an open fire or on an iron spit. Breakfast usually was piñole or roasted maize with milk. Or it might be beans alone, or fried meat, often cooked with chili, onions, tomatoes and beans. This repast held body and soul together until 4:00 or 5:00 in the afternoon. Knives, forks, and spoons such as those commonly used today were seen only infrequently. Horn spoons and forks were used, and often a piece of tortilla served as fork and spoon for meat and beans.

The Californios preferred beef and veal, particularly barbequed ribs. They varied this meat diet with mutton, chicken and egg dishes. Bear meat and pork were not to their liking. Pigs were generally thought of only as providing fat for making soap. An unwritten law allowed a hungry traveler to kill a beef for necessary meat, so long as he hung the hide where the coyotes could not get at it and where the owner could find it.

The Dons, like the padres, preferred chocolate to coffee as a beverage. On infrequent occasions trading ships brought green coffee beans, which were prepared by being roasted over a low fire and ground on a metate. Coffee was made by adding one tablespooon of the roasted ground grains to each cup of cold water, bringing it to a boil and allowing it to settle. This beverage was often quite bitter; however it gradually found its way into the menus of Mexican rancheros. When the Americans came they brought small coffee mills which soon replaced the metate and aided in the growing popularity of coffee among the Californios. Coffee or chocolate was sometimes brought to the bedrooms of distinguished guests as an hospitable gesture.

Californios learned from the Indians that the yucca plant had many uses. The fibrous thread peeled from the green saber-like leaves was used for embroidering leather saddle pads of the horsemen. The tender green shoots served as food, the taste resembling that of artichokes. By mixing in ground yucca with corn flour, tortillas could be prepared in drying ovens so they lasted for months. Called *totopo*, these tortillas were furnished to campaigning soldiers. The dried yucca stalk was trimmed, scraped, hollowed out and fitted with sheep-gut strings to fashion a crude musical instrument.

The First Families of California consumed great quantities of olives and olive oil. Processing methods were similar to those employed at the missions, though smaller quantities were needed by individual families on the ranchos. Green corn was a favorite dish whether roasted, baked or boiled. It also was an important ingredient of *puchero*, a dish of boiled meat and vegetables, introduced from South America and the equivalent of a New England boiled dinner.

In spite of having vast cattle herds, the rancheros used little milk, butter or cheese, as the cows were raised primarily for breeding. However, in early spring when the grass was green, wives of the rancheros made *asaderas*, small flat cakes of fresh cheese, which had to be eaten the same day. Three men were required to milk one of the wild cows, as she would have to be lassoed fore and aft. Milk pails were unknown. If several cows were milked at one time, the milk was stored in bowls, tumblers, teacups, or any other containers at hand.

A water supply was obtained from open trenches called *zanjas*, leading from the nearest river, which usually had been laid out by the padres and built by the Indian neophytes. Lack of house-keeping conveniences and cooking aids did not dim the spirits of the senoras and senoritas. Washday, for example, was often an excuse for a fiesta. A group of ladies would repair to the river, taking along not only the laundry but an ample supply of food and wine. In the evening they would be joined by their menfolk for a barbeque and fandango.

Certain essential household needs could be met only by the household itself. Laundry soap was one of these necessities. Pork fat was preferred for making soap; bear grease was a poor second choice. Fatty portions of the hog were tried out, or rendered, in a large kettle over a slow fire. The unreduced portions, or cracklings, were munched on by the children. The soap-making process was quite like that followed by the missions, but woe be unto the housewife who found it necessary to boil the soap mixture in her kitchen. It scorched easily and emitted a most disagreeable odor which permeated the surrounding atmosphere. This "smell" could be dispelled only by setting a pan of vinegar to simmer on the stove.

With the assistance of Indian servants, the busy senora dried fruits for winter. Grapes, peaches, apricots, apples, pears, figs and tomatoes dried very well. Bunches of grapes were dipped into a lime bath and hung from the rafters to dry. Peaches, apricots, and tomatoes were halved; pears were left whole. After being dipped into a lime bath they were laid on grass mats supported by bamboo-floored scaffolds and placed in the sun to dry. They were later stored in Indian-made bushel baskets for future use.

Wine making at the individual ranchos was not as complicated as the procedure followed by the missions, and possibly the wine was not as good either. The ranchero set his Indian servants to the task of crushing enough grapes to fill an open fifty-gallon barrel, utilizing the Americans' newly invented hand press. The pulp was stirred once a day with a long paddle, making sure the grapes at the bottom of the barrel were brought to the top. Care was taken to prevent the pulp which rose to the top from being exposed for more than six hours, as the air soured it and spoiled the entire barrel. By the tenth day all of the roughage was massed at the bottom. The liquid was drawn off and strained into a smaller barrel, and with the top covered it was allowed to stand uncorked. The bunghole was covered with cheese cloth and the contents were allowed to ferment for ten days, making sure the barrel was not moved. Then the clear liquid was siphoned into a clean charred barrel and tasted to make sure it was sweet. If it met the test it was sealed well for at least three months before being used.

LOVE OF HAPPY OCCASIONS

Nothing delighted a ranchero more than having his sons and daughters, sometimes as many as fifteen, their wives, husbands and offspring, drop in for a visit of a week, or even a month. When the climate was favorable, the women slept indoors and the men bedded down outside under the stars, with a serape for a blanket, a saddle for a pillow and the good earth for a bed.

Family groups of as many as fifty people would go to visit neighboring ranchos. Indian tortilla makers were kept busy day and night, and a bullock slaughtered one day would be almost entirely eaten that same day, leaving barely enough for breakfast the following morning.

Picnics in the country were frequent and joyous occasions. Several families would join in the outing, contributing chickens, stuffed turkeys, tamales, stuffed peppers, and a fat calf to be killed on the spot. One or more carts of provisions would be taken to the designated spot in advance. The elderly and married couples would go on horseback on separate horses while young women rode together with the young men. Each young lady rested her foot in a straw stirrup, and her young man, seated behind her, placed an arm around her for support, with his hat on her head, leaving his own head bare or covered with a handkerchief.

The slaughtered calf was hung up under the nearest tree and a fire was kept burning. When a ranchero became hungry before or after the feast, he cut a steak to his liking and cooked it to his taste. Chickens and turkeys were rather scarce and were valued as special treats.

The ambitious Yankees who fell under the spell of charming senoritas and married into Spanish or Mexican landowning families usually Latinized their names and embraced the

Sport of Tailing a Steer

LAND OF SUNSHINE, ED BOREIN SKETCH

41

Catholic faith. Although they did not invade the kitchen, as increasing numbers of husbands are prone to do today, it is safe to assume that their wives were influenced to try American dishes, using foods and seasonings purchased from the trading ships.

A wedding presented an occasion for a celebration which lasted several days. When the families were prominent socially, a special wedding arbor was constructed in which the wedding feast could be enjoyed in comfort. The table was set with a fine cloth, china plates and cut-glass decanters. Delicacies of all kinds were prepared days in advance. The usual beef or calf was hung for roasting over the main fire, and smaller fires were at hand for cooking other dishes. Toasts in flowery language were offered and the guests danced until daylight to the throbbing music of guitars and violins.

In 1843 the officers of a United States military squadron gave a ball in Monterey at the Government House. The stewards of their messes prepared many dishes which were new to the ladies of Monterey, including cake and mince pie. The supply of Madeira wine ran out and the stewards substituted whiskey toddy, which the ladies enjoyed immensely, so the story goes.

Much as the people of New Orleans still do, the Californios really cut loose on the pre-Ash Wednesday celebration which lasted three glorious days. In preparation for this occasion, eggs would be emptied of their contents by blowing through small holes pierced in each end of the shells and refilled with cologne. The holes were sealed with wax. Acquaintances greeted one another by crushing these *cascarones*, as they were called, on each other's head. Sometimes the eggshells were filled with confetti and broken over the heads of guests at balls on festive occasions, which was not so messy as the cologne-filled shells, and just as much fun!

TRADE WITH THE YANKEES

Though heavy penalties once had been levied on smugglers in an attempt to control trade with foreigners, the Californios could not depend on supplies from Mexico. In time regulations were relaxed and a great deal of profitable activity was carried on, with Americans in particular, as the Yankee sea traders coveted the hides and tallow from Mexican ranchos. A trading ship in port was like a department store. Once the senoritas and senoras learned about the fancy food items, the dry goods, dishes, and furniture to be had from the East Coast, they clamored for them.

The men folk were eager to obtain iron, hardware and farm implements. Despite the superabundance of hides, the lack of skilled shoemakers necessitated shipping tanned hides to Boston and purchasing finished shoes from the traders.

In his famous book about the California hide trade entitled *Two Years Before the Mast*, Richard Henry Dana described a Boston ship cargo as consisting of everything under the sun, including spirits, tea and coffee, sugar, spices, raisins, molasses, hardware, crockery, cutlery and tinware, as well as clothing of calicoes, cottons, crepes and silks; shawls, scarves, necklaces, jewelry, combs, furniture "… and everything that can be imagined from Chinese fireworks to English cart-wheels."

A typical rancho breakfast provided by a Don to his Yankee trader guest included spit-turned beefsteak, onions, eggs, beans, tortillas, and pea coffee. Some guests were unkind enough to complain about the tough beef steak. On rare occasions, white yeast-rising bread might have been offered.

Even in the late years of Mexican rule livestock was still inexpensive. A fat beef cost $5, a sheep $2, hogs were $6 each, and milk cows $8. One hundred pounds of sugar cost $20, five pounds of butter $2, a bushel of

Arrival of the Edward Everett *at Sacramento*

wheat $3, a bushel of maize or peas $1.75, and a bushel of beans $2.50.

Through sea traders and overland trappers the promise of agricultural riches of sunny California came to the attention of restless American pioneers who were moving west. Captains and crewmen deserted their ships and along with early adventurers by land, married into California families, or gained permission from Mexican authorities to settle in the rich valleys which were still wilderness areas.

John Sutter, who reached California in 1840 and bought out the Russian establishment at Fort Ross, planted a colony and strong military fort in the Sacramento Valley. He was an influential agent in the influx of American emigrants. Overland routes both from the south and the north converged at Sutter's Fort, where half-starved and exhausted wayfarers found food and shelter after their long journey.

At a lavish Christmas dinner Captain Sutter entertained several guests. His cook, an English cockney and ex-ship's cook, rashly promised a meal "which would rival Delmonico's best efforts," despite the fact that the larder consisted wholly of beef, frijoles, unbolted flour, Mexican panoche sugar about the color of natural beeswax and of about the same consistency, with an abundance of red chili peppers, plenty of salt, black pepper, coffee and tea. There were no spices, butter, milk, eggs or raisins on hand, from which the cook could concoct the "real John Bull plum pudding" which he promised, though there were small black wild grapes, just "a little more sour than concentrated vinegar."

The first course was "beef soup, garnished with frijoles, chili and garlic; the second course was roast beef; the third course was baked beef pie; the fourth course was stewed beef; and the fifth course was fried beef, accompanied by black bread," all of these dishes being well-garnished with the available condiments.

The cook brought on the pudding, and the narrator of the incident commented that "it is doubtful if another to compare with it has ever been or ever will be concocted." The mixture of beef tallow and sour grapes had been liberally seasoned with chili, black pepper, salt and garlic, and the sauce was made of the panoche sugar and tallow, also generously seasoned with chili and black peppers. Unable to restrain himself further, a guest, swallowing in anguish, asked, "Cook, what is it?" "Why sir," replied the cook, "It is a regular Christmas plum pudding, Mexican style." The guests gave up, as did Captain Sutter.

Another Sutter treat was waffles made with wild duck eggs and home-ground flour, baked on a crude cast iron waffle iron.

In 1845 Thomas O. Larkin, the first United States Consul in the Mexican capital at Monterey, said "the whole foreign trade of California is in the hands of Americans." He advised prospective settlers who were California-bound to provide themselves for a family of five or six persons with one good wagon, four or five yokes of oxen, three or four cows, three horses, and for each person two hundred and fifty pounds of bacon, thirty pounds of coffee, fifty pounds of sugar, twenty pounds of rice, two good blankets and a few cooking utensils.

Unfortunately, Larkin did not take into consideration the long and treacherous overland trail through deserts and mountains and rain and snow. Many families were forced to abandon some or all of their supplies along the way and to kill their stock for survival, arriving in the promised land destitute and hungry. Larkin further advised emigrants to find land without delay and begin sowing wheat from December to February and beans, peas and corn in April or May; also to procure cows two years old, worth from $4 to $5 each; a young bull at $2 or $3; thirty or forty mares at $5 or $6 each, a stallion at $15 to $20, and a few sheep at $2 each.

During the spring and summer of 1846 when the tension of war between the United States and Mexico was felt in Texas as well as California, Lieutenant John C. Fremont and his party of rugged volunteers, who were in California supposedly on a mapping and exploring expedition, moved his troops too near the coast in violation of a pledge to Mexican authorities. In the midst of a flurry of threats, counter threats and excited rumors, alarmed American settlers in the Sacramento and Napa valleys took the moment to revolt and raised a crude bear flag in proclamation of the Republic of California. Though the republic was short-lived, the Bear Flaggers played a vital role in the state's final annexation by the Union.

Recipes

ROAST TURKEY
Ave Rellena Adobada y Asada
When Don José Arguello entertained Baron Rezánov, the Russian nobleman, the lavish menu included this feast dish, which was reserved for special occasions. Turkeys were not as meaty then as those we are familiar with today and had cavities large enough for a tempting stuffing such as this one which combines cooked beef with olives and raisins. Ana Begue Packman printed a recipe for this noble bird in her book *Early California Hospitality.*

1 large turkey (about 18 pounds)
2 pounds shoulder beef
Giblets

2 tablespoons fat
4 green onions
1 dry onion
1 tablespoon vinegar
1 teaspoon sugar
2 tablespoons toasted breadcrumbs
Salt and pepper
½ cup pitted ripe black olives
¼ cup raisins
2 eggs

Singe, draw and wash turkey. Rub well inside and outside with salt and pepper. Prepare stuffing as follows: Cook beef and giblets in 1 quart of water until tender. Reserve stock and when giblets are cool, chop fine. Place fat in skillet with minced onions and fry until onions are limp and golden. Add vinegar, sugar, breadcrumbs, salt and pepper, olives, raisins, and 1 cup of reserved meat broth; mix well. Stuffing should be crumbly–not watery. Remove from fire and cool slightly. Add beaten eggs and mix well. Stuff fowl and bake 4½ to 5 hours in moderate oven (325°) or until done.

Basting Sauce:
6 dry red chilies
1 cup boiling water
1 tablespoon vinegar
Salt and pepper
2 cloves garlic, minced
¼ teaspoon crushed oregano

Wipe chilies clean, stem, slit, remove seed veins and seeds. Steam in 1 cup boiling water until soft, about 30 minutes. Rub through sieve and mix with vinegar, salt and pepper, garlic and oregano. Add remainder of meat stock. Baste turkey with this puree every 15 minutes, after skin has browned.

TURKEY WITH MEXICAN SAUCE
Mole de Guajolote

The reader who might consider the preceding early recipe for roast turkey a bit on the elaborate side should first scan the following one which has long been popular in Mexico and naturally was imported to California. It is a variation of turkey with mole sauce, a lavish concoction of chili pulp and ground seeds, with the characteristic Mexican chocolate added. It was a great chore to make in early

days but now happily can be prepared in a blender.

1 18-pound turkey
½ pound pasella peppers
½ pound broad peppers
¼ pound brown peppers
4 to 10 chilies
3 cups olive oil or butter
1 tablespoon sesame seeds
½ cup squash seeds
½ cup pumpkin seeds
½ cup peanuts
2 tablespoons piñon nuts
1 piece stale tortilla
½ slice white bread
3 to 6 garlic cloves
3 tomatoes, chopped
1 sprig of marjoram
1 sprig of thyme
1 bay leaf
3 cloves
1 teaspoon cinnamon
1 tablespoon aniseed
½ teaspoon ginger
½ cup raisins
1 ounce Mexican chocolate

Disjoint turkey, cover with cold water, and set aside while sauce is being prepared. Remove seeds and veins from peppers and chilies and fry in plenty of oil. Fry turkey in pepper-flavored oil until brown on all sides. Arrange turkey pieces close together, preferably in an earthenware baking dish, cover with salted boiling water, and cook gently until nearly tender. Toast sesame seeds by shaking over heat in a dry pan. Fry squash and pumpkin seeds but do not brown. Roast peanuts if not already roasted. Fry tortilla and bread until crisp, then crumble. Finally, grind sesame, squash and pumpkin seeds, peanuts, piñon nuts and bread crumbs. Also, grind peppers and chilies together. Slowly fry garlic without browning. Add tomatoes and fry until tomato pulp thickens. Assemble all of these prepared flavorings in one pan and mash or work mixture until smooth. Add strained oil from various fryings to herbs, spices and raisins; mix thoroughly, seasoning to taste with salt. Simmer and stir with wooden spoon, then add turkey and its broth and finish cooking, moving pieces about once in a while with a wooden spoon to prevent sticking. Add grated chocolate at the last moment and take up when melted and blended.

BARBEQUED BULLOCK'S HEAD
Cabeza de Tatamada
Well-liked from California's earliest days, this barbeque method has retained its popularity among the nostalgic-minded. Back then when diners were less finicky, the cleaned head was wrapped in green leaves from the handiest tree. This recipe appears through the kind permission of Katherine Ainsworth, who tells us this method was used by Bill Magee, a descendant of one of California's proud old rancho families. The head is buried in coals overnight and makes a delicious breakfast dish.

Clean the beef head thoroughly, including teeth, mouth and esophagus. Dig a pit at least 2½ feet deep by 2 feet wide–large enough to fit the head in with a little room to spare. Cover bottom of pit with fair-sized igneous rock, approximately 3 to 6 inches. Fill pit half-full of oak wood and burn for at least 2½ hours. Wrap beef head in three thicknesses of burlap and place on the rock, first removing any unburned pieces of wood. Cover the wrapped head with coals, lay a tin or iron plate over it, and cover the metal with hot ashes. Let cook for nine hours or overnight. Exhume, peel off skin and serve.

BARBEQUED BEEF
Carne Tatamada
Cookouts today often are overseen by the man of the family under controlled conditions of a carefully regulated charcoal fire, but more than a century ago were as temptingly done in a barbeque pit.

Choose a cut of choice beef large enough to allow about one pound per person. Season with salt and pepper. Wrap in leaves or gunny sack and cook in a pit the same way as for bullock's head. Serve with red chili and black olive sauce, green chili pepper sauce, or your own favorite barbeque sauce.

TRIPE
Menudo
Tripe is the inner muscular lining of the stomach of meat animals, that of beef stomach, white and honeycomb in appearance, being the most delicate. This dish became popular among the Indians during mission and rancho days.

2 pounds honeycomb tripe
½ teaspoon salt
½ teaspoon sugar
2 cloves garlic, sliced
⅔ cup chopped onion
1 small hot red chili
Hot sauce

Wash tripe several times in water, cut into thin strips and cover with cold water. Bring to boiling point and add salt and sugar. Cover pot and simmer about 2 hours. Add garlic, onion and red chili pepper. Simmer until tender. Serve with or without hominy, and include a dash of hot sauce.

PORK SAUSAGE
(See cautionary remarks in Foreword)
Chorizo
Each family had its favorite method of preparing pork sausage; recipes differed only slightly in the degree of taste-bud tolerance, which depended on how many red-hot chili peppers were added to the meat. A number of recipes for chorizo have been noted in old California cookbooks; this recipe follows Ana Begue Packman's directions, which are similar to those of Mildred MacArthur's.

4 pounds ground lean pork
1 pound dry red chilies
½ cup vinegar
1 tablespoon salt
1 teaspoon black pepper
1 teaspoon oregano
2 cloves garlic, mashed
½ cup toasted bread crumbs

Wipe chilies clean and remove seeds. Place in pot and pour one cup of boiling water over them. Steam until soft, then rub through a sieve to separate hulls from pulp. Add pulp to meat and mix thoroughly with vinegar, salt, pepper, oregano, garlic and crumbs. Stuff into sausage casings and store in cool place.

BOILED DINNER
Puchero

This one-dish meal is a Mexican-Californian version of a New England boiled dinner, as recorded by Ana Begue Packman in her charming story of colonial days entitled *Early California Hospitality.* Ingredients can vary but usually include two or more meats plus vegetables.

1 large knuckle bone
2 pounds veal
2 pounds beef
3 ears corn
3 sweet potatoes
1 cup garbanzo beans
2 whole onions
3 dried tomatoes
2 green chili peppers
1 pound green string beans, tied in bunches
1 bundle kohl leaves
3 small summer squash
1 hard apple
1 hard pear
2 teaspoons salt
½ teaspoon pepper

Cover knuckle bone and meat with cold water. Bring to boil and skim. Place all vegetables, fruit and seasonings over bone and meat, in the order given, so they will cook whole. Simmer over a slow fire until done, about 2 hours. Today's cook may prefer to add vegetables and fruit during the last 45 minutes of cooking so they will be tender but still retain good shape and color.

MEXICAN STEW
Estofado

Wine cookery was appreciated in early California days, just as it is today. A stew such as this one, which is basically a meat dish, particularly benefits from the addition of a little spirit. A variation of this recipe is one of the favorites in my personal file. It can be prepared with beef or veal, but is equally good with venison, rabbit, pheasant or chicken.

3 pounds veal or beef shoulder
2 tablespoons fat
2 onions
1 clove garlic
1 red chili

1 teaspoon salt
½ teaspoon pepper
1 bay leaf
1 pint red wine
1 tablespoon vinegar
1 cup ripe black olives

Cut meat in 2-inch cubes. Heat fat in iron kettle and brown meat, onions, garlic and chili. Add salt, pepper, bay leaf, wine, vinegar and 1 cup water. Simmer for 3 hours, or until tender. When ready to serve, stir in olives and heat through.

CARNE CON CHILE

Because meat was the principal ingredient of this very popular dish in early California days, it was called *carne con chile*—meat with chili sauce—instead of chili con carne which is familiar today. California restaurants still offer a choice of chili with or without beans. Variations of the dish are too numerous to count, but this one is a very old recipe. Tortillas were a usual accompaniment.

2 pounds beef chuck
2 tablespoons fat
Salt and pepper

Cut meat in 1-inch cubes. Heat fat in large iron skillet and add meat, salt and pepper. Cover and simmer until tender, about 1 hour. Add sauce and heat through. Garnish with olives and serve. If beans are included, pour meat mixture over heated beans.
Sauce:
¼ pound dry red chilies
2 tablespoons fat
1 tablespoon flour or 2 tablespoons
  toasted bread crumbs
1 clove garlic, well mashed in salt
1 tablespoon vinegar
1 cup ripe black olives

Remove stems and slit chilies. Wipe clean. Toss into kettle and cover with one quart of boiling water. Cook until pulp separates from hulls. Drain, cool, and rub through sieve. This should make about 1½ pints of thick red puree. Heat fat in iron skillet. Add flour or crumbs and garlic. Cook until light golden color, stirring constantly. Add chili puree and vinegar and simmer 15 minutes longer.

TONGUE SALAD
Escabeche de lengua

A special dish of rancho days, often marinated in a vinegar dressing and served cold, was pickled tongue or tongue salad. Anna Begue Packman called it a dish to whet the appetite. However, it also was served hot with horseradish sauce.

1 medium-sized beef tongue
1 teaspoon salt
1 teaspoon pepper
1 clove garlic
1 small laurel leaf
1 small hot red chili

Place tongue in deep kettle, cover with cold water, add seasonings and cover tightly. Simmer until tender, or about 2 to 3 hours. When cool, remove skin and bones, slice and serve hot with horseradish. Or, if preferred, chill and serve with vinegar and onion dressing, made as follows:

4 tablespoons olive oil
3 tablespoons vinegar
1 tablespoon salt
1 sliced onion

Blend ingredients well and pour over sliced tongue. Allow to stand overnight in a cool place and serve cold.

MEAT-STUFFED CHILIES
Chiles Rellenos con Picadillo de Carne

Californians are well-acquainted with this popular Mexican dish of stuffed green chilies, which was also enjoyed in rancho days. One version with a beef filling was found in a cookbook of old family recipes compiled by the Ladies Social Circle of a Los Angeles church.

6 large green chilies
1 pound beef shoulder
* (yields 2 cups ground cooked meat)*
2 slices toasted bread
2 or 3 green onions, minced
2 tablespoons fat
½ cup ripe olives
1 teaspoon salt
Pepper
1 tablespoon vinegar
3 eggs
2 tablespoons flour

Roast chilies in oven until skins blister. Peel, and remove stems and seeds, taking care not to tear the chilies. Boil meat until tender, drain, and chop fine, with the toast. Fry the green onions lightly in fat. Add chopped meat and pitted olives. Season with salt, pepper and vinegar, mix well and simmer for five minutes, then stir in one egg which has been beaten to a froth. Stuff chilies with this mixture. Beat remaining 2 eggs, roll stuffed chilies in flour and then in beaten eggs; fry in deep fat. Drain well and place in warm casserole until ready to serve with sauce.

Sauce:
2 tablespoons fat
2 green chilies
1 onion
1 cup ripe tomatoes
½ teaspoon salt
¼ teaspoon pepper

Chop green chilies and onion and fry lightly in hot fat. Add tomatoes, salt and pepper, and simmer 10 minutes. Pour over stuffed cooked chilies and set in warm oven for 5 minutes before serving.

TAMALES

The name for this dish comes from the Aztec word *tamalli*. It has been made in Mexico for centuries and of course arrived in California via the Spanish explorers and Mexican colonists. The basic ingredient is masa with a variety of meat or cheese fillings steamed in corn husk wrappers. This old recipe gives instructions for making the masa as well as a beef filling.

Masa:
5 pounds corn
2 quarts water
2 tablespoons lime
2 tablespoons lard
1 teaspoon salt
Corn husks

Boil corn in lime water until tender. Wash thoroughly. Mash to mushy consistency and add lard and salt.

Filling:
5 pounds beef
25 green chilies
1 clove garlic, minced

1 pound raisins (optional)
1 onion, chopped
1 quart olives, chopped coarsely

Cut meat in small pieces, add water to cover, and cook until tender. Steam chilies, remove pulp and discard seeds and skin. Add pulp, garlic, raisins, onion and olives to meat. Spread masa on corn husks, using three leaves for each tamale. Place a large spoonful of the meat mixture on the corn layer and roll the husks around it tightly. Tie both ends with strips of husks. Steam one to two hours.

GREEN CORN TAMALES
A delectable way to cook fresh sweet corn, highly recommended by Genevieve Golsh of Pala.

Remove husks and silks from tender young corn, saving outer husks. Grate corn from cob, add grated onion and enough milk to form a paste. Shape into cigar-like portions about 3 inches long and 1 inch thick. Wrap tightly in husks and tie securely with strips torn from left-over husks. Place in container over boiling water and steam until done.

ROASTED SWEET CORN
Maiz Tierno
This fun way of roasting sweet corn is great for a picnic, such as the rancheros frequently enjoyed. *Maiz tierno* translates simply as "tender corn."

Strip husks about halfway down the ear of corn and remove as much of the silk as possible. Pull husks back in place and press tight. Bury the ears in hot ashes of a wood fire for about 25 minutes, or until done. Remove husks and season with salt and pepper. Add butter if desired.

STRING BEANS
Ejotes
Menus of the Mexican rancheros were not noted for including garden fresh vegetables. However, here is a recipe for *ejotes*, green string beans, with the delightful flavorings of tomatoes, chilies and garlic added.

2 pounds green beans

3 tablespoons olive oil
2 tomatoes, chopped coarsely
1 onion, sliced
2 green chilies, chopped
1 small clove garlic, minced
1 teaspoon vinegar
1 teaspoon salt
¼ teaspoon pepper

String, snap and wash beans. Heat oil in kettle, add beans and mix well. Add tomatoes, onion, chilies, garlic, vinegar and salt and pepper. Simmer slowly for 20 minutes, or until beans are tender. As tomato juice is absorbed add boiling water.

FRIJOLES
Beans, or frijoles, were no more foreign to the Mexican ranchero than they are to the Mexican cuisine today, and easily found their way into almost every meal, in one form or another. Frijole often refers to the popular pink bean used today in many Mexican dishes, or to the pinto, so-called because it is mottled in appearance, though the "spots" disappear during cooking. This recipe is a way to prepare the dried beans, but they can be purchased today already cooked in cans.

Pick over 2 cups of pink beans, discarding imperfect ones. Wash well. Place in a deep kettle and add cold water to cover with 3 inches to spare. Simmer for 3 hours or until beans are soft, adding boiling water when needed to cover beans. Mash beans with fork, leaving part of them whole. If beans are dry, a little broth may be added.

NOPAL CACTUS CUBES
California Indians introduced Mexican colonists to the thick pulpy leaves of the nopal cactus. As a vegetable it is considered delicious by some, but there must be a word of warning to those who wish to gather it fresh —care must be taken to avoid the tiny thorns on the skin. The leaves can be handled with tongs for peeling.

1 pound young, tender, thorn-free cactus leaves
1 teaspoon salt
¼ teaspoon pepper

¼ teaspoon fat
1 onion, minced
1 clove garlic, crushed
1 green chili, minced
2 tomatoes, chopped

Cut cactus leaves into ½-inch cubes. Add salt and pepper, cover with boiling water and cook slowly until tender. Drain and set aside. Heat fat in heavy skillet or kettle, add onion, garlic, chili, and tomatoes. Cook until limp. Combine with cactus cubes, cover and cook for 30 minutes or until tender.

CHEESE CAKES
Asaderas

Accounts differ as to how this soft fresh-milk cheese was produced in rancho days. The fact that wild cows were difficult to milk seemed to discourage extensive making of cheese. This recipe, described by H. H. Bancroft, is similar to the *schmierkase* made by my own German grandmother.

1 gallon fresh blood-warm milk
1 tablespoon cuajo, or one commercial rennet tablet
1 teaspoon salt

Stir rennet into milk and allow to cool, to form clabber. Pour clabber, an inch thick into a shallow pan. Place over a slow fire and while it is heating, press out the whey and form into a solid cake. When cheese is firm, lift onto a cloth-covered dish to drain and cool. Add salt, fold as turnover and serve fresh.

RENNET
Cuajo

To make rennet, the stomach bag of an unweaned calf was used. The bag was washed thoroughly, rubbed well with salt and hung out to dry. As needed, a finger-sized strip was cut off, dropped into a cup of warm water, and set aside for 24 hours. Later commercial rennet tablets became available.

COOKED WILD GREEN SALAD
Ensalada de Verduras

Greens of purslane, known as *verdolagas*, were chilled after cooking and marinated in a vinegar and oil dressing. Other edible native greens enjoyed by the rancheros were wild amaranth, lamb's quarters, sour dock, wild mustard, and frog greens.

1 pound verdolagas or other greens
1 medium-size onion, sliced
3 tablespoons olive oil
2 tablespoons vinegar
½ teaspoon salt
¼ teaspoon pepper

Wash greens thoroughly, removing discolored and coarse leaves. Cook until tender in one quart of salted water, and drain well. Serve well-chilled, with a dressing made of olive oil, vinegar, salt and pepper. Garnish with sliced onion.

GREENS AND EGGS
Quelites y Huevos

A favorite Lenten dish, these greens are simmered lightly in olive oil and served with a garnish of hard-boiled eggs.

4 cups cooked mustard or other greens
2 green onions, minced
1 clove garlic, mashed
2 tablespoons olive oil
6 hard-boiled eggs

Drain greens well and chop fine. Add onion and garlic and fry in olive oil until limp. Stir in greens and simmer 10 minutes. Salt and pepper to taste. Garnish with eggs cut in slices or halves, and serve.

OXEYES—EGGS IN CHILI
Ojos de Buey

An attractive, filling Lenten dish, with lots of "bite".

12 eggs
12 dried red chilies
2 tablespoons suet or lard
3 tablespoons toasted breadcrumbs
1 tablespoon vinegar
1 clove garlic, mashed
1 teaspoon salt
1 cup pitted ripe black olives
1 tablespoon chives, minced

Wipe chilies clean, split, and remove stem, seeds and veins. Toss into pan, cover with boiling water and steam for about 15 minutes. Drain well, saving about ½ cupful of the liquid. Rub chilies through colander, adding a little of the reserved liquid to help remove the pulp from the skins. Heat fat in skillet, stir in breadcrumbs, and brown lightly. Add salt, garlic, chili puree and vinegar, and simmer for 15 minutes. Pour puree into a baking dish, drop in eggs one at a time, and set in warm oven for 15 minutes or so, until eggs are firm. Garnish with olives and minced chives, and serve while hot.

WATERCRESS SALAD
Berro

Watercress was relished as a salad, with a simple dressing of oil and vinegar, or as an attractive garnish for cold meats.

FRIED SWEET TORTILLAS
Buñuelos

These unusual sweet-treats are formed like cooky balls, pressed out like tortillas, fried like fritters or doughnuts, and served with a sweet syrup like pancakes. They still are popular at Christmas time as they were in the days of the Dons. Sometimes, as a joke, women would fill them with cotton wool and send them to their friends.

3 cups flour
1 tablespoon sugar
½ tablespoon salt
1 egg
1 teaspoon baking powder
½ cup milk
2 cups fat

Sift flour, salt, baking powder and sugar into bowl. Add well-beaten egg and milk, a little at a time. Turn onto a well-floured board and knead until elastic. Divide dough into 2-inch balls and roll out into thin cakes about 5 inches in diameter. Prick with fork. Fry in deep fat one at a time until golden color. Serve with sauce, made as follows:

Sauce:
1 cup sugar
2 cups water
2 teaspoons aniseed

Bring water and aniseed to boil. Add sugar, stir until dissolved and boil until slightly thickened.

SWEET TAMALES

The familiar masa is used with a luscious fruit filling to make a special dessert.

8 cups masa
1 pound lard
3 tablespoons plus 1 teaspoon baking powder
5 cups sugar
½ cup raisins
8 ounces crushed pineapple
2 teaspoons crushed stick cinnamon or aniseed
½ pound corn husks

Mix masa, lard and baking powder well, in a large bowl. In another bowl, combine sugar, raisins, pineapple, and cinnamon and stir until sugar is dissolved. Blend with masa mixture. Spoon onto cleaned corn husks, fold husks around mixture and tie each end with husk strips. Steam about 45 minutes, or until husks can be removed easily from the tamales.

ANISEED COOKY
Puchitas

The tangy flavor of lime or lemon juice is added to aniseed in this cooky.

2 cups white flour
1 teaspoon salt
1 teaspoon baking powder
1 cup sugar
½ cup lard or other shortening
1 egg
1 teaspoon aniseed
½ cup water
Juice of 1 sweet lime or ½ lemon.

Boil juice, water and aniseed. Sweeten with 1 tablespoon of sugar. Cool. Sift flour, salt, baking powder and sugar into a bowl. Add shortening and mix. Stir in well-beaten egg and aniseed water. Knead until smooth and form into marble-sized balls. Place balls on baking sheet and flatten out with fork or mold. Bake in hot over (400°) until light golden brown.

CORN MEAL CUSTARD
Jiricalla

A milk and egg custard includes corn meal and is topped with a meringue.

6 eggs
1 quart milk

1 cup sugar
Dash cinnamon and nutmeg
½ cup masa
½ cup water
Separate eggs. Beat yolks lightly. Scald milk and add to yolks, with sugar, cinnamon and nutmeg. Dilute masa with ½ cup of water and strain. Add to egg mixture and cook slowly until thick. Beat egg whites until fluffy and spoon onto custard. Sprinkle lightly with sugar and place in oven to set meringue. Cool before serving.

FLAN

This delicate molded custard is one of California's all-time favorite desserts, from Spain by way of Mexico. Flavorings vary but the ceremony of serving it with flaming brandy is the only dramatic way to present it.

1¾ cups sugar
3 egg whites
8 egg yolks
3¼ cups rich cream
2 teaspoons vanilla
6 tablespoons brandy
Pour 1 cup of sugar into a baking dish or pan in which custard is to be baked. Place over heat and stir sugar constantly until it melts and turns golden. Remove from heat and tip pan around to coat entirely with caramel, then cool while making the custard. Beat egg whites and yolks together well and add cream, remaining sugar, and vanilla. Beat until sugar dissolves, then strain custard into caramel-coated pan. Place baking pan in a larger pan containing 1 inch of hot water. Bake in moderate oven (350 °) for about 1 hour, or until a knife inserted in the center comes out clean. While still hot, turn out on a serving platter so the caramel does not stick to the pan. Chill thoroughly. When ready to serve, pour brandy over pudding and set aflame.

CANDIED PUMPKIN
Dulce de Calabaza

This conserve was to the Dons what pumpkin pie was to the Pilgrims. Banana squash may be treated in the same manner.
Peel a small pumpkin, cut into finger-sized strips and place in a crock or kettle. Pour over it 1 gallon of water in which 2 heaping tablespoons of unslaked lime have been dissolved. Let stand overnight. Next day drain the pumpkin and wash well in fresh water, to remove the taste of lime.

Drop strips into a syrup made by boiling 2 quarts of sugar, 1 lemon and 2 teaspoons of aniseed in 2 quarts of water for 10 minutes. Cook until pumpkin is transparent but firm. Remove from fire, drain and chill before serving.

CHAMPURRADO

A traditional gruel-like Mexican drink is concocted of masa, rich cream and chocolate.
1 pound masa
1 cup brown sugar
5 cups water
1 square Mexican chocolate, crushed
1 teaspoon crushed cinnamon
¼ teaspoon salt
1⅔ cups rich cream
Dissolve masa and sugar in water, mix in chocolate, then strain. Add cinnamon and salt, place over low heat and stir until mixture boils. Add cream and simmer for 5 minutes, stirring constantly.

MEXICAN CHOCOLATE

Although this recipe is a trifle more elaborate than the one which appears in the mission section, the chocolate is the same and can be purchased in Mexican groceries today.

3 quarts rich milk
18 squares unsweetened chocolate
1 teaspoon cinnamon
5 eggs, separated

Heat milk to boiling point in heavy kettle or in top of a double boiler. In another heavy pan dissolve chocolate in 4½ cups of warm water, stirring constantly until hot. Add cinnamon. Slowly pour boiling milk into heated chocolate and let mixture boil 5 minutes. Beat whites and yolks separately until very light. Add chocolate mixture slowly to egg yolks while stirring. Fold in egg whites and beat all together for 1 minute. Serve immediately.

Chapter IV

The Bear-Eating Gold Seekers

Oh, Sally, dearest Sally!
Oh, Sally for your sake,
I'll go to Californy
An' try to raise a stake.
— JOE BOWERS FROM PIKE

Pioneer Mining in California

For a couple years after the American acquisition of California as a result of the war with Mexico, there seemed to be little change in the way of life in the golden land. California might have developed gradually as an agricultural state if James Marshall had not discovered all that gold when he did. Marshall, who had drifted westward, sharpening his skill as a carpenter as he went, was employed by Captain Sutter in 1847 in the building of a sawmill near the present site of Coloma on the South Fork of the American River.

The electrifying news of his find circled the globe, and conditions being what they were, one of the great migrations in history was under way within a few months. Miners and would-be miners poured into the Mother Lode country from every state in the Union and from almost every country in the world. They lived a hard life and some of them died young. A fortunate few made their pile and had the good sense to return to their native hearth or move to San Francisco and go into business, or invest in California land and lend their energies and talents toward developing the state's future.

When the big news broke, in spite of his efforts to keep the discovery at his mill secret, John Sutter turned to the business of supplying food and equipment to the oncoming horde of gold-seekers, but before long his land was overrun and his establishment destroyed.

A depression in France following the Revolution of 1848 had left thousands unemployed and created an economic and political upheaval which lasted until the mid-1850's. Excited by news of the gold discovery, many foot-loose men headed for California, which had been widely advertised in France. Of the several emigration companies created, the most famous was the Societé du Lingot d'Or, under whose auspices nearly four thousand men arrived in California. Other Frenchmen came at their own expense, not only from their native land but from Chile, Peru, Tahiti, Mexico and Louisiana.

By 1851 more than 20,000 Frenchmen could be found in California and in the mines near Placerville, Marysville, Columbia, Mokelumne Hill, Coloma, Sonora and Auburn. They made little effort to become citizens or to master the English language. Many of them complained of suffering injustice at the hands of Anglo-Americans and were quite unhappy with life in the rough camps. The more or less frequent clashes with other groups, coupled with the dwindling supply of easily accessible gold which made surface mining unprofitable, hastened their departure for San Francisco and elsewhere, to engage in activities better suited to their temperament and talents.

The ghosts of the people of many nationalities who grappled for the precious yellow metal haunt the few towns remaining in the Mother Lode country. Every one of these towns has its museum, displaying the pathetic souvenirs of that legendary era, salvaged from cabins, saloons and junk heaps. As the casual visitor strolls down the streets of Placerville, or Coloma, or Columbia, or Sonora, or one of a dozen others, he feels the presence of those long-dead, tired, hungry, gold-crazed argonauts peering over his shoulder and mute lips trying to say "this is how it was, here is where the big vein was, this is where I almost made my pile." Names of other once-lively towns tell their own sad tales: Mokelumne Hill, Chinese Camp, Bidwell's Bar, Grizzly Flat, Lousy Level, Whiskey Slide, Poverty Flat, Spanish Flat, Poker Flat, Jackass Hill, Irish Creek, Stag Camp, Fleatown, Rough and Ready, Port Wine Diggins, Canada Hill, Kanaka Flat, Lost Hill, Gouge Eye, Our Chance, New England, Hell's Half Acre, Brandy City, New Chicago, and so on *ad infinitum.*

The Gold Rush did indeed change California. In fact, it changed the whole world. Perhaps the earlier Mexican settlers were wiser in letting well enough alone. Juan Baptiste Ruelle, the French-Canadian (or Francisco Lopez, a Mexican laborer—take your choice—my sources are evenly divided), had discovered gold in Placerita Canyon northeast of San Fernando Mission in Southern California in 1841, the same year the Russians abandoned Fort Ross. The find was not hailed with any great excitement. About $8000 worth of gold was panned out but the news of the discovery did not circulate outside the state. The Indians had known about it, and they also knew there was gold in the Sierra country, but until they saw the inordinate value placed on it by the white man they paid little attention to it. However, the fever that seized so much of the world also affected Mexico, and hundreds if not thousands of Mexicans came up from Sonora and Sinaloa and other states of Mexico, and many left their bones to bleach in the sun in the great deserts which they tried to cross in the summer. But all were overpowered by the Americans.

During the span of less than a decade the Tortilla Culture had waned and the Wheat Culture was in ascendancy. Wheat is a superior cereal grain, makes finer bread, is more widely grown, and was preferred by the Americans of western and northern European ancestry who came to make California their home. The almost bewildering variety of fancy and exotic foods demanded by the polyglot mixture of world citizens with ample means to indulge their tastes, accelerated the sophistication of California's cuisine at a dizzying pace.

THE HUNGRY CROWD

Between April and December in 1849, seven hundred ships unloaded their human cargoes in San Francisco. All who could walk or ride headed for the diggings, where they met the tide of Easterners, Midwesterners, Southerners, or Mexicans and others who swarmed over the Sierra in covered wagons, oxcarts, on horseback or across the desert afoot—many suffering brutal hardships every mile of the way.

Visions of food obsessed the goldseekers, judging from contemporary accounts. One Forty-niner on the Lassen Trail in a transport of rapture, P. A. Chalfant, member of Bruff's Washington Company, wrote about his breakfast at the Davis Ranch on Davis Creek near the Pit River in north central California:

"A snow-white table cloth, sure enough queensware dishes, not a speck of dirt on one of them, biscuits and broad slices of light bread, coffee and cream and milk, beefsteak and milk gravy, and potatoes and butter, for a fact. It was the climax of a civilized breakfast."

Along the roads to the diggings, rough and ready establishments provided the simplest of fare, which was later improved with the addition of tinned oysters and sardines, bottled sour cucumber pickles, and more or less ancient cheese which was worth its weight in gold. There were no tablecloths and each individual was expected to provide his own tin plate, cup, knife and fork. The man with the longest reach got the best service and finished his meal first. Cooking was done on a cast-iron range or in an open fireplace. Of course there was no running water, except that from the nearest stream.

A healthy percentage of the early arrivals were college graduates, representing the professions, accustomed to a genteel way of life and eager to make their fortunes and get on with their life's work. But mining was rough and hazardous. Miners used their boots for pillows, not only because they had no better,

The Pioneer

The Miner

The Englishman

The Irishman

The Jew

The Negro

The Hybrid   *Chinese*   *Sandwich Islander*

Chilians   *The Hindoo*   *Mexicans*

but in order to prevent them from being stolen during the night.

The usual diet of the newly arrived miner was bacon and flour, and he was glad to get that. Gradually he was able to obtain beans, onions, potatoes and rice, for variety, as well as wild game and salmon, at $2.50 a pound, from the Sacramento River. On rare occasions he indulged in luxuries such as a small can of sardines for $2, or vinegar and olive oil from the south of France at $3 for less than one and one-half pint.

A tongue in cheek list of the "necessaries of life" for an eight-day trip into the mountains for four people, was published in the Mariposa Star. It called for six pounds of potatoes, one bottle of whisky, one bottle of pepper sauce, one bottle of whisky, one box of tea, nine pounds of onions, two bottles of whisky, one ham, eleven pounds of crackers, one bottle of whisky, one-half dozen sar-

dines, two bottles of brandy, six pounds of sugar, one bottle of brandy, seven pounds of cheese, two bottles of brandy, one bottle of pepper, five gallons of whisky, four bottles of whisky, one small keg of whisky, and one bottle of cocktails designed for a starter.

If a miner had a fairly good week he might travel to San Francisco, bringing back some fresh bread, a bottle of brandy, a bottle of wine, and a bag of dried fruit at $1 a pound. Who can recall the name of the hungry, inventive soul who built an outdoor oven of adobe bricks in the Gold Rush country? Others were put up forthwith, and the bread problem was more or less solved.

One person remarked that "Americans either bake bread, using baking soda to make it rise, or make flapjacks." They cooked their beefsteak by twisting a piece of an old iron hoop into a serpentine form and laying it on the fire for a grill. "Makes a first-rate grid-

The German

The Russian

The Italian

dle on which a man could cook his steak to his own taste," according to one who knew how to do it. Natives of New South Wales dined at their Hangtown camp on beefsteak, "damper," a kind of biscuit, and tea. Wheat bread was made with flour ground on the premises.

Later, pack mule trains began to come in more or less regularly over the mountains, which were impassable for wheeled vehicles. Thirty to fifty mules were utilized in this manner and Mexicans excelled at this occupation. The mule trains brought fresh meat and there was no fear of famine for those who had the price. Dark cured hams, salt mackerel, barrels of rusty pork, canned oysters, and plenty of flour could be purchased.

WAGONS, WOMEN AND HOPES

There were few women in the diggings, but some enterprising ones opened boarding houses as the hordes of men continued to inundate the area, and never lacked for customers. A Madame Penn ran a boarding house, in addition to working at her rocker, a cradle-like device for washing gold. In the 1850's a Madame Salandie opened a butcher shop in Sonoratown, now Sonora, and conducted a money-lending business on the side. It is said that some of the numerous "soiled doves" married miners who struck it rich, moved to other locations and achieved a high degree of respectability.

On observing the primitive living conditions in the predominantly male population in the camps in 1849, one hardy emigrant lady from New England observed, "It is no more extraordinary for a woman (in California) to plough, dig and hoe with her own hands, if she have the will and strength to do so, than for men to do all their household labor for months." This was Mrs. D. B. Bates who later wrote a book on her experiences

entitled *Incidents on Land and Water*, or *Four Years on the Pacific Coast*. After wives began to arrive from the East, there were cook stoves in the Gold Mines in short order.

English-born James Hutchings, who came to California, made and lost a fortune, and founded California's earliest illustrated magazine, later operated a hotel of sorts, the Hutchings House in the Yosemite Valley. The informal accommodations and services were a standing joke among all those who visited the valley; however, the food was so delicious and the conversation so stimulating that the guests did not mind searching out their own silverware and serving themselves.

FARE AT HANGTOWN

> They suddenly stopped on a very high hill,
> And with wonder looked down upon old Placerville;
> Ike sighed when he said, as he cast his eyes down,
> Sweet Betsy my dearest, we've got to Hangtown.
> —Sweet Betsey from Pike

Old Dry Diggings, so called because of the rich waterless deposits, became known as Hangtown after a few examples of frontier justice had been meted out. As the population became more stable and prosperous, civic-minded citizens urged that the name be changed to Placerville. This was done, but the old picturesque moniker persisted for a long time thereafter. The town's population in 1858 was 5,000.

An 1850 bill of fare in Placerville's El Dorado Restaurant included soup for $1 or bean soup (oxtail) for $1.50; roasts of wild beef for $1.50; beef, upalong, for $1.00; beef with one potato (fair size) for $1.25; baked beans plain for 75 cents; baked beans greased for $1; and two potatoes for 75 cents. Sauerkraut was listed at $1; hash (low grade) for 75 cents, and hash (18 carat) for $1. Game included grizzly roast for $1 and whole jackrabbit for $1.50. Two codfish balls were 75

Troubles of a Forty-Niner.

GRIMES MADE HIS "PILE" THE FIRST YEAR.   THE SECOND, SENT FOR HIS DEAR WIFE.

Receives her on the wharf.   Very plain woman.

Wife becomes expensive.—Too many bills.

Wife wants to go to a ball.   Grimes objects.

She does go to ball, in spite of Grimes.

Deserts Grimes next day, for "cruelty." Threatens divorce.

The last of poor Grimes.—Desperate case of Suicide.

Troubles of a Forty-Niner

Early Life in California's Mother Lode

cents. Rice pudding plain was 75 cents, rice pudding with molasses was $1, and rice pudding with brandied peaches was $2. One square meal was $3, all payable in advance. "Gold scales at end of bar."

OTHER WAYS TO MAKE A STRIKE

One enterprising newcomer, Jacob Wright Harlan, sized up the supply situation upon his arrival in San Francisco and invested his funds in goods which he sold in his log-cabin store in Coloma for prices that netted a handsome profit. Flour was sold for $1 a pound, sugar for 75 cents a pound, beans for 50 cents a pound, bacon for 75 cents a pound, coffee for $1.50 a pound, tea for $3 a pound, and pilot bread for $1.25 a loaf. Dried beef was $1 a pound. Whisky was $8 a bottle. Coarse boots sold for $25 a pair, common

blankets for $32 a pair, shovels and picks for $16 or one ounce gold, and tin pans for $8 each.

These prices quickly doubled as the great influx of miners continued. Mr. Harlan later abandoned his store and took up farming. An acre of potatoes netted him $1250, as he sold them for 25 cents a pound.

A bronze plaque marks the site of John Studebaker's blacksmith shop in Placerville. Arriving there in the early 1850's with 50 cents in his pocket, he was hired within the hour to make wheelbarrows for the miners. A local restaurant owner trusted John and a friend for their first dinner at $3 each, which included hot roast beef and potatoes, baked beans, cold rabbit, bread, coffee and rice pudding with molasses. In a few years John returned to his native Indiana with $8000,

62

which he invested in his brothers' wagon manufactory. This later became the Studebaker Auto Manufacturing Company—one man's realization of the American Dream.

Boarding-house keepers in Hangtown, where the diggings were exceedingly rich, made their fortunes by feeding forty to fifty hungry miners three times a day on an oilcloth-covered table. The menu was salt pork, greasy steaks and pickles. Average eating time was three minutes.

When they had gold in their pockets food-obsessed miners indulged in the most expensive food and drink. Bayard Taylor, a writer who contributed to a popular magazine called the *Overland Monthly*, observed one group of miners who apparently had never before thought of luxury beyond a good steak and a glass of whisky, but were drinking champagne at $10 a bottle, eating tongue and sardines, while warming tin cans of turtle soup and lobster in their smoke-blackened camp kettle.

A man named Fash, operator of the only stove in Mokelumne Hill, charged miners a $1 fee for cooking on his large sheet-iron model. He had a ready market for all of the apple pies he cared to make, at a standing price of $2 each. He ran out of apples one day, but as he had an ample supply of beans on hand he made a bean pie. Touting it as a "novel and delicate luxury," he sold it quickly.

Eggs were in extremely short supply in the mining camps and on occasion the price reached $9 a dozen. Oysters were scarce and expensive. They were shipped from the coast up the Sacramento River.

Etienne Derbec, a traveling French journalist, reported from the gold fields in 1850 that bears were sought after and were worth 2000 francs, or $400 each. He also reported "they appear only on the tables of the wealthy, and are, along with some game birds,

which are worth their weight in gold, the *ne plus ultra* of a sumptuous feast."

THE NICETIES OF LIFE

An appetizing home-cooked meal, served on a clean white cloth, with adequate dishes and silver, was something to be remembered fondly as men worked in the wet, cold mines. It is reported that one hapless miner spent everything he earned on food. Oh, it was a cruel country in those wild, riproaring, rough and tumble, hazardous times.

Louis Fairchild, son of a prominent Wisconsin family, who labored six years in the gold fields before making a small fortune, wrote in his diary:

"My partners are good boys and we live very comfortable together, being situated nicely to live, having a good tent on logs for a store room and a good large fireplace, good large stone bake oven, fine brush house and sleeping room. Oh! we live up to the nines on pork and bread with few of the luxuries of life, but the staples taste well with a good appetite after a day's work."

If one had the wherewithal, one could enjoy most of the conveniences of ordinary life in the town of Sonora, which was named for the large number of miners from the Mexican state of Sonora. Ice cream and sherry cobblers were obtainable, snow being packed in on mules thirty or forty miles from the Sierra Nevada. Cocktails were well iced, and consumed in enormous quantities. The residents of a town which became known as French Corral, after a Frenchman who had built a corral there for his mules, also demanded and got ice cream.

Not all arrivals in California found conditions displeasing. The intrepid Louise Amelia Knapp Smith Clappe accompanied her physician husband to California and her letters back to New England, written under the pen name of Dame Shirley, earned her a secure niche in the history of the gold fields. Dame Shirley wrote enthusiastically about the fine dinner prepared for her and her doctor husband on their arrival at Rich Bar in 1851. It consisted of oyster soup, fried salmon caught from the American River, roast beef and boiled ham, fried oysters, potatoes and onions, mince pie, pudding made without eggs or milk, Madeira raisins, nuts, claret wine and champagne and coffee. Ned, the cook, had laid out this feast handsomely on a white cotton cloth, bordered in branches of white pine, to hide the inadequate length of the cloth. Napkins were of diaper cloth, fringed, folded and placed in tumblers.

Breakfast at the home of a ranchero in 1851 consisted of canned peaches, watermelons from the garden, oysters, salmon, beef roasted over the coals, chicken, vege-tables, tea, coffee, chocolate, champagne, claret, port wines and stronger spirits for those who wished them. Indian burro meat was regarded as a delicacy by the miners (well, some of them). Most meats were garnished with frijoles, as the observant reader has already noted.

Since boredom was the *bête noir* of the camps, it followed that gambling became the most popular pastime. Bull and bear fights provided exciting diversion, and in due time, traveling theatrical companies and popular entertainers toured the camps. Lotta Crabtree, Lola Montez, Adah Isaacs Menken, the Booths, prominent opera stars and minstrel troupes were among those who graced the rough boards in culturally starved outposts.

Downieville had its theater, and concerts

Miners' Ball in the Gold Fields

brightened the evenings. It also boasted billiard rooms, a daily newspaper, facilities for warm baths, and restaurants where men in red flannel shirts with bare arms spread a napkin over their muddy knees and studied the bill of fare for half an hour before they could make up their minds what to order for dinner.

The tame performing bear of Jackson's Camp, usually staked in front of Jackson's leading restaurant and saloon, was moved to a corner of a pigpen. Apparently resenting this indignity the bear avenged himself by killing a couple of the fat shoats. When the pig's owner called this deed to the attention of the bear's owner, the latter attempted to drag the bear away by his chain, but the bear rose up on his hind legs and hugged his master so tightly that he died three days later. Those who attended the wake were served bear steaks.

The Miners' Ten Commandments, composed and circulated by James Hutchings in leaflet form in 1853, were so well received that his profits from the sale of the leaflets netted him sufficient capital to begin publication of Hutchings' California Magazine in 1856. His commandments to California wives, also published in leaflet form in 1855, failed to catch on; however numbers IV and VII of these admonitions are pertinent to the theme of this book and we quote them here:

"IV. Thou shalt not starve thyself and family twenty-nine days out of thirty, to feast thy circle and give a party; nor by the purchase of expensive gewgaws and finery keep thyself and husband poor..."

"VII. Thou shalt not substitute sour looks for pickles; nor a fiery temper for stovewood; nor cross words for kindlings; nor trifling talk for light bread; nor tart language for dessert; nor excuses for anything..."

CHINESE IN CALIFORNIA

The face of California was altered by the arrival of shiploads of Chinese laborers who brought their strange customs and stranger food to this new land. While the Californios knew about rice and included it in their menus, corn was the favored staple. The Chinese composed their entire meals around rice, as their forefathers had done before them. Rice is mentioned in Chinese records as far back as 2800 B.C.

Chinese laborers were imported to the gold diggings under the sponsorship of companies formed for the express purpose of exploiting them. The recruits were mostly young, single men who hoped to accumulate a modest fortune which might enable them to return to their homeland, acquire a wife and lead their own free lives. This was a distant dream of most of them as the bulk of their earnings was turned over to their sponsors. However, some of the lucky ones "made their pile" and returned to China bearing their fortunes in tin boxes. Most, however, remained.

Thousands worked at Chinese Camp under the auspices of a group of Englishmen. Chinese Camp was east of present-day Placerville in the Southern Mines area. Marysville was heavily populated by Chinese, and the joss house, or temple, which remains there, is a popular tourist attraction to this day. Hostility of other miners was so fierce that the Chinese were not permitted to own claims in some places and had to content themselves with picking over claims abandoned by others. Many became discouraged and fled to San Francisco, opening restaurants or laundries, engaging in fishing for shrimp or becoming servants in the homes of the newly rich. By the end of 1853, there were approximately 17,000 Chinese in the state. Many had filtered into Southern California, Nevada, and other Western states where they

The Cradle and Manner of Using It

were treated with kindness.

The Chinese gold seekers who arrived at the diggings in the early days subsisted for a time on the roughest and plainest sort of food—beans, fish, rice, with little meat and no fresh vegetables—their diet differing little from that of the Caucasians. Invoices of the period of 1851-1854 show that they soon resumed their traditional eating habits as shipments bound for San Francisco from China included Chinese oranges, dried oysters, abalone, squid, shark fins, shrimps, cuttle fish, dry bean curd, dried mushrooms, bamboo shoots, yams, sugar, sweetmeats, peanut oil, salted cabbage, and the sauces to which they were accustomed. Each immigrant was permitted to bring two jars of ginger to California for his personal use.

Because of the prejudice against them the Chinese kept to themselves, clinging to their national costume of baggy black cotton trousers, rough blue tunics, "queer little black soft hats" or plaited bamboo, wide-brimmed hats, and hair in long black queues. They celebrated Chinese New Year and the Feast of the Dead with solemn ceremony. The dead were kept in leaden coffins and stored in a vault until they could be shipped back to China for burial. The New Year was celebrated with gifts, typical of which were the narcissus or Chinese sacred lily bulbs, in low bowls of water. Sweetmeats of litchi nuts, candied fruits and coconut, tangerines, chunks of sugar cane and jars of preserved ginger were given to friends, as well as fireworks of all kinds. More expensive gifts for special friends included plain and brocaded silk squares, Chinese slippers, fans, beautiful vases and bowls, figurines and hair ornaments.

Hop Loy, one gold seeker who gave up mining to run a laundry in Hangtown, sent his customers' laundry to China to be washed, requiring a six month's wait for its return. This practice was followed by other "launderers" in the mining camps and San Francisco. Those who did the actual work locally took the clothing to the nearest river and beat it on stones and boards. The clothing was ironed beautifully, but the beatings were hard on the fabric.

Another of the Chinese, Ah Date, was an enormous eater, and though he liked to work in the mines, he chose to become a cook for a wealthy family because of easy access to pork chops, thick juicy steaks and other good things to tempt the appetite. One evening his mistress requested hot cakes for the following morning breakfast, forgetting that she had not taught him how to make them American style. To her great surprise and that of her family, Ah Date served plain cake hot from the oven.

In the 1860's when the Central Pacific began construction of a railroad, the call went out again for Chinese workers and thousands

Ceremonial at a Chinese Grave

were imported from southern China for the dangerous, grueling labor of laying the tracks through the snow-packed Sierra Nevada. Caucasian laborers refused to do the work and the phrase "not a Chinaman's chance" was coined about this time, in reference to the hundreds of hapless Chinese who failed to survive the ordeal of building the road through the mountains in the broiling summer heat and the bone-chilling winter cold. Prosperity, and the anticipation of linking the East and the West by means of the railroads, brought peaceful coexistence between Orientals and Caucasians; however, when the railroad was completed in 1869 and the 15,000-odd Chinese turned out into the labor market again, violence flared up as it had a decade previously.

When the second wave of immigrants arrived for work on the railroads, supplies of their accustomed Chinese foods were shipped to a company store kept in several cars at the end of the track, so that they could acquire foods to their liking and prepare them as they wished. Charles Nordhoff reported in his book, *California, a Book for Travelers and Settlers*, that the Chinese had a better diet than the "beef, beans, bread and butter, and potatoes of white laborers." He mentioned also that the railroad store sold pipes, bowls, chop-sticks, joss paper and Chinese writing paper, Chinese shoes, and scales—"for the Chinaman in particular, who re-weighs everything he buys as soon as he gets it to camp."

The hard-working, ancestor-worshipping Chinese have added color and flavor to California, and their somewhat exotic cookery lends piquancy to the cuisine. San Francisco's Chinatown, a city within a city, is one of the most publicized popular attractions of that Western Mecca.

Recipes

HOME MADE YEAST

The amazing ability of certain yeast plants to change sugar into carbon dioxide led to their use in leavening bread to cause a mixture of flour and yeast to "rise." In a proper atmosphere of moisture and warm temperature yeast plants multiply rapidly. Pioneers in Gold Rush days knew well how to grow an active colony of plants; then the mixture could be cooled and kept for weeks ready to use as a bread starter.

Boil 2 ounces of hops in 1 gallon of water for a half-hour. Strain mixture into an earthen bowl and cool to the warmth of new milk. Add ½ pound of brown sugar and a small handful of salt (about two tablespoons). Stir well. Take part of the liquid and beat with one pound of flour until smooth and free of lumps. Add rest of liquid and mix well. Set aside in a warm place and let stand for two days, stirring often, after which time add three pounds of boiled and mashed potatoes. Keep in a warm place for another day, stirring often. On the fourth day, strain, pour into a bottle and cork tightly. The yeast can be used on the sixth day. Shake bottle well before using.

SOURDOUGH STARTER

In earlier days homemade yeast was used to create a sponge of fresh active yeast and was always kept on hand. This starter is made with commercial yeast, readily available today in any grocery.

2 cups flour
2 cups lukewarm water
1 yeast cake or package of dry yeast

Mix flour, lukewarm water and yeast thoroughly. Set overnight in warm draft-free place. By the following morning the mixture should have a bubbly surface and pleasant yeasty odor. It is ready for use.

SOURDOUGH BREAD

Not too long ago bread was baked as needed and often was a daily chore.

Starter sponge
4 cups flour
2 tablespoons sugar
1 teaspoon salt
2 tablespoons lard, melted

To starter add equal quantities of flour and lukewarm water to make about 3 cups of sponge. Let stand 6 to 8 hours or overnight in a warm location. It should bubble and emit a yeasty odor. Take out 2 cups of this sponge, leaving remainder for next starter. To these two cups of sponge add flour, sugar, salt and lard, and mix until a soft dough is formed. If dough is stiff, add a little milk; if too soft, add more flour. Knead for 3 or 4 minutes on a clean floured surface. Shape into 2 loaves and place in well greased loaf pans. Cover and set in a warm place until loaves have swelled to double size. Bake 50 to 60 minutes in a preheated moderate oven (350°). Bread is done when loaves are golden brown and shrink away from sides of pan. Turn out on rack and rub top surface with butter or lard.

INDIAN BREAD

This early 1850 version of a steamed quick bread combines equal portions of wheat flour and corn meal or masa, called Indian meal. The saleratus called for is, of course, baking soda.

2 quarts buttermilk
⅔ teacupsful molasses
1 tablespoon saleratus
1 teaspoon salt
Indian meal
Wheat flour

Mix batter as thick as can be stirred, with equal parts of Indian meal and wheat or graham meal. Let stand in warm place ½ hour to rise. Steam it 2½ or 3 hours. Makes 2 loaves in 2 quart basins.

SOUR MILK CORN BREAD

The corn tortilla was firmly implanted in the Mexican tradition but many of the newcomers from the eastern and southern states preferred the corn bread and muffins to which they were accustomed.

2 cups water-ground corn meal
2 teaspoons baking powder
½ cup flour
1 teaspoon soda
1 teaspoon salt
2 cups sour milk
2 tablespoons bacon drippings
1 unbeaten egg

Set square baking pan in hot oven (400°). Mix dry ingredients with milk, beating well to remove all lumps. Stir in egg and drippings. Remove hot pan from oven and pour batter into it. Bake 15 minutes.

FLAPJACKS

Flapjacks, or pancakes, were a great standby in the gold diggings or on the emigrant trail, when a quickly made bread would satisfy the appetite. This fancy recipe uses eggs but there are ample records that they often were unavailable.

Pulverize two level teaspoons soda very fine before measuring and thoroughly mix with one quart of flour. Make a batter of this flour, a quart of sour milk and three egg yolks, beaten, and a tablespoon of butter or lard. Add whites of eggs which have been whipped, just before baking on griddle. These cakes may also be made without eggs.

DAMPER

A "down-under" recipe for bread, requiring only flour and water, was a method used by Australian miners.

Work flour and water into dough, adding a pinch or two of salt. Rake down a good hardwood fire, place dough on hot ashes, and smother in more hot ashes to a depth of two or three inches. Pile more still-burning embers on top. In a few minutes, feel crust to determine whether it is sufficiently cooked.

SPANISH CHICKEN PIE

Blending of cuisines is plainly evident in this casserole-type dish of chicken or other fowl, fortified with sausage, peppers and wine, and presented in the favorite American pie fashion.

Take one pint of cold chicken, duck, or any game, cut it into flakes and place it in a pudding dish which has been lined with a thin crust. On the layer of meat place a layer of sweet red peppers, seeds removed and cut in slices; next a layer of thinly sliced bologna sausage, and so on until the dish is full. Over this pour a glass of claret into which has been rubbed two tablespoons of flour. Cover with a thin crust of pastry and bake until crust is brown.

MEXICAN CHICKEN BALL SOUP
An American adaptation of an old California dish, this recipe from the mid-1800's uses green pepper in place of chili peppers.

1 chicken
1 small clove garlic
2 small onions
½ green pepper
1 teaspoon spearmint
1 egg
2 teaspoons salt
1 teaspoon black pepper
3 tablespoons flour
1 teaspoon lard

Cook chicken until tender. Remove meat from the bones and chop very fine with the garlic, one onion, green pepper and mint. Mix with other ingredients and roll in balls about the size of a pigeon's egg. Mince remaining onion, fry in fat until it browns in a saucepan, add two quarts of boiling water, drop the balls in and let boil for an hour. These may also be made of veal or lamb.

FRIED ABALONE
Abalone, one of California's native shellfish, found its way into the repertoire of home cooks, as indicated by this contribution to the *California Farmer*.

Remove meat from shell and cut all black part away with a very sharp knife. Remove entrails. Trim off part that adheres to rock. Slice ¼ inch thick, lay on wooden board, and pound until meat becomes soft. Dip in egg batter, then in cracker crumbs, and fry about

1½ minutes in butter, bacon drippings or olive oil. Do not overcook. Salt while frying.

OYSTER STEW
A familiar dish which was pronounced a "royal stew," is made here without cream or milk.

Drain liquid from oysters into saucepan, let boil, skim, and season with butter and pepper. Add oysters, let come to a boil only, season with salt and serve.

STEAMED OYSTERS
Food was of the coarsest kind out in the gold diggings, and those miners who recalled better days and a softer life "back East" dreamed constantly of good things to eat. Oysters were a favorite delicacy. This recipe gives two methods for preparing steamed oysters.

Lay some oysters in the shell in an airtight vessel, placing the upper shell downward so the liquor will not run out when they open. Set them over a pot of boiling water where they will get the steam and boil hard for 20 minutes. If the oysters are open they are done; if not, steam till they do open. Serve at once and eat hot, with salt and a bit of butter. Or, wash and drain one quart of select oysters, put in pan and place in steamer over boiling water, cover and steam till oysters are plump with edges ruffled; place in heated dish with butter, pepper and salt, and serve.

HANGTOWN FRY—OYSTER OMELET
Considerable legend has grown around this recipe as to its origin. One story has it that a hairy, unkempt miner from Shirttail Bend blew into Hangtown, now Placerville, tossed a handful of gold nuggets on a table at the Cary House and demanded the most expensive meal the cook knew how to prepare. The cook, without batting an eye, allowed as how eggs and oysters best met these specifications, and set about putting together a masterpiece. Using the small Pacific Coast Olympia oysters and good eggs, the following dish was set before the famished customer.

12 oysters
9 eggs
3 tablespoons butter

Flour
Fine cracker crumbs
Salt and pepper

Drain oysters well on clean cloth, then dip each one in flour seasoned with salt and pepper, then in well-beaten egg and then in cracker crumbs. Fry in heated butter until nicely browned on both sides. Beat remaining eggs with salt and pepper and pour over oysters. Cook until eggs are set. Turn with a large spatula and cook for a couple minutes longer. Serve immediately. Will fill up one famished gold miner or four ordinary hungry diners.

HANGTOWN FRY WITH BACON

Some cling to the Hangtown-Fry-with-Bacon theory. Here is a version currently served in the Blue Bell Coffee Shop, a Placerville restaurant.

3 Eastern oysters
2 strips of bacon
2 large fresh eggs

Dredge oysters with flour, dip in beaten egg, then coat with fine bread crumbs. Place in hot greased skillet and fry. In another skillet, fry bacon, drain, and return to skillet, placing strips about one or two inches apart.

Beat eggs lightly and pour over bacon. Cook until almost done. By this time the oysters should be browned on both sides. Place over egg-bacon mixture, folding over each end to make a 3-fold omelet. Serve with a lemon wedge. Serves one.

PICKLED OYSTERS

Oysters, oysters—as Ettrick Shepherd wrote in 1828, "There's really no end in natur to the eatin' of oisters."

Drain the juice into a dish and save. To one can of oysters put two quarts of water, made as salt as common brine. Then put as many oysters in a stewpan as will cover the bottom and let them scald until the fringe around the oyster begins to curl up. Repeat until all are done. Put into crock, first one layer of oysters, then of mace and cloves. Add vinegar to the juice to suit taste, and pour over oysters.

Use an ounce of mace, an ounce of cloves, and a few grains of pepper to make spice mixture.

BAKED SALMON

It was a happy miner who chanced to feast on this dish.

3 or 4 pound salmon
½ cup olive oil
3 onions, sliced

Pour olive oil into baking pan and heat. Season fish well with salt and pepper and place in pan. Lay sliced onions on top and cover with heavy paper. Bake in hot oven for 45 minutes. Remove paper, pour ¼ cup sherry over fish and continue baking until brown.

VENISON RIBS

These ribs are best lightly done; otherwise they become tough, dry and tasteless.

Cut ribs into 3-inch squares and broil in medium-hot oven, basting frequently with lard, butter or drippings. Serve when lightly browned, adding salt and pepper to taste.

BEAR STEAKS

The California bear population had increased over the years because of an over-supply of free-ranging mission and rancho cattle. The bears in turn became prey of hungry gold hunters and others, who relished fresh bear steak, done rare, and paid premium prices for it.

Cut the steaks fairly thin. Place on a hot broiler. When partly cooked, turn, and add salt and pepper. Do not overcook.

BEAR PAWS BOILED

A favorite of the Mountain Men.

2 pounds skinned front bear paws
¼ pound salt pork
Salt and pepper

Clean paws well and marinate in vinegar if available, as it is a good tenderizer. Place in a deep pot, cover with water, add salt and pepper, and simmer for about 8 hours. Add more water if needed during cooking. Slice and serve.

JACK RABBIT STEW

A native of western America, the jack rabbit had healthy long legs and fine dark meat which was prized for stews.

Cut up rabbit and soak in salted water for several hours. Slice an onion and brown lightly in butter or lard. Brown rabbit in this, season with pepper and salt, cover with water and simmer gently until tender.

CHINESE ROAST DUCK

Chinese gold diggers brought their traditions and food with them. Roast duck was a dish served on holy days, New Year's, at marriages and other special occasions. This recipe features a stuffing of Chinese vegetables and dried black mushrooms.

Dress a 5 to 6 pound tame duck and chop off the wings close to the breast. To prepare stuffing, mix one cup of dry Chinese vegetables, one cup of black mushrooms which have been soaked in hot water for 30 minutes, and add enough vegetables to moisten. Rub inside and outside of duck with Chinese soy sauce, salt, and a little pepper. Stuff with dressing and fasten with skewers. Roast for an hour in a hot oven (400° to 425°) basting several times while cooking. Serve with steamed rice and Chinese tea.

CHINESE KIDNEY FLOWERS

This dish with a flowery name is said to have been introduced in San Francisco by an unidentified Chinese cook.

2 pig kidneys
6 water chestnuts, sliced
1 cucumber, sliced
1 Chinese onion, chopped
Soy sauce
Yellow wine
Bean starch
Salt
Sugar

Soak kidneys in salt water for an hour. Dice and simmer in wine until tender. Add water chestnuts, onion and cucumber and cook for 10 minutes. Blend in bean starch, sauce, salt and sugar, heat through, and serve.

SPICED TONGUE, CHINESE STYLE

Despite their preference for pork, the Chinese knew what to do with the always-plentiful beef in California.

1 beef tongue
2 medium onions, sliced
6 whole cloves
1 teaspoon ground cinnamon
6 whole peppercorns
3 tablespoons sugar
¼ cup raisins
3 tablespoons flour
Vinegar
Juice of 1 lemon
Salt

Simmer tongue with onions, salt and peppercorns until tender. Peel off skin and remove small bones. Make sauce by simmering vinegar, raisins, cloves, sugar and cinnamon until raisins are soft and puffy. Thicken with flour, add lemon juice and simmer 5 minutes longer. Slice tongue, place on platter and pour sauce over it.

HONGKONG ROAST PORK

A spicy treatment of pork which would be suitable today for cocktail tidbits or as the main course, with vegetables.

3 pounds lean pork loin
4 tablespoons Chinese soy sauce
1 tablespoon strong prepared mustard

Cut pork into long strips about 2 inches thick, removing all fat. Mix soy sauce and mustard, roll pork in this sauce and place in a roasting pan. Cook in a hot oven until brown, turning and basting every 10 minutes.

AMERICAN BAKED HAM

Hams available in the mining camps were not the pink, oozy, anemic-looking ones which are sold in today's supermarkets. In those days hams were rubbed well with salt and hung in the meat-house, to be cured by hanging over a slow-burning apple-wood fire, or hung in the chimney for a month or so. The texture was fine, the meat a rich, dark red, the taste substantial. It might have been a bit salty if the meat had not been properly treated before cooking.

Pour boiling water over ham and let it stand until cool. Scrape clean with a coarse hairbrush used for this purpose. Place in a clean boiler with cold water enough to cover; bring to the boiling point and then place on back part of stove to simmer steadily for six or seven hours, or till tender when pierced with a fork. Be careful to keep water at boiling point and not to allow it to go much above it. Turn ham once or twice while cooking. When done, take up and put into baking-pan. When cool enough to handle, remove skin by dipping hands in cold water, taking the skin between your fingers and peeling as you would an orange. Set in a moderate oven, placing the lean side of the ham downward, and if you like, sift over pounded or rolled crackers. Bake one hour. Baking brings out a great quantity of fat, leaving the skin much more delicate. If desired, the ham may be glazed with strong meat jelly or any savory jelly at hand, boiled down rapidly until it is like glue. Brush this jelly over the ham when cool and it makes an elegant dish. The nicest portion of a baked ham may be served in slices, and the ragged parts and odds and ends chopped fine for sandwiches, or by adding three eggs to one pint of chopped ham a delicious omelet may be made. If the ham is very salty, it should lie in water overnight.

POTATO-ONION CASSEROLE

Here is one of my own treasured heirloom recipes from yesteryear, and it always seems to be well-liked. There is never any left over. It may be close to the one written about so glowingly by Dame Shirley (Louise Clappe) upon her arrival in California from New England.

4 large potatoes (cobblers are best)
2 medium onions
5 tablespoons butter (or ham fat)
Salt and pepper

About an hour before you are ready to cook, slice onions very thin and soak in water to which two tablespoons of salt have been added. When ready to use, drain well, patting with towel to remove all moisture. Put in a heavy skillet with 5 tablespoons of butter

or ham fat, and cook until onions are soft and faintly golden. Peel potatoes and slice paper thin. Place a layer of potatoes in a shallow two-quart baking pan, well buttered. Cover with a layer of the onions which have been well drained, and season with salt and pepper. Repeat layers, adding seasonings after each one, ending with a layer of potatoes on top. Pour the liquid from the onions over the potatoes and dot liberally with butter. Add just enough hot water to barely cover potatoes. Bake in a preheated oven (375°) for 30 minutes, or until done.

GOLD NUGGET PORK AND BEANS

Miners who did not have ovens could still bake a pot of beans by placing the pot in a hole beneath the camp fire, though it may have required a little time and patience to keep the fire going. This recipe for a dark golden brown pot of beans approximates one in the collection of old family recipes compiled by the Ladies of Columbia Church of the '49ers. It came from New England.

1 quart white navy beans
½ teaspoon soda
½ pound salt side pork
Molasses (about 1 cup)
Salt and pepper

Boil beans with soda for 30 minutes. Drain. Wash pork and place in earthen bean pot. Add beans, salt, pepper and molasses. Cover with boiling water, set lid on pot and bake in moderate oven (350°) for six hours or until done. If necessary, add a little more water. Remove lid about 45 minutes to an hour before serving time and add more seasonings if desired.

MINER'S BAKED BEANS

American immigrants became partial to the good Mexican flavorings of tomato, chili, and green peppers, featured in this slowly baked bean pot.

2 cups pinto beans
¼ pound salt pork, diced
2 onions, diced
1 can tomatoes
½ ounce chili powder

2 garlic cloves, minced
1 green bell pepper, sliced

Wash beans well, discarding imperfect ones. Combine with all ingredients except pepper and place in large earthen pot. Cover with about 5 cups of water. Arrange pepper rings on top, cover pot tightly and cook in slow oven (325°) until tender. Add more water during cooking, if needed. Serve with sourdough bread.

SPANISH RICE
Arroz de California

The dish known as Spanish rice is distinctly Californian, not Spanish or Mexican but a blend. This recipe includes the Spanish staple of rice and the familiar Mexican ingredients of tomato and chili. As with most recipes there are variations even in the cooking method. The dish can be prepared on top of the stove but this recipe calls for baking in the oven.

1 cup raw rice
1 small onion, chopped fine
½ clove garlic (optional)
2 green chilies, minced
¼ teaspoon pepper
2 large ripe tomatoes
2 tablespoons olive oil or drippings
1 teaspoon salt

Wash and drain rice. Heat fat in skillet, add rice, and cook over low flame until golden, stirring frequently. Add onion, garlic and chilies and cook 5 minutes longer. Chop tomatoes, stir in with salt and pepper and cook 5 minutes. Pour into an earthenware baking dish, cover tightly and bake in moderately hot oven (375°) for about an hour. Stir once with a fork while rice is cooking and if it seems dry, add one or two tablespoons of boiling water. Rice should be dry and fluffy when done.

EGG NOODLES

One of the stand-bys of yesteryear is homemade noodles. Generally considered German in origin, they are a substantial accompaniment to soups, stews and roasts. Some modern cooks still "roll their own."

2 eggs

⅛ teaspoon salt
1 cup flour

Beat eggs until frothy, add salt and mix in flour, adding more if necessary to obtain a stiff dough. Let stand for an hour. Roll dough into paper-thin sheets and spread them out on cloths to dry. Before sheets are too dry to handle, roll them into cylinders and cut into strips. Separate strips and allow to dry thoroughly. Drop into boiling water and cook for 20 minutes.

SAUERKRAUT

One of the many ways we are pampered today is in food preparation. This recipe is a reminder of the laborious process needed to prepare foods such as sauerkraut, which needed careful attention. The wooden beetle mentioned here is a pestle.

Slice cabbage fine on a slaw-cutter. Line the bottom and sides of an oaken barrel or keg with cabbage leaves, put in a layer of the sliced cabbage about six inches in depth, sprinkle lightly with salt, and pound with a wooden beetle until the cabbage is a compact mass. Add another layer of cabbage, repeating the operation, pounding well each layer, until the barrel is full to within six inches of the top. Cover with cabbage leaves, then a cloth, next a board cut to fit loosely on the inside of the barrel, kept well down with a heavy weight. If the brine has not raised within two days, add enough water, with just enough salt to taste, to cover the cabbage. Examine every two days, and add water as before, until brine raises and scum forms. Lift off cloth carefully, so that the scum may adhere, wash well in several cold waters, wring dry and replace, repeating this operation as the scum rises, at first every other day and then once a week, until the acetous fermentation ceases, which will take from three to six weeks. Up to this time keep warm in the kitchen, then remove to a dry, cool cellar, unless made early in the fall, when it may be at once set in the cellar. One pint of salt to a whole barrel of cabbage is a good proportion; some also sprinkle in whole black pepper.

GINGERBREAD

An all-time favorite, especially when served with whipped cream or hard sauce.

½ cup lard or butter
½ cup sugar
1 egg
2½ cups flour, sifted
1½ teaspoons baking soda
1 teaspoon cinnamon
1 teaspoon ginger
½ teaspoon cloves
½ teaspoon salt
1 cup molasses
⅛ cup hot water

Cream shortening until light and fluffy, add sugar and beat until smooth. Beat in egg and continue beating until light. Sift together flour, soda, cinnamon, cloves, salt and ginger. Combine molasses and water and add to batter in thirds, alternating with dry ingredients. Beat until smooth, pour into greased pan and bake in moderate oven (350°) for 50 to 60 minutes. Cool for 10 minutes before turning from pan.

SODA CRACKER PIE

One California pioneer who came to the state as a child later recalled that in 1852 apples were a dollar a pound, and "we young people all craved a piece of mother's apple pie to appease our homesick feelings." Mother complied with a deception, concocted of homemade soda crackers, heavily soaked in citric acid. The recipe became popular and numerous variations have been found in old recipe books. It should be noted that soda crackers of 1852 were quite different from the crispy thin varieties of today. Those of yesteryear were huge stick-to-the-ribs, no-nonsense crackers.

Break 4 soda crackers into an earthen bowl. Pour over them a pint of cold water, made very tart with citric acid. When soft, but not mashed, remove the soda crackers to your pie plate, with the under crust already on, then sift over them two tablespoons of light brown sugar, with a little allspice and cinnamon added for flavor. The brown sugar and spices supply the requisite color. Cover with a prettily perforated top crust and bake in a very quick oven for a few moments.

WALNUT RAISIN COOKIES

Walnuts and raisins became plentiful crops in California in later days, but in the Gold Rush period often had to be imported.

1½ cups brown sugar
1 cup lard or butter
3 eggs
2 cups flour
1 teaspoon soda
1 teaspoon cloves
1 teaspoon cinnamon
1 cup walnuts, chopped
1½ cups raisins
½ teaspoon vanilla (optional)

Cream butter well and add sugar, beating until batter is smooth. Whip eggs lightly and add alternately with dry ingredients which have been sifted together. Stir in walnuts. Drop by teaspoonfuls onto greased cookie sheet and bake in moderate oven 12 to 15 minutes.

CARAMEL PUDDING

The basic ingredient of this interesting pudding is bread, and the cooking procedure demonstrates how cooks managed to get by without fancy kitchen equipment, and maybe even ovens.

4 slices bread (lightly buttered)
⅔ cup brown sugar (firmly packed)
2 eggs, beaten with a fork
2 cups milk
½ teaspoon salt
½ teaspoon vanilla
¼ cup raisins

Cut bread into small cubes and place in heavy saucepan. Sprinkle sugar and raisins over the top. Mix eggs and milk with salt and vanilla and pour over bread mixture. Do not stir. Cover and cook very slowly for an hour.

FRUIT PUDDING

We are reminded that pudding was on the menu of the feast enjoyed by Dame Shirley, prepared by the master cook at Rich Bar in the gold fields. She offered no description of it except that it contained neither eggs nor milk. It may have been similar to this recipe.

Stew dried apples, apricots or other fruit,

until tender. Drain. Make a rich soda-biscuit dough, roll to half an inch thick. Spread sweetened fruit on dough, roll up, tuck ends in and prick deeply with a fork. Lay in a steamer and place over a kettle of boiling water. Cook for an hour and three quarters. Or, wrap in a cloth, tie up the ends and baste up sides, put in a kettle of boiling water and boil an hour and a half or more, keeping the water boiling constantly. Cut across, and eat with sweetened cream or butter and sugar.

CREAMY RICE PUDDING

To be served hot or cold, this old-fashioned pudding is slowly baked, then served with good maple syrup.

1/4 cup raw rice
4 cups rich milk
1/2 teaspoon salt
1/2 cup brown sugar
1/4 teaspoon cinnamon

Stir three cups of milk into rice. Mix salt, cinnamon and sugar, and add to rice, stirring until sugar is dissolved. Pour into buttered baking dish and bake in slow oven (300°) until rice is very soft (about 3 hours) adding remaining cup of milk as needed. Serve hot or cold, with maple syrup.

CRYSTALLIZED CHINESE ORANGES

The Chinese do not top off their meals with cakes, pies, ices or other desserts as we do in the Western world. Candied fruit is served throughout the year, most particularly at New Year's. Crystallized orange is taken to Chinese temples as food offerings. The plethora of California citrus fruit is a boon to the cook who wishes to try this recipe.

Take oranges not quite ripe, cut off the colored part of the rind carefully with a sharp knife, cut a hole where the stem has been, sufficiently large to take out all the inside. Be careful not to change the form of the orange. When the oranges are clean inside and outside, cover them with water and salt for 24 hours. Change the water, but this time omit the salt. Do this for 5 or 6 days, or until all the bitterness has disappeared. Drain, place oranges in boiling water and boil for 20 minutes. Remove from pan and drop into cold water immediately, allowing them to drain while preparing the syrup. The syrup is made by putting equal quantities by weight, of sugar and fruit in enough water to give the consistency of ordinary syrup. Boil the fruit in the sryup over a slow fire until the syrup attains the consistency of honey. Take the fruit out and let it dry in a convenient place.
NOTE: Small lemons or limes are crystallized by the same process, except that they are simply cut in two before being placed in the brine.

COFFEE

Who will try this distilled brew?

Put ground coffee into a wide mouthed bottle overnight. Pour rather more than 1/2 pint of water upon each ounce and a half, and cork bottle. In the morning, loosen cork, put bottle into a pan of hot water, and bring the water to boiling. The coffee is then poured off clear and the latter portion strained; that which is not drank (sic) immediately is kept closely stopped and heated as wanted.

SHERRY COBBLER

Here is a pleasantly fizzy drink made with sherry.

1 part good dry sherry
2 parts water
Orange slices
Lemon peel
1/2 teaspoon baking soda

Mix sherry and water gently and pour over ice in pitcher or tall glass. Drop orange slices into glass and place twist of lemon peel on edge of glass. Add soda and stir vigorously. Serve immediately.

HANGOVER REMEDY

Highly recommended for heavy heads is a soothing, thickened milk brew, with a dash of brandy and nutmeg.

Put two tablespoons of flour in a frying pan and cook until golden brown. Add a quart of milk and stir well. Cook a few minutes, then add salt. Put in a scant jigger of brandy and allow to cool. Season with a little nutmeg and eat with a spoon.

Chapter V

The Birth of
Cities and Cuisines

*They come from the East, from the North
and the South,
A look in the eye and a set to the mouth,
Joining the others of epoch and plain,
Taking their place in the wagon train . . .*
—GORDON W. NORRIS

Donner Party on the Way to the Summit

An Evening at Sea Enroute to California

A Rolling "Pioneer Palace Car"

The strong westward push of the adventurous itchy-footed Americans, coupled with the increasingly numerous printed accounts praising the climate, fertility and spaciousness of California, had begun to gain momentum before the Gold Rush. John Bidwell organized a colonizing expedition to California in 1841 and his successful journey encouraged many who were hesitant about starting out. However, the tragic account of the ill-fated Donner party, which was stranded for the winter in the Sierra Nevada where nearly all perished, winnowed out the timid and cautious. The hardships of the long trek were very real and awesome. Those who fell on the way rested in rude graves hastily dug and roughly marked, soon to be obliterated by time and the elements.

J. Goldsborough Bruff, who came over the Lassen Trail, made notations in his diary of the Gold Rush days of many of these lonely markers and took care to copy the epitaphs. One of them was composed by Bruff himself after assisting a bereaved mother and her daughters when the father and three sons were crushed to death in their sleep by a falling tree:

> *Their journey is ended, their toils are all past,*
> *Together they slept, in this false world, their last.*
> *They here sleep together, in one entombed,*
> *Side by side, as they slept, on the night they were doom'd.*

Nevertheless, glowing reports of the richest, most beautiful, and healthiest country in the world, and the vast possibilities of the granary of the Pacific, encouraged optimistic friends and relatives to hasten their departure for this Promised Land. Those who had read in their geography textbooks in the early 1850's that "the soil and climate of California were not adapted to agricultural purposes," lived to snicker at the ignorance of the authors.

The blending of the Corn, Wheat and Rice cultures began, gradually at first, but after the Gold Rush soon exploded into fantastic acceleration. Those emigrants who had arrived prior to 1848 began to prosper beyond their wildest imaginings. The tremendous upsurge of demands for food, clothing, and other necessities of life in the mines provided a ready market for anything the ranches could produce. The merchants found they could sell anything edible, wearable and usable, with buyers clamoring for more, more, more. The state's 100,000 population of 1849 zoomed to over 380,000 by 1860—proof that aside from the phenomenal growth during the height of the Gold Rush, there were thousands of willing believers in California's great future.

FOOD FOR NEWCOMERS

In January of 1847, Edwin Bryant, author of a much-read volume entitled *What I Saw in California*, stayed overnight with a group of travelers in a private Los Angeles residence. He was quite interested in the tortilla-making procedure of an Indian girl and related:

"An Indian muchacha crushed wheat between two stones, after which the ranchera cleansed it of chaff, dust and insects by tossing the grains in a basket, after which she sifted it through a coarse sieve. Water was added to make dough, and the dough was kneaded by the muchacha. An iron plate was placed over a rudely constructed furnace and heated. The dough was shaped by hand into tortillas which were slapped onto the red-hot plate and cooked."

The tortillas were served to Bryant and his party with stewed jerked beef with chili seasoning, milk, and cheese cakes.

J. Goldsborough Bruff described in his

diary one meal he shared with a cultured California-bound family who were camped in the shadow of the Sierra Nevada in 1849. They served him venison potpie, piñole, bread, coffee, grape pie, grapes, poetry and botany.

Following the Constitutional Convention of 1849, a grand ball was held in Monterey. The ladies were richly dressed in velvets, brocades and satins; the gentlemen's attire showed considerable variety, and one fancy dresser laid out $50 for his second-hand patent leather boots. The midnight supper did ample justice to the historic occasion. Tables were laden with roast turkey, roast pig, beef, tongue, patés, wines, liquors of various kinds, and coffee in abundance to clear heads after the rigors of the meeting. Convention delegates were still laughing at the discomfited military officer who had misun-derstood "free-holders" to mean "frijoles" during that day's proceedings, and asked why food entered the discussion.

California inns were few and far between before the Gold Rush, but stopping places sprang up swiftly between 1849 and 1860, offering various degrees of comfort and cuisine. In 1850 the City Hotel in San Jose offered eggs for breakfast at 50 cents and potatoes as the main dinner course at $2 a plate. Not until the mid-1850's did that city boast of several hostelries where guests could obtain choice wines, liquors, cigars and good food. In 1851 the Crescent Hotel in Sacramento served breakfast by candlelight. The meal did not do justice to the romantic setting, however, as it consisted of beans, venison and coffee.

Sir Henry Huntley, an English nobleman, wrote his impressions of his journey from

A Festive Family Dinner in 1857

Making Picnic Chowder at the River

Sacramento to Placerville in 1852, entitled *California: Its Gold and Its Inhabitants.* An American family with whom he dined served roast duck and oyster pie, gooseberry tart, cheese and preserved ginger. On another day his supper at Hickman's ranch in the gold country consisted of stewed tripe, pork chops and "good fresh butter."

The January 5, 1853 issue of *California Farmer* carried an editorial addressed to the question, "Is California Fit for a Home?" The writer stated that newcomers were so struck with wonder and astonishment at the splendor of California's general appearance that they went back home at once and had their families join them.

Some food prices in 1855 were salmon for 12½ cents retail, potatoes for 2½ cents a pound, pork for $16.50 a barrel, and flour for $11 to $13 a barrel. Butter was 45 to 50 cents a pound and lard in thirty-pound tins was 14 cents per pound.

The visitor from back East was often quite surprised to find ornate Victorian residences, or old-style bungalows, as he traveled around the new state. During the prosperous 1850's many homes were built by newly arrived carpenters, who were unfamiliar with California architecture. Lumber being scarce, those able to afford it ordered houses pre-cut and ready for assembling, and had them shipped around the Horn. Charles Dickens, who had visited the United States first in 1841 and had commented derisively on

American manners, fourteen years later toured parts of California and reported on the iron houses which were manufactured in Belgium and shipped to San Francisco:

"They are too hot in the sun, cool too rapidly, and toward dawn are ice houses. When warm the anti-corrosive paint on them emits a sickly smell, the rain falls on the roof noisily like small shot, and if such houses become implicated in a fire they first expand and then collapse, and tumble down with astonishing rapidity."

LUXURIES OF STAGE TRAVEL

There's no respect for youth or age,
On board of a California stage,
But pull and haul about for seats,
As bedbugs do among the sheets...
–J. Hutchinson

The Pony Express in the north and the Butterfield Overland Stage in the south served as links between East and West at a crucial time when the Union was splitting apart. While it is doubtful that favorite recipes were exchanged by mail, at the prevailing rate of about $5 for one-half ounce, it is reasonable to assume that news of the fabulous variety of fruits and vegetables available for experimentation by the home cook was passed along to family and friends back East.

Traveling journalists, ladies enroute to join their sweethearts or husbands, adventurers, and others drawn to California, complained bitterly about the rigors of stagecoach accommodations. In due time, the luxurious, for that day, Concord coaches were obtainable from the East, and Wells-Fargo, leading transportation company, laid down the *Stagecoach Riders' Nine Commandments*, intended to eliminate some of the minor annoyances. It was stated that adherence to the following rules would insure a pleasant trip for all:

1. Abstinence from liquor is requested. If you must drink, share your bottle; otherwise you will appear to be selfish and unneighborly.

2. If ladies are present, gentlemen are urged to forego smoking cigars and pipes, as the odor of same is repugnant to the gentle sex. Chewing tobacco is permitted, but spit with the wind, not against it.

3. Gentlemen must refrain from using rough language in the presence of ladies and children.

4. Buffalo robes are provided for your comfort during cold weather. Hogging robes will not be tolerated and the offender will be made to ride with the driver.

5. Don't snore loudly while sleeping or use your fellow passenger's shoulder for a pillow. He (or she) may not understand and friction may result.

6. Firearms may be kept on your person for use in emergencies. Do not fire them for pleasure or shoot at wild animals as the sound riles the horses.

7. In the event of runaway horses, remain calm. Leaping from the coach in panic will leave you injured, at the mercy of the elements, hostile Indians and hungry coyotes.

8. Forbidden topics of discussion are stagecoach robberies and Indian uprisings.

9. Gents guilty of unchivalrous behavior toward lady passengers will be put off the stage. It's a long walk back. A word to the wise is sufficient.

Frank Marryatt, a visiting English journalist, complained that Concord stage coach travelers were required to eat at specified hours, dining on tough beefsteak, boiled potatoes, stewed beans, dried-up apple pie, and the ever-present jug of molasses. In the manner of his countryman, Charles Dickens, Marryatt caustically reported that the American diner would taste the food with the point of his knife before digging in.

Corner of San Francisco's Plaza in 1850   *CENTURY MAGAZINE,* CALIFORNIA STATE LIBRARY

The First Hotel at San Francisco   *CENTURY MAGAZINE,* CALIFORNIA STATE LIBRARY

By 1850 there were numerous stage lines linking the towns of northern California but most of them had only one vehicle. One stage driver, Clark Foss, capitalized on the shortage of adequate table fare. He took his hungry passengers, bound for San Francisco, on a detour to Calistoga above San Francisco on the Napa River, for the meals prepared by his wife at his hotel there, and the passengers had no regrets. She offered chicken, game, fruits, vegetables and tasty desserts, pure fresh mountain water, and coffee.

Another stage driver, Charlie Parkhurst, who was New England-born, rough, tough, and one of the "select whips" of the gold region, hid the fact that "he" was a woman. The discovery was made after her death in 1879.

During these years the admonition to "Go West, Young Man," came into wide circulation through the efforts of the famed *New York Tribune* editor, Horace Greeley. However, Greeley had taken the phrase from an editorial by John L. Soule in the *Terre Haute, Indiana Express,* and received credit for originating it. When Greeley followed the suggestion himself and shook, rattled and rolled along in Hank Monk's stagecoach enroute to Placerville in 1859, he probably wished he had never ventured off the sidewalks of New York. Mark Twain's account of that ride was reprinted during Greeley's campaign for the presidency in 1872, and Greeley blamed his failure to receive the nomination on this hilarious account of the episode.

SOUTHERN CALIFORNIA CUISINE

Southern California's population was centered in the Spanish communities of San Diego, Los Angeles and Santa Barbara until the 1850's. A few disappointed gold seekers drifted down that way to raise cattle, paving the way for the multitudes that followed.

Fire-eating Southern Democrats settled El Monte in 1851, the first American settlement in the area. In 1857 a group of San Francisco German families formed the cooperative community of Anaheim. About the same time the Mormon leader, Brigham Young, sent a colonizing group to San Bernardino, but recalled them to Utah a few years later. Santa Barbara was predominantly New England in taste and origin. Pasadena and Los Angeles attracted Chicagoans and Hoosiers from Indiana, while Iowans flocked to Long Beach.

In the 1850's John Schumacher owned a grocery and bar in a German neighborhood on the west side of Spring Street near First Street in Los Angeles. He was locally famous for his peach brandy and honey, considered by the good burghers to be an effective prevention and cure for colds. He is reputed to be the first Angeleno to import lager beer.

Hundreds of English families graced the southern scene. Although the English had lost out in their early colonizing efforts in California, their influence in the realm of cookery is very evident. Those who came here to make their homes were usually members of well-to-do families, who brought along Mrs. Beeton's *All About Cookery* as well as their own favorite family recipes. They entertained frequently and well, thus spreading the influence of English cooking.

A certain Dr. Carter, an Englishman living in Los Angeles, is credited with introducing the Christmas tree to Southern California. He provided the tree and his neighbors, who lived in the adobe house on Main Street between First and Second streets, helped trim it. To celebrate the advent of the festive season, Dr. Carter presided as Santa Claus and joined in songs, dancing and games.

About the same time King Kamehameha IV of Hawaii learned about Christmas celebrations while visiting in Britain and in 1856 issued a royal proclamation declaring Christmas, as well as Thanksgiving, legal holidays, both to be celebrated in the Islands on December 25. Because of the number of nationalities represented in the Islands, the variety of holiday foods is infinite.

Hawaii is well represented in California cooking, as well as in its history. The Kanakas were expert sailors and served as crew members on trading ships plying between China and the Pacific Coast. Some of them liked what they found in California and remained. John Sutter had brought with him twelve Islanders, including two women, when he established his fort and trading post in the Sacramento Valley. Coconut punch, whole roast pig and pineapple are typically Hawaiian. Pineapple and coconut are important ingredients in numerous California dishes.

As early as 1766 the crews of British ships in the harbor of Waimea Bay celebrated Christ's birthday in a way that would be considered typically Hawaiian today—with feasts of coconut punch and roast pig. A ship's officer went ashore on Christmas Eve and distributed small gifts to Hawaiian women and children. The following day Hawaiian officials reciprocated with porkers and vegetables.

During the pre-Christmas period in 1861 the Los Angeles River rose to such a height that it could not be forded, presenting transportation problems to those who wished to visit friends. The Andrew Boyle family was invited to Mat Keller's for Christmas dinner, but as they were unable to reach the host's home and also being without groceries for their own use, Mrs. Boyle sent her servant Jesus along with a note of regret and a grocery list. Jesus swam across the swollen river, delivered the missive, was given some goodies, purchased the groceries from a store, wrapped them in a large canvas and fastened

the parcel to a good-sized board. With the aid of this improvised raft, he swam back across the river, arriving home with his burden dry and in good condition. It is a matter of record that he received his full share of the holiday dinner he had risked his life to deliver.

The Anglo-Saxon custom of celebrating New Year's Day was introduced about 1855. The English residents of Los Angeles held Open House, some entertaining hundreds of guests. A few of the native Californians adopted this pleasant custom with great enthusiasm. Turkey and cranberry sauce were served, accompanied by plum pudding, mince pie, eggnog, wine, and other holiday refreshments. Accounts have it that there were those who partook too liberally of the liquid refreshments.

The Cinco de Mayo celebrations of the Mexicans also were elaborate affairs in Los Angeles, with grand parades, spirited music by native musicians and lavish picnics at which the tables groaned under their loads of food and drink.

Los Angeles was a town of innovation, even then. One pleasant custom of the 1850's and 1860's was that of inviting all and sundry to a feast on the opening of a new business venture. By his own admission, Harris Newmark introduced finger bowls to Los Angeles and in his book about his sixty years in Southern California from 1853 to 1913 he wrote:

"To show the provincial character of Los Angeles fifty years ago...in the metropolis (New York) I had found finger bowls in common use, and having brought back with me such a supply as my family would be likely to need, I discovered that it had actually fallen to my lot to introduce these desirable conveniences to Los Angeles."

Records indicate that the first ice cream parlor in Los Angeles was opened in the Temple Block in 1871, when ice was then manufactured in the city.

In 1861 the *California Farmer* commented on the spirit of change, but stressed a concern for proper diet and nutrition as follows:

"Reforms of every description are at present engaging the attention of contributors to the press, but I do not think there is any of them of more importance to our generation than the cooking reform....It ought to be our constant aim to learn to prepare food so that it can be partaken of without detriment to our health."

Prior to the Civil War efforts were made to organize the southern counties into a separate territory. Southern sympathizers did their best to swing California to the slavery side. Failing in that effort, they made their presence felt in their customs and cookery. In the north, however, in 1863 efforts were made to convert the huge surplus of beef in the state into jerky for use by the Union Army as a relief from the diet of fat pork of uncertain vintage.

One Californian wrote in 1870 that the general sentiment of the people in the state was opposed to the use of any coin less than a 10-cent piece; they liked high wages and high prices, and the introduction of half-dimes and cents would make them feel poor and bring about lower wages. Even the candy and fruit retailers refused to take the half-dime.

A certain Los Angeles restaurant in the 1870's advertised "all you can eat for 25 cents." An immigrant German entered the restaurant and proceeded to consume trayful after trayful of food, carried to his table by several increasingly unhappy waitresses. In desperation the proprietor took down his sign, declaring that the diner had eaten food worth $7 or $8. Later the owner learned that his ravenous customer was a professional eater, whose inordinate appetite had attracted world-wide medical attention.

In 1875 Mat Keller, a leading wine-maker of the area, invited one hundred and twenty-five guests to share a dinner to commemorate the Harvest Home celebration. This was a European custom, in this case presumably imported from Germany. The elaborate menu included mock turtle or oyster soup, fish, oyster patties, blanquette of veal and breaded veal cutlets, steak and kidney pudding, curried pigs' feet with rice, macaroni and cheese, rumpbeef corned with cabbage, leg of mutton, lamb, pork with sage and onion, and pig with applesauce. Desserts and beverages were English plum pudding, apricot pie, mince pie, blackberry pie, green-gage pie, apples, pears, grapes, nuts, mixed candies, fresh strawberries, and tea, coffee and wines of claret, Eldorado, Madeira, Angelica, white wine, Sherry, Port, Riesling and Muscatel.

The famed Pico House led Los Angeles in observing the National Centennial in 1876. On July 4th the biggest celebration in the town's history took place. The restaurant greeted its guests with this message:

"To the patrons of the Pico House, may you live 100 years; no North, no South, no East, no West—a Fourth of July for all—Independence Day, a welcome for our guests."

In September of the same year the Pico House prepared a feast for two hundred and fifty guests to celebrate the completion of the railroad track connecting San Francisco and Los Angeles. Los Angeles was not to be intimidated by the sophistication of San Francisco, and the menu did justice to the occasion. While French language purists may wince at the mishmash of fractured French employed in what was probably a souvenir menu, we can hope that the culinary creations were not impaired in any way by the flaws in their description. This notable menu, copied verbatim from Maymie R. Kryth's

Stage Arrives at the Pico House   JOHN DAWSON

article "Pico House: the Finest Hotel South of San Francisco" which appeared in the June 1955 issue of the Southern California Historical Quarterly, included "consomme royal; filet of salmon; hors d'oeuvres of olives, shrimps, anchovies, apple sauce, cranberry sauce, and pickles." Salads were "mayonaise de homards monte, mayonaisse de chicken à la Italiene and German salad." Some of the ornamental dishes were "noix de veal a la Montmorency a la jelly, turkey galatine en belle vue, pates de foies au attele belle vue, and pates de quail a la jelly." Roasts included "ham de Mayence roast a la jelly,

turkey truffles aux papilettes, smoked tongue en arcade, chicken bards a la gelee, quail piques de cores, chaux froids de chicken decorated, quarter de vension veal a la creme, aspic financiere belle vue, and preces de flanc."

Among the pastries and desserts were "English plum pudding and maraschino sauce, fruitcakes, glace blaue, ladies kisses, mushroom meringues, cakes a la genoise diversee, vanilla souflee, macaroons," several pies, "nougat baked garnie with fruit caramel, champagne jelly a la rese, vanilla ice cream, and blanc mange punache." The feast was accompanied by several wines.

Fancy Pullman Dining Car

Cakes a la genoise diversee probably were what we today describe as petits fours, or more literally translated, assorted little cakes. Because of the various inaccuracies we can only guess at some of the other culinary masterpieces.

A great boon to housewives in California, as well as to the entire world, was the discovery of borax in Death Valley in 1882. Until the twenty-mule team wagons started hauling it out of the desert it had been quite expensive, costing as much as 25 cents an ounce. The bill of fare for the drivers of these ponderous wagons included bacon, bread and beans "with every variety of canned goods known to the grocery trade for the upper strata." The cooks carried Dutch ovens for baking, pans for frying, and tin kettles for stewing.

During the land boom of the 1880's, emigrants were lured to Los Angeles by enticing advertisements:

"In no place on this side of God's great footstool can one obtain so good a 25-cent meal as right here in the Angel City. Excellent 15-cent dinners can be had at some restaurants, including wine and fruit, and a bountiful breakfast for 10 cents."

In 1887 when the Santa Fe Railroad completed its transcontinental line to Los Angeles, over one million potential homemakers visited the state. A rate war among the railroads reduced the fare so drastically that for one day that year the lucky traveler could go from Kansas City to Los Angeles for $1. No one knows how many people took advantage of this almost-free transportation.

In the 1890's the short-order departments of the wholesale grocery business were called upon to supply items outside the standard line. One customer requested "a good house cat." Another customer out in the desert ordered a coffin for a recently deceased relative. One can't help wondering where the remains of the deceased were stored while awaiting delivery of the coffin.

As roads in the vicinity of Los Angeles improved toward the end of the century, cycling clubs became popular. Picnic runs with lunch in Glendale or Monrovia were favored by bicycle buffs. During the late summer season the "watermelon run" to El Monte was the *in* thing, or perhaps a trip to Baldwin's Ranch at Santa Anita, where saddle horses, fruit and wine could be had, or a jaunt to the San Gabriel Mission and winery.

The water shortage in the fast-growing City of the Angels threatened its very existence, but as the 20th Century approached, this problem was to be solved with the completion of a monumental system of aqueducts which would bring water from the Owens Valley below the eastern slopes of the Sierra Nevada. Strenuous opposition by Owens Valley residents was futile against the pressure of Southern Californians.

By the 1890's the voice of the California cook was heard throughout the land. The October 1896 issue of *Delineator*, a ladies' magazine, published details, written by Charlot M. Hall, of a "Ramona luncheon." The luncheon, announcing the engagement of an Eastern girl to a boy of Spanish descent, was inspired by a visit of the fiancee's mother to Southern California, where she had heard much about Helen Hunt Jackson's romantic novel, *Ramona*.

Ramona sandwiches contained figs, dates, raisins, citron, "and any candied fruits and a very little candied peel" with melted loquat jelly poured over the mixture. After the mold had been thoroughly chilled, slices were cut off and served between two slices of bread as sandwiches. Oh, what heinous crimes were committed in the name of "California cookery" in behalf of those dainty ladies' luncheons at the turn of the century.

Dining at Delmonico's in San Francisco, 1853

RESTAURANTS OF SAN FRANCISCO

Poets have rhapsodized, song writers have lyricized, novelists have romanticized, and journalists have idealized San Francisco. It was the mecca of the gold miners, eager to exchange their new-found riches for a giddy whirl in the light-hearted, anything-goes metropolis.

The Bay City's Bohemia has harbored many prominent men and women of letters. California brides have regaled their granddaughters with reminiscences of their San Francisco honeymoons. Its restaurants won world-wide fame in the glorious decades from 1850 to 1900. San Francisco's only rival as the most colorful city in the United States was New Orleans.

The menu of an unnamed San Francisco restaurant in the Gold Rush days of 1850 included mock turtle and St. Julian soup, boiled salmon trout with anchovy sauce, leg of mutton with caper sauce, corned beef and cabbage, and ham and tongue. Entrees were listed as fillet of beef with mushroom sauce, breaded veal cutlets, mutton chops, lobster salad, sirloin of venison, baked macaroni and beef tongue with sauce piquante. If one used some discretion a complete dinner cost $5.

During the 1860's a great many San Francisco residents lived in hotels or lodging houses and ate their meals in restaurants, a carry-over from Gold Rush days when the population was predominantly male. Consequently, the city was blessed with a wide variety of eating places, ranging from unpretentious establishments serving meals family style for 25 cents, to the famed Palace Hotel. One visitor wrote that it was possible in San Francisco to dine in any language, and travelers were impressed with the great variety of foods. A few choices available were duck, quail, roast venison, grizzly steak, crab, shrimp and abalone.

The French continued to exert an influence in California by catering to an affluent society. Frenchmen who came to hunt gold found the rough life of the camps displeasing and soon departed to San Francisco, where they found opportunities particularly as hoteliers, importers or restaurateurs. Some of their restaurants achieved world-wide fame. The center of the French colony lay north of Market Street not far from today's Embarcadero. At least two French restaurants courted American patronage by naming their establishments Jackson House and Lafayette.

Vioget's House served a menu for the rough and ready palate and featured Ameri-

As J. Ross Browne Saw Diners in 1864

can pancakes, unsalted native butter, wild honey, corn tortillas, tamales, beef, venison, antelope and bear steaks, wild ducks and geese, fish, and a variety of vegetables which included frijoles, all to be washed down with brandy, whiskey, coffee or tea.

Although original structures of favorite eating houses were destroyed by the 1906 earthquake and fire, and other changes have occurred through the years, a few of the names of famous restaurants have survived, such as the Poodle Dog, Sam's Grill, and the Tadich Grill. Others, such as Trois Freres, Cafe de Paris, Maison Riche and the Fly Trap are only memories.

To whet the appetite, Hotel de France served appetizers of celery, radishes and young onions, bowls of fruit and long loaves of crisp, freshly baked French bread. The meal began with thick cabbage soup, followed by sand dabs or sole or fried smelt. There was an entree of fried chicken on Sunday and roast or boiled beef on weekdays from which each diner carved off a piece to his liking; dishes of vegetables; and bowls of salad mixed by the owner. The meal ended with fruit in season, which might have been apples, oranges, peaches, pears or grapes. A pint of red wine was included of course. All of this cost 15 cents on weekdays and 25 cents on Sundays. In the 1890's prices were increased to 25 cents and 35 cents.

San Francisco's Chinese restaurants were easily identified by their long three-cornered yellow silk flags. They were liked by Americans because of their excellent preparation and the fact that meals were $1 each, without regard for quantity. Kong Sung's near the water, Whang-Ton's on Sacramento Street, and Tong-Ling's on Jackson Street were favorites. A variation of the popular oyster loaf was a specialty of the Chinese cook at Gobey's saloon in San Francisco in the 1870's, and was made with large transplanted

Eastern oysters. The ready-to-eat loaf was wrapped in brown paper. The Chinese served chow-chow and curry, besides many English dishes, and it was said their tea and coffee were unsurpassed.

Chow-chow is of uncertain origin and composition. Generally it is accepted as a term in pidgin English with which the Chinese referred to a miscellaneous mixture. One recipe suggests that "chow-chow" was a preserve of mixed peel and ginger, while another holds that it was made of chopped mixed pickles in mustard sauce. Two Chinese authorities, however, told me that chow-chow, which they pronounced "tsau-tsau," referred to any kind of food, particularly meat or vegetables, chopped fine, mixed and stir-fried in a wok, a special round-bottomed pan used in Oriental cooking.

Luna's, a Mexican restaurant frequented by artists and writers in the 1890's, served hot Mexican sausages, enchiladas, frijoles, fritas, chiles rellenos, pickles and sweet tamales. The cost was 50 cents on weekdays or 75 cents on Sundays.

Queen of them all, and symbolic of the good life enjoyed by San Francisco's society, was William Ralston's luxurious Palace Hotel. The original Palace, world-famed for its lavish appointments and cuisine, was host to heads of state, generals and royalty from all over the globe. They were served artisitc creations by master chefs on the fabulous Gold Service. The original Palace was destroyed in the earthquake and fire of 1906 but was promptly rebuilt along the same elaborate lines and continues to dazzle visitors, especially with its famous Palace Court salads.

While the French and the Chinese excelled as restaurateurs, Italian, German, Scandinavian, Yugoslav and Russian names appeared on signboards as proprietors of businesses. One traveler commented, "a visitor to San

Grand Entrance of the Palace Hotel in San Francisco, about 1882 CALIFORNIA HISTORICAL SOCIETY

Francisco is saved a trip around the world because of the many nationalities found there ... this combination of races produces bright, intelligent children."

The city was blessed with several very good American theaters, one French theater and an Italian opera. Also popular were the masquerades held in gambling saloons.

Out-of-state visitors congregated at San Francisco's elaborately decorated bars where the thirsty could choose a punch, sling or cocktail, requiring various combinations of whisky, gin or brandy, combined with sugar, bitters, peppermint, absinthe or curacao and garnished with lemon peel or mint. The oblig-

ing bartenders exercised their ingenuity in devising new drinks to suit the popular taste. Fancy names were invented to suit the brew, such as Stone-fence, Queen Charlotte and Pulkey Sangaree.

Free lunch was offered those who bought drinks at a restaurant and saloon named the Palace of Art, the *in* place during the last decade of the 19th Century. Ladies were admitted to the restaurant adjoining the bar, but were forbidden to enter the *sanctum sanctorum*. A struggling young lawyer or architect, a junior clerk or an impecunious playboy could gorge himself at the groaning board for the price of a couple beers.

Recipes

BREAKFAST FOOD
As a healthful way to start the day an 1855 issue of the *California Farmer* recommended wheat meal mush and wheaten grits to be eaten with milk, syrup, or cream and sugar. Alternates were listed as rye, corn or oatmeal, nice baked potatoes, and cold good bread, with a little butter and a glass of water.

GERMAN PANCAKES
An 1853 recipe is made with sweet milk and lots of well-beaten eggs.

1 pint flour
6 eggs
2 cups sweet milk
1 teaspoon salt

Separate eggs. Beat whites until stiff and set aside. Sift flour and salt together and pour milk slowly into flour while beating hard with a wire whisk to remove lumps. Beat egg yolks until frothy and add to batter. Beat hard. Fold in egg whites. Fry on buttered griddle.

NO MATTERS
It is a mystery what the title meant to the person who contributed this recipe for large pancakes to the *California Farmer* in 1856. The healthy-sized cakes are made with buttermilk and served up with apple sauce in a manner so popular with Germans.

To three teacupsful of buttermilk, add three tablespoonsful of rich cream, and a small quantity of sugar. Stir in flour until it is of the consistency of paste for doughnuts. Roll out size of a large breakfast plate, and fry in lard to a rich brown color. As each cake comes from the fire, cover with apple sauce made from tart apples sweetened to taste, and spiced with nutmeg or cinnamon, and continue the process till the plate is well heaped.

POTATO MUFFINS
Potato muffins, or rolls, are as popular with hearty eaters nowadays as they were in 1859 when this recipe first appeared in *California Farmer*. Of course, yeast in cake or powder form is used at present instead of the old-fashioned yeast starter.

One pint of milk, six large potatoes mashed, one egg, a desertspoon (2 teaspoons) of butter, and one gill (½ cup) of good yeast. Mix well and let set a while, then pour into muffin tins and bake till done.

SOUTHERN BEATEN BISCUITS
Cooks from the Old South brought favorite hot bread recipes to their new home in California. This one required a strong arm for beating the batter.

Work 1 tablespoon of lard into 3 cups of flour and 1 teaspoon of salt. Stir in equal parts of milk and water to make a dough as stiff as can be handled. Lay dough on wooden block and beat steadily for 15 minutes with a rolling pin. Cut into round cakes, prick with fork and bake in a quick oven (400°).

CORN STICKS
Heavy iron pans and skillets were put to many uses. Corn bread batter was sometimes baked in special molds, for variety. Each cornstick resembled a small ear of corn.

2 cups water-ground corn meal
1 whole egg
1 cup sweet milk
1 teaspoon sugar
½ teaspoon salt
2 teaspoons baking powder
1 tablespoon melted lard or bacon drippings

Mix all ingredients well, in order given. Pour batter into corn stick pan and bake in hot oven (450°) for 20 minutes, or until golden brown. Makes 1 dozen.

CHICKEN-HAM SOUP
Large American families enjoyed this rich supper dish which sounds luscious with the good flavors of chicken, ham and celery stewed in milk, fancied up with tiny dumplings and delicately flavored with nutmeg and mace.

Cut up 2 large fowls as if for carving for table. Wash pieces in cold water. Add ½ dozen thin slices of cold ham to chicken in soup-pot. Season with very little cayenne, a little nutmeg, a few blades of mace, but no salt, as ham will furnish salt. Add 1 head of celery, cut in bits, ¼ pound of butter, divided into two and rolled in flour, and pour over all 3 quarts of milk. Set soup pot over fire and let boil slowly, skimming well. When it has boiled an hour, put in some small round dumplings, made of ½ pound of flour mixed with ¼ pound of butter. Divide dough into equal portions, roll in your hands into little balls about the size of hickory nuts. Soup must boil until flesh of the fowls is loose on bones, but doesn't break off. Stir in, at the last, the beaten yolks of 3 or 4 eggs, and let soup remain about 5 minutes longer over fire. Take soup off fire, cut fowl off bones, cut up slices of ham, mince livers and gizzards–put bits of fowl and ham in bottom of large tureen and pour soup over them.

BOUILLABAISSE

A traditional French soup of fish, crab and other shellfish was introduced into the mid-century California cuisine, and benefitted by the addition of olives and red pepper.

Clean well 3 pounds of mixed fish (several kinds), a crab or lobster, and ½ pound of other shellfish. Lay aside the best fish after removing heads and tails and cutting into portions. Throw inferior fish scraps and bones into 2 quarts of boiling salted water and boil to pieces. Strain broth through cheesecloth, squeezing it hard to extract all fish juice. Fry 2 large onions and a sprig of parsley, all chopped fine, in two large spoonfuls of olive oil until they color, then add a sprig of thyme, a can of tomatoes, a red pepper, a pinch of Spanish saffron, and salt, and boil until well incorporated. Crack the crab or lobster claws, remove the shell, sand bag, etc., and cut into pieces. Add to the broth with the pieces of fish and shellfish and simmer until all are done. Pour into a large deep dish over pieces of toasted French bread.

MOCK TURTLE SOUP

Calf's head or pigs' feet were major ingredients of this favorite Old South recipe. A California version includes them but suggests veal as a preference.

4 pigs' feet
2 pounds veal with bone or 1 calf's head
1½ teaspoons salt
5 carrots
3 medium sized onions
2 lemons
¼ teaspoon each powdered marjoram,
   thyme, allspice and grated nutmeg
1 teaspoon cloves
1 teaspoon mace
½ cup flour
1 cup dry sherry or Madeira wine
Salt and pepper to taste

Place veal in large kettle, add 2 teaspoons of salt and cover with cold water. Bring to boil and simmer until meat is tender. Remove meat from kettle and add enough water to stock to make 4 quarts. Grind carrots, lemons and onions with meat, add to soup stock and simmer for 1 hour. Make a thin paste of flour and water, add to wine and stir into soup. Simmer ½ hour longer. Garnish with sliced hardboiled eggs.

If calf's head and pigs' feet are used, boil until very well done–about 3 hours. Remove head from water, take out meat and brains and set aside separately. Chop meat and season with spices. Remove feet, take out bones, and replace gelatinous meat and ground vegetables in pot. Boil for 2 hours longer, then set aside until the next day. An hour before dinner, set stock over fire, add meat which has been cut into small squares and simmer over low fire. Make a thin paste of flour and cold water, adding brains which have been mashed, and the wine. Stir this into the stock, bring to a boil, and simmer for 30 minutes.

ITALIAN ONION SOUP

Onion soup is popularly associated with French cookery; however, this old recipe has been handed down in an Italian family.

Cut 3 or 4 large onions in thin slices and fry until transparent in ½ cupful of butter. Simmer gently for nearly an hour. Pour over them a quart of rich, clear stock and bring to a boil. Have ready a hot tureen in which has been placed two or three slices of bread

toasted a golden brown. On this pour the soup.
Add half a cupful of Gruyere cheese and serve.

BORSCHT

The Russian colonists at Fort Ross preserved their national traditions in cooking favorite dishes, including borscht, still popular today. Ingredients usually varied, and when little meat was on hand, a "thin" soup was bolstered by a cooked grain cereal, called *kasha*, and served with thick slices of dark bread. This is a rich version with plenty of beef.

4 raw beets
4 medium-sized onions
½ head small cabbage
1 tablespoon fat
1 quart beef stock
1 tablespoon flour
2 pounds stewing beef
1 small ham hock
6 tomatoes
1 quart water
1 bay leaf
Salt and pepper to taste

Peel and shred three of the beets and chop onions and cabbage. Cook in fat until soft. Stir in flour and cook for 2 minutes longer. Add stock, meat, bay leaf, water, salt and pepper, and cook slowly for 1 hour. Chop tomatoes and toss into pot. Simmer for 2 hours longer, or until meat is tender. Cool. Skim off fat. Lift beef and ham hock from pot and cut into serving pieces, removing bone from ham. Grate the remaining beet, add a little stock and simmer for 3 minutes. Add to the soup, with the meat, and heat through. Serve with a spoonful of sour cream on top. Boiled potatoes usually accompany this dish.

SAUERKRAUT SOUP

Most Russian soups included cabbage, either fresh or as sauerkraut. This recipe calls for both, as well as tomatoes and onions, plus a generous helping of beef to be served separately.

3 pounds beef shoulder or short ribs
3 marrow bones
3 cloves garlic, minced
2 onions, minced
6 large tomatoes

1 large firm head cabbage
1 teaspoon pepper
3 teaspoons salt
¼ cup sugar
2 tablespoons flour
1 pound sauerkraut, drained
½ cup sour cream
¼ cup vinegar

Place meat and bones in deep kettle with garlic, onions and tomatoes. Add 3 quarts of water, bring to a boil and skim. Shred cabbage, discarding core. Add to soup with salt and pepper and cook slowly for 1½ hours. Stir in vinegar and sugar and cook 30 minutes. Mix flour with 2 tablespoons of water and blend until smooth. Pour into soup, stirring constantly to prevent lumps from forming. Add sauerkraut and cook until meat is tender. More salt, pepper and sugar may be added if needed. Garnish with a spoonful of sour cream. Serve meat separately.

FISH STEW

Italian fishermen introduced this dish, called *cioppino*, to San Francisco where later and somewhat more elaborate versions have become famous.

2 pounds halibut, rock cod or sea bass
10 dried mushrooms
1 stalk celery, sliced thin
2 carrots, peeled and sliced thin
1 parsnip, peeled and sliced thin
2 teaspoons salt
1 teaspoon pepper
3 tablespoons butter
1 onion, chopped fine
1 cup tomato sauce
1 tablespoon capers, drained
10 ripe olives
1 fish head

Cover mushrooms with water and soak for 2 hours. Drain carefully, rinse and slice. Wash fish and head and slice. Place cleaned fish head in deep kettle, add celery, carrots, parsnip, salt, pepper and 2 quarts of water. Boil for 45 minutes. Strain. Melt butter in large saucepan, add chopped onion and cook for 10 minutes, stirring frequently. Add fish and brown lightly on both sides. Stir in tomato sauce, capers, olives, and fish stock.

Cook over medium heat for 35 to 40 minutes, or until fish is cooked. Add more salt and pepper if desired. Serve in deep soup plates, garnished with lemon slices and parsley.

SOFT SHELL CRAB

Here is a recipe which came to California from an Italian monastery.

Wash carefully 6 live, soft-shell crabs and throw them into a bowl containing 1 pint of milk and 3 beaten eggs. Let them stand until they have consumed the liquid, then roll in fine cracker crumbs and fry in boiling lard. When done, serve with bunches of fried parsley.

DEVILED CRAB

Two California crabs equal a dozen Eastern crabs. Here the cooked meat is combined with mushrooms and baked in the shell with a topping of cracker crumbs.

12 crabs
1 onion
1 dozen mushrooms
1 teacup cracker crumbs
1 teacup cream
1 egg
1 lemon
Butter, pepper, cayenne

Boil the crabs half an hour, then pick out flesh and fat, discarding the dead man's fingers. Heat in a saucepan a lump of butter the size of an egg. Chop one onion fine and fry until brown. Add the prepared crab meat and mushrooms. Moisten the cracker crumbs with the cream and the egg yolk. Add lemon juice, salt to taste and a thick sprinkle of cayenne. Stuff the crab shells, cover with crumbs, putting a small lump of butter on top of each, and bake 20 minutes in moderately hot oven.

FRIED FROG LEGS

An out-of-the-ordinary treat at the turn of the century, and still popular.

Remove skin from the hind legs (the only part used). Dip in crumbs, seasoned with salt and pepper, then in egg, and again in crumbs. Wipe the bone at the end. Put in a basket and fry one minute in smoking hot fat. Drain and serve. Some people parboil them in boiling salted water and a little lemon juice before frying.

OYSTERS KIRKPATRICK

San Francisco's Palace Hotel was worthy of its name and famed for its elegant cuisine. An original recipe for baked oysters on the half shell was named for the first general manager, John C. Kirkpatrick.

12 oysters in the half shell
1 cup catsup
1 cup chili sauce
1 teaspoon Worcestershire sauce
½ teaspoon A-1 sauce
½ small green pepper, finely chopped
1 teaspoon chopped parsley
4 strips bacon, each cut in 3 pieces
½ cup grated Parmesan cheese

Place oysters on a silver oyster tray or on a bed of rock salt. Cover with the sauce, which has been well mixed. Place bacon pieces on top and sprinkle with cheese. Bake in a moderately hot oven for 12 minutes. Serves 2.

CALIFORNIA OYSTER OMELETTE

A fancy, flamed oyster concoction served in omelette form with cream sauce was one of the earliest Palace dishes to attain international renown.

12 Olympia oysters
1 cup cream sauce
4 ounces butter
½ jigger sherry
3 eggs
½ cup cream
1 teaspoon grated cheese
Salt, pepper, paprika

Sauté oysters in a little butter and paprika. Add sherry. Flame. Add one-half of the cream sauce with salt and pepper to taste. Beat eggs and add a dash of cream. Heat omelette pan with butter. Make a fluffy omelette. Fold in oyster mixture. Place on oval platter and cover with light cream sauce, using the remaining ½ cup with some cream added. Sprinkle with grated cheese and brown under salamander.

OYSTER LOAF

Samuel Dickson, a lyrical admirer of San Francisco, says this dish was invented in that fascinating city. However, a 1739 edition of E. Smith's *Compleat Housewife* contained a similar recipe, called "Penny Loaves."

Cut a round piece, say six inches across, from the top of a well-baked round loaf of bread, and remove the inside from the loaf, leaving crust half an inch thick. Spread outside of this shell lightly with melted butter and bake in a moderate oven (350°) until it is golden brown. Make a rich oyster stew as follows: Drain 1 pint of oysters, reserving liquid. Melt in a saucepan 2 tablespoons of butter. Add 2 tablespoons of flour and stir until blended. Stir in slowly 2 cups of oyster liquor, and season with ½ teaspoon of salt and ⅛ teaspoon of paprika. When sauce is smooth and boiling, add drained oysters. Remove from heat and pour part of sauce over 4 egg yolks, beating constantly. Blend egg mixture into oyster mixture, set over fire and cook for about one minute longer, stirring constantly. Remove from fire, add 1 teaspoon of lemon juice or 1 teaspoon of sherry and pour into prepared shell. Place cover over top and set in oven for a few minutes. Serve at once, garnished with chopped parsley.

OYSTER SALAD

This interesting recipe from the mid-1800's includes celery and nut meats with the ever-favorite oysters, and is served with an old-fashioned boiled dressing.

1 quart oysters
Lemon juice
1 bunch celery, chopped fine
1 cup chopped nuts

Cook oysters. Drain and cut into small pieces. Pour lemon juice over pieces and set in a cool place. When quite cool, add celery and nuts. Season to taste and serve with dressing. To make dressing, beat 1 egg lightly and set aside while heating 1 cup of vinegar and 1 tablespoon of butter to boiling. Remove from stove and stir in egg. If too thick when cold, thin with sweet cream. Salt to taste.

OYSTER PIE

The person who gave directions for this mid-century recipe no doubt was a good cook, but sketchy as to directions. If read with imagination one finds here a very clever way of baking a top crust for a pie before the filling is added by holding up the crust with stale bread. The writer uses the word "paste" for pie dough. Even though it is recommended that the dish be served promptly, it also is suggested that it can be reserved to serve cold for picnics or traveling.

Line a pie-dish half-way up with good pie-crust, fill the dish with pieces of stale bread, place a cover of paste over this, and bake about twenty minutes in a brisk oven. Take off crust, have ready some oysters prepared as for patties and fill the shell with them. Replace top crust and serve at once.

Or, line dish with a good puff-paste, place an extra layer around the edge, and bake in a brisk oven. Fill with oysters, season with pepper, salt, and a tablespoon of butter, sprinkle lightly with flour and cover with a thin crust of paste. Bake quickly. When the top crust is done the pie will be ready to take up. Serve promptly, as the crust quickly absorbs the gravy. Some like this cold for picnics or traveling.

STEWED PIGEON

Such a prosaic title certainly belies its name because this is a most sophisticated manner to present pigeon.

Truss young pigeons and place side by side in pan, breasts uppermost. Add a sliced carrot, an onion with a clove stuck in it, a teaspoon of sugar and chopped parsley. Lay bacon slices on top, add boiling stock, cover tightly and simmer till tender, adding stock if needed. Serve on buttered toast with a border of spinach.

CHICKEN CHAUD-FROID BLANC

A recipe for chicken in the best haute cuisine French tradition offers two sauces.

Clean and singe a 3-pound chicken. Lay bird on its side in a roasting pan and spread with 2 tablespoons of butter. Add ¼ cup of hot water to pan. *Roast in a moderately hot oven (375°) for 20 to 25 minutes, turn bird and roast for 20 to 25 minutes longer to brown both sides. Baste frequently with pan juices and add a little more water if necessary. Turn chicken on its back to brown breast. When chicken is done, drain juices from cavity into the pan. Remove bird to a platter and set aside to cool, while making sauces.*

Jellied White Sauce:
Soften 2 tablespoons of gelatin in ½ cup of cold water. Bring 2 cups of sauce veloute to a boil and dissolve gelatin in sauce. Strain sauce through a fine sieve. Just before it congeals use sauce to coat cold chicken.

Sauce Velouté:
Melt 2 tablespoons of butter in a saucepan. Add 4 tablespoons of flour, blend until smooth and cook slowly, stirring until it starts to turn golden. Gradually add 3 cups of boiling hot white chicken stock, stirring vigorously with a wire whip. Add 3 white peppercorns, a little salt and a sprig of parsley; also ½ cup mushroom peelings and stems, if available. Simmer sauce, stirring frequently, for 1 hour, or until it is reduced to two-thirds the original quantity and is as thick as heavy cream. Skim occasionally. Strain it through a fine sieve and season to taste.

CHICKEN SALAD
Although this dish was published in *California Farmer* as a chicken salad, it could be served warm as an entree.

Take one chicken, boil tender with a small piece of salt pork, chop fine without the pork, adding one head of chopped celery. For the dressing, use the yolks of four hard-boiled eggs rubbed to a paste, add one-fourth tablespoon of cayenne pepper, one teaspoon of black pepper, two tablespoons of prepared mustard, one gill of vinegar, one-half cup of melted butter. Pour this over the chicken and celery and stir well. Chop the whites of two of the eggs with the chicken. Slice the whites of the remaining two in rings, place on top of the salad after it is in the dish ready for the table, and in each ring place a little sprig of the green top of the celery.

CHICKEN CROQUETTES
Made with stewing chickens and cream, this simply written recipe suggests an extremely rich dish.

Boil two fowls weighing five pounds each till very tender. Mince fine, add one pint of cream, a half-pound of butter, salt and pepper to taste. Mold in oval shape. Fry in lard like doughnuts until golden brown. Serve with or without white sauce.

CHICKEN OR LAMB CASSEROLE
An interesting dish which came from Chile as *cazuela*, includes onion, tomatoes, green peppers, peas, string beans, potatoes, rice and sweet corn, to be served in a tureen in which an egg yolk has been whipped with a little vinegar.

Cut up a young chicken or 1½ pounds of lamb in 2-inch pieces and fry until a light brown, in some lard in which a chopped onion has been fried. Add 2 peeled tomatoes and 2 chopped green peppers. Put all of this in a large saucepan, cover with 3 quarts of water, and simmer 2 hours. Then add 1 cupful of green peas, ½ cupful of string beans, 1 large green pepper cut in slices, with seeds removed, 2 potatoes cut in quarters, 1 tablespoon of raw rice and 2 ears of corn chopped in 1-inch lengths. Season with salt and pepper to your taste. Boil until tender and add 4 or 5 stalks of young mint. Into the broth stir the white of an egg and pour all into a tureen in the bottom of which is the yolk of the egg mixed with a tablespoon of vinegar. If the broth is too thick add a little boiling water.

CHILI COLORADO
One nostalgic Californian living in Nevada contributed this recipe to the compiler of an early California cookbook. The Mexican manner of using chilies adds a pungent flavor to the dish.

Take 2 chickens and cut up as if to stew. Simmer until tender, and add a little green parsley and a few onions. Remove seeds from ½ pound of pepper pods. Cover with boiling water and steam for 10 or 15 minutes. Pour off water and rub them in a sieve until all the juice is out. Add the juice to the chicken. Let it cook for half an hour, then add a little butter, flour and salt. Place a border of rice around the dish before setting on table. Note: This dish may also be made of beef, pork or mutton. It is to be eaten in cold weather.

STEAK AND KIDNEY PIE

The famous English cookbook author, Mrs. Beeton, included a recipe for this dish in her early cookbook which English pioneers brought to California. My own family likes it so well I make it frequently, with a few embellishments here included.

2 beef kidneys, diced
1 pound round steak, diced
1 small onion, diced
½ pound fresh mushrooms, sliced
1 tablespoon Worcestershire Sauce
1 teaspoon tabasco sauce
2 tablespoons drippings
1 cup burgundy
½ cup flour
Salt and pepper to taste

Melt fat in a heavy skillet, add kidneys and steak which have been well coated with the flour. Sear meat on all sides and remove from skillet. Place onions and mushrooms in skillet and sauté for about 5 minutes, turning them often. Return meat to skillet, add remaining ingredients, cover, and simmer for about 2 hours, stirring from time to time. Remove from heat and cool, then skim fat from surface. Preheat oven to 400°. Put the meat mixture in a heavy baking dish, cover with pastry, and bake until brown, about 30 to 35 minutes.

Pastry:
2½ cups flour
1 cup shortening
½ teaspoon salt
2½ teaspoons baking powder
½ cup milk

Combine ingredients as for biscuits and pat out to about ½ inch thick. Cover casserole. Brush the top with 1 beaten egg and 1 tablespoon cream combined.

ROAST BEEF WITH YORKSHIRE PUDDING

An old English favorite introduced by English cooks. The pudding is very simple and easy to put together and is a hearty, flavorful accompaniment to the roast.

A sirloin or rib roast is best. Have the bones removed. Roll the meat and fasten in shape with skewers or tie with piece of string. Place on a rack in a dripping pan and put it in a very hot oven to sear it over in order to retain the juices. Keep the oven closed for about 10 minutes, then open, dredge roast with flour, salt and pepper, and baste with the gravy. Turn the meat when necessary, and baste often. Bake a six-pound roast one hour if liked rare, and an hour and a quarter if liked well done. Serve with gravy made from the drippings of the meat; or any favorite sauce.

Yorkshire Pudding:
1 pint sweet milk
4 eggs
2 cups flour
2 teaspoons baking powder
1 teaspoon salt
Drippings

Beat whites and yolks separately. Mix the ingredients into a smooth batter. Pour drippings from the roast into a baking dish, add the batter, and bake 20 minutes. Serve immediately. It is not good except it be hot. This is better than the old way of baking in the pan with the roast.

BEEF CASSEROLE
Kavillolani

A late 19th Century recipe which is essentially Hawaiian acquired rice, tomatoes, and chili peppers when it reached California.

1½ quarts roast beef
1 quart cooked tomatoes
½ pint boiled rice
1 medium onion
2 chili peppers
1 pint gravy

Chop beef, peppers and onions very fine. Season with salt and pepper. Spread in shallow baking dish, cover with tomatoes, then rice, then gravy. Add tabasco sauce to taste. Bake 1 hour in moderate oven (350°).

SHEEPHERDER STEW

Hearty lamb stews, well fortified with garlic, characterize Basque cookery. This stew recipe blends the lamb with a variety of herb flavorings, a little wine, onions and peas.

3 pounds lean lamb, cut in 1-inch cubes
⅓ cup flour
3 tablespoons olive oil
1 tablespoon salt
½ teaspoon pepper
½ teaspoon basil
½ teaspoon marjoram
2 cloves garlic, mashed
2 medium-sized onions, chopped fine
¾ cup dry red dinner wine
1½ cups water
1 cup garden peas, cooked

Dredge lamb cubes with flour. Heat oil in heavy kettle and brown lamb. Add remaining ingredients except peas, bring to a boil, and simmer for 30 minutes, or until meat is tender. Add peas and cook 10 minutes longer.

GERMAN ROUND STEAK

A delicious way to cook round steak with little white onions and carrots was found in the *California Farmer*, where it was entitled "German Soup."

1½ pounds round steak cut in 1-inch cubes
3 carrots cut in 1-inch pieces
12 small dry onions left whole
2 tablespoons lard
1 tablespoon butter
2 tablespoons flour
Salt
Pepper

Melt lard and butter in iron skillet. When hot, add meat, onions, carrots, flour, salt and pepper. Stir constantly until browned. Add one quart of boiling water and bake 1½ hours in slow oven. Add more water while cooking if needed.

TOAD IN THE HOLE

Such a venerable English recipe hardly needs

explanation due to its continued popularity. It combines cooked minced beef with a popover mix, and was brought to California in 1890 by Doris Loewnau's father.

1 cup flour
1 cup milk
2 eggs
½ teaspoon salt
⅛ teaspoon pepper
1 tablespoon melted butter
Ground beef, cooked

Chill batter. Meanwhile spread ground beef over bottom of baking dish. Pour chilled batter over meat, and bake in hot oven (425°) for about an hour, or until toad is well risen, puffy and brown. Serve immediately.

ROAST MUTTON WITH CAPER SAUCE

Another recipe from the English cuisine, this time with an interesting basting sauce.

Rub roast well with salt and pepper. Place on rack in roasting pan, add a cup of boiling water and set in hot oven (400°). After 15 minutes of cooking time, reduce heat to moderate (350°). Allow 15 minutes per pound, basting every 10 minutes with sauce.

Caper sauce:
½ cup capers in vinegar
½ pint boiling water
Butter size of an egg
1 tablespoon flour

Pour water over capers and bring to boil. Add butter and stir in flour rubbed smooth in a little water. If not sour enough, add a little more vinegar.

ROAST LEG OF LAMB

A simple but classic Basque recipe with slivers of garlic inserted into the meat, which is roasted with a basting of vinegar and oil slightly flavored with more garlic.

1 5-pound leg of lamb
2 cloves of garlic
2 teaspoons salt
½ teaspoon pepper

Peel garlic and cut into thin slivers. Stick these into the roast, dust with salt and pepper, and place in roasting pan. Cook in moderate oven (325°) basting occasionally with a sauce made by mashing 1 clove of garlic in 2 tablespoons of vinegar and 2 tablespoons of vegetable or olive oil. Should be done in about 2½ hours. Serve with gravy made from pan drippings.

SHISH KEBOB

A typical Armenian manner of preparing lamb, which has retained its popularity among home barbeque buffs and restaurants.

3 pounds boneless lamb, cut from leg.
2 onions, chopped fine
1 green pepper, minced
6 stalks celery, chopped
1 bunch parsley, chopped
½ cup red wine
½ teaspoon pepper, freshly ground
Basil
Salt

Cut lamb into 1½ or 2-inch cubes and place in a deep bowl. Combine onions, pepper, celery and parsley and mix with meat. Add basil, salt, pepper and wine, stirring well. Marinate for 3 hours. When ready to cook, remove meat from marinade, thread on skewers and grill over coals. Serves 6.

ROULETTE OF VEAL

French haute cuisine is evident here in this recipe for thin, rolled veal steaks, lightly seasoned.

Small thin veal steaks; bacon, parsley, and onion. Spread steaks with finely minced parsley and onion, roll and fasten them with toothpicks. Let them stand for two or three hours. Brown thin slices of bacon in a hot sauce pan. Put in the veal, cook it very slowly for one hour, adding a little water if required. Take out the veal when done, and make the gravy by creaming one tablespoon of flour with 1 teaspoon of butter, pouring into it little by little some of the hot gravy in which the veal was cooked, then pouring this slowly into cream, when it is ready to serve.

CALF'S LIVER EN BROCHETTE

A simple skewer method of broiling liver; also recommended for kidneys.

Cut thin slices of liver and of bacon, into pieces 3 inches square. Put alternate slices of liver and bacon on skewers, and broil over coals until done and brown. Season with salt, pepper, butter, and a little lemon juice.

SPARERIBS AND PINEAPPLE, HAWAIIAN STYLE
Poh Loh Pai Kwut

Chinese influence is reflected here in the blending of soya, pickled vegetables and ginger root with pineapple.

1½ pounds pork spareribs or back bones, cut in 2-inch pieces
½ teaspoon salt
1 tablespoon soya
¾ cup pickled vegetables or mixed pickles
1 teaspoon cornstarch
2 tablespoons peanut or salad oil
½ tablespoon fresh or dried ginger root soaked in 1 tablespoon of water
3 tablespoons sugar
4 slices canned pineapple
¼ cup vinegar
1 cup water
2 tablespoons flour
¾ cup pineapple juice

Soak spare ribs in soya for 5 minutes, or longer if desired. Heat oil very hot, and fry the spare ribs for 5 minutes. Add flour to the rib mixture and stir into the fat, making a smooth paste. Add ginger, pineapple juice, salt, 1½ tablespoons of sugar, vinegar, and water. Simmer for 45 minutes, or until meat is tender. Make a smooth paste by combining the cornstarch with 1 tablespoon of water, add to the pork mixture and stir well. Cut the pickled vegetables into thin slices. Cut each slice of pineapple into 8 pieces. Add vegetables and pineapple to pork, bring mixture to the boiling point and simmer for 2 minutes.

EGGS A LA BONNE CUISINE

A fancy late-century French way to prepare deviled eggs gets a flourish of pureed spinach garnish.

Cut 4 hard-boiled eggs in half. Scoop out the yolks and rub to a paste with 1 tablespoon of butter and 1 teaspoon of anchovy paste, 1 pinch of curry powder and 1 teaspoon of chutney. Fill whites of the eggs with this. Fry some rounds of bread a golden brown and when cold spread with the remainder of the paste. Place a half egg on each round and with a pastry tube, garnish with a little cooked spinach that has been rubbed through a sieve with a little butter.

POLENTA

A happy marriage of corn meal and cheese, this Italian dish began to appear in California recipe collections during the late 1880's and is still popular. A cold, sliced corn meal mush is layered with cheese in a casserole dish and baked.

Melt a large spoonful of butter in 1 quart of boiling water. Wet 1 pint of corn meal with a very little cold water. Add 1 teaspoonful of salt, then stir slowly in boiling water and bring it to a boil, stirring continuously until the meal is cooked and has lost its raw taste. It should be thick enough to make into a ball. Lay aside to cool. When quite cold, cut into thin slices and put a layer on the bottom of a pudding dish, dot it with butter and thin slices of cheese, then more mush, cheese and butter until the dish is full. Make the last layer cheese, and bake in a quick oven for 20 to 30 minutes.

BAKED MACARONI WITH CHEESE AND TOMATOES

It is hard to believe that this thoroughly American and still popular dish was first served in the 14th Century to England's King Richard II.

1 cup macaroni, broken into ½ inch pieces
⅔ cup cracker crumbs
Cheese
Tomatoes
Milk
Butter
Salt and pepper

Place macaroni in a kettle of boiling salted water and cook rapidly for ½ hour. Put in a baking dish a layer of macaroni, then a layer of grated cheese, topped with a layer of tomatoes, repeating until a sufficient quantity is used. Pour over this mixture enough milk to cover, and season with salt, pepper

and butter. Cover the whole with cracker crumbs, moistened in melted butter. Bake until the crumbs are a light brown.

HOT POTATO SALAD

A turn-of-the-century manner of serving this typically German dish.

Boil potatoes in jackets. Peel and slice while hot. Layer in bowl with alternate layers of raw mild white onions, sliced thin. Add salt, white pepper and chopped parsley. Serve with dressing made of 1 part lemon juice to 2 parts olive oil.

ONIONS

The clever trick of cooking strong-flavored vegetables like onions and cabbage in milk was not new in 1856.

Boil onions in milk and water; it diminishes strong taste of vegetable. Good way to serve onions after boiling: chop them, put in a stew pan with a little milk, butter, salt and pepper, and let them stew about 15 minutes.

SWEET POTATOES

Authorities are not agreed as to whether the sweet potato was native to tropical America or the East Indies. A popular Hawaiian way of fixing them, called *koele palau*, was made by mashing the cooked potatoes and reheating them with the milk of shredded coconut. The recipe thrived in California, as reflected in directions for this 1854 dish, minus the coconut.

Boil two large sweet potatoes, rub them through a sieve; then add a piece of butter the size of an egg, a little salt, one pint of buttermilk, a teacupful of sugar, and a tablespoon of saleratus dissolved in warm water. Bake in an earthen dish. Serve up with cold cream.

POTATOES A LA CANNES

The story of this potato-puff recipe has it that the delayed arrival of a French king at an inn in Cannes created a kitchen crisis, and the flustered chef accidentally concocted the puff from the lowly potato. The king was delighted and thus the dish was preserved for posterity. Naturally the recipe found its way to San Francisco.

Wash 6 medium-sized potatoes and peel. Cut them endwise in slices 1/4 inch thick and stand in salted water 15 minutes. Dry them and simmer till tender in warm fat (not boiling hot) about 10 minutes. Take them from the fat and drain. Make the fat boiling hot, put a few pieces at a time in a drying-basket and plunge into the fat. They should puff out to about twice their original size.

RICE PILAF

Armenians have added many of their native dishes to the California cuisine. This is a basic one made with rice instead of the preferred bulgur wheat.

1 cup long grain rice
1/4 cup fine egg noodles
4 tablespoons butter
2 cups boiling chicken broth
1 tablespoon olive oil
Salt and pepper

Heat oil in an earthen casserole and cook noodles until golden. Add rice, salt, pepper, butter and broth and stir until butter is melted. Cover tightly, set in moderate oven (325°) and bake 30 minutes, or until all liquid has been absorbed. Remove casserole from oven, take off lid, and cover with a thick kitchen towel. Set lid on top of towel and let stand for 5 minutes. Serve.

COLACHE

The vegetable dish we call succotash is similar to this 1860 Americanized version of a Mexican recipe which uses fresh green summer squash and corn, with the addition, of course, of chilies and tomatoes, and a smidgen of onion.

Peel squash and cut in cubes. Add green beans, fresh corn cut from the cob, green chilies, tomatoes and onions. Simmer until tender. Season with salt, pepper and drippings or butter.

EGGPLANTS

Connoisseurs of eggplant will be happy with this 1854 treatment, which many agree has a taste almost equal to oysters.

Peel the fruit and cut into thin slices. Boil in salt and water until quite tender. Drain off the water and add sweet milk. Thicken with toasted bread crumbs, and while simmering gently, add butter and pepper, etc., and break in three of four fresh eggs. Take up before the eggs cook hard, and you will have a dish almost equal to stewed oysters. To fry eggplants they should be peeled, cut into thin slices, parboiled, then dipped in batter which has been highly seasoned, and fried in butter or lard. Either way they are delicious.

STEWED CELERY

Here is a simple way to make a delicately creamed vegetable.

Cut the blanched or white portion of the celery stalks in pieces about an inch in length and put them in a saucepan over the fire, with milk and water, in equal proportions, barely sufficient to cover them. Add a little salt and let them stew gently until perfectly tender. Then take out the celery, add a piece of butter to the liquor it was boiled in, thicken it slightly with flour, pour it over the celery, and serve it up.

ALMOND CREAM SOUP

A fine puree of stewed celery and almonds makes this taste-tempting soup of Spanish derivation.

Mince a small onion and two stalks of celery fine, add a cup of blanched almonds, chopped. Cover with cold water and cook slowly until soft, then rub through a sieve. Stir the puree into a quart of chicken broth, or hot milk, and pour it slowly over the beaten yolk of an egg. Heat in a double boiler, season with salt and cayenne and serve with a spoonful of whipped cream in each plate.

FRIED ARTICHOKES

An Italian cook contributed this recipe for marinated and deep-fried artichokes, in the late 1800's, when this fancy vegetable had proved it would thrive in California. Summer squash and cauliflower may also be cooked in this manner.

Wash well 4 tender young artichokes, cut off the stems and all the tough, outside leaves and thorny points. Cut in quarters, or if large, in eighths and marinate in French dressing. Dip in batter and fry in boiling oil until brown.

PLAIN COLE SLAW

A simple cole slaw is recommended by a mid-century cook as an accompaniment to fried oysters.

Slice cabbage very fine. Season with salt, pepper, and a little sugar. Pour over vinegar and mix thoroughly. Nice served in the center of a platter with fried oysters around it.

JERUSALEM ARTICHOKES
EN CASSEROLE

This native plant of North America has nothing whatsoever to do with Jerusalem and is not a globe artichoke. Eastern American Indians cultivated the plant for its potato-like root and it came to California via a European route, presumably from seeds acquired in 1605 by a French explorer, Samuel de Champlain. They were promoted vigorously in California in the late 1850's.

Select large smooth artichokes, scrape clean and drop at once into cold water to keep them from turning dark. Drain, pack into a baking dish, sprinkle with salt and pepper, dot with butter, cover and bake in a moderately hot oven for 45 to 60 minutes or until artichokes are tender. Add no water. Serve in the casserole.

COCONUT CAKE

Fresh coconuts were brought over by ship from the Hawaiian Islands. This is a three-egg layer cake which calls for yeast powder, and is put together with a grated coconut filling.

Two cups powdered sugar, one half cup butter, one cup milk, three cups flour, three eggs, two teaspoonful yeast powder. Sift sugar, flour and yeast powder together. Cream butter, add eggs and beat well. Add milk alternately with dry ingredients and beat until well blended.

Bake in two layer cake pans in moderate oven. When cool, put together with filling:

One grated coconut. To one-half of this add whites of three eggs and one cup of powdered sugar. Lay this between the layers. Mix with the other half of grated coconut four table-spoonful powdered sugar and strew thickly on top of cake.

TIPSY CAKE

Ancestry of this cake dates back to 17th Century England and has been a notable New Year's favorite. It is made with layers of sponge cake, jelly and almonds, all soaked with plenty of sherry, then served with a chilled soft custard poured over the top. This was a favorite of Doris Loewnau's mother, who brought a collection of her family's recipes from England in the 1890's. It tastes divine!

Line a glass bowl with stale sponge cake cut in slices. Spread with raspberry jam or currant jelly. Stick full of blanched almonds, quartered. Repeat layers until cake is used up. Moisten nicely with good sherry, about a cup. Let set for about an hour, then pour over it a a nice soft custard. Serve very cold, garnished with dabs of jam or jelly, and whipped cream, if desired.

Soft Custard:
2 cups milk
6 egg yolks
½ cup sugar
¼ teaspoon salt
Grated peel of ½ lemon
1 teaspoon vanilla

Scald milk in top of a double boiler. Beat egg yolks and combine with sugar, lemon peel and salt. Add milk. Cook and stir over hot water until mixture thickens and coats a metal spoon. Cool, add vanilla and chill.

SPANISH HEDGEHOG

Spain's answer to England's Tipsy Cake, using sweet Spanish wine.

Thoroughly saturate a round sponge cake with sweet Spanish wine. Stick all over surface blanched almonds cut in strips. Just before serving, pour around it a cold, rich Spanish cream which is made of six eggs, one pint of milk, one teacupful of sugar, and one stick of cinnamon, boiled until thick.

ANNIVERSARY CAKE

I hope the lucky husband for whom this cake was prepared was appreciative—it takes a full day to prepare. However, the yeast-raised cake, heavily laden with currants, citron and raisins, will keep for weeks and improves with age. Early California raisins were sold with stems attached, but this recipe calls for the firm-packed type, called layer-raisins, which came onto the market later.

Take two quarts of lukewarm milk, with flour and yeast, and set a sponge, as in the receipt for bread. When sufficiently raised, stir in the following: one pound of Zante currants, three-fifths of a pound of prepared citron, three-fifths of a pound of layer-raisins, stoned and chopped, and four teacups of sugar. Mix well and set to rise as before; when raised, stir it down and put into a pan for baking. If it should prove too thin (it needs to be stiffer than ordinary stirring cake) add a little flour as you stir it down. Let it rise the third time, and when raised, bake in a very slow oven for three hours. When done, turn from the pan bottom side up, and apply a frosting, made in the following manner: Beat the whites of three eggs till you have a stiff froth, then add two teacups of the best pulverized sugar. Mix well, and with a knife spread it on the bottom and sides of the cake while warm. This cake should be eaten when cold, and, indeed improves with age for five or six weeks. It should be kept in a dry, cool place and not in a jar.

SCRIPTURE CAKE

There are several variations of this recipe. A particular one with King James Bible references has been used by four generations of California cooks since the day it came across the mountains.

1 cup Judges 5:25 (butter)
2 cups Jeremiah 6:20 (sugar)
3½ cups I Kings 4:22 (flour, sifted)
2 teaspoons Amos 4:5 (baking powder)
3 cups Samuel I 30:12 (figs and raisins)
1 cup Genesis 43:11 (almonds)

1 cup Exodus 3:8 (milk)
5 Isaiah 10:14 (eggs)
½ teaspoon Leviticus 2:13 (salt)
1 teaspoon Exodus 30:23 (cinnamon)
¼ teaspoon each II Chronicles 9:9
  (cloves, allspice, nutmeg)
1 tablespoon Genesis 24:20 (water)

Follow Solomon's advice for making a good boy (Proverbs 23:14) and you will have a good cake. Loosely interpreted: Cream butter and sugar and beat in eggs one at a time. Sift dry ingredients together and blend into creamed mixture alternately with milk. Fold in chopped blanched almonds, figs and raisins. Bake in a 10-inch tube pan which has been generously greased and dusted with flour, for 1 hour and 10 minutes, in moderate oven (325°). Cool 10 minutes. Turn on to cake plate and drench with syrup, made as follows:

Melt 1½ cups Jeremiah 6:20 (sugar) in a heavy skillet over low heat and cook until it forms an amber syrup. Add ½ cup Genesis 24:20 (water) and cook until quite dark and smooth. Remove from heat, add ¼ cup Genesis 18:8 (butter) and stir until well blended and butter is melted. Cool, pour over cake and serve.

BUTTERNUT CAKE

Good mid-century cooks sometimes guarded their cooking secrets, or took for granted that other cooks knew how to put a cake together. There was only one line of directions given here.

2 cups of sugar
1 cup butter
3 cups flour
1 cup sweet milk
1 cup raisins
4 eggs
2 teaspoons cream of tartar
1 teaspoon soda

Beat sugar and butter to a cream. (That's all! However, you can obtain an excellent cake by proceeding as follows: Sift flour before measuring. Resift with cream of tartar and soda. Add eggs to butter-sugar mixture and beat until light and fluffy. Beat in milk alternately with dry ingredients. Stir in raisins last, and if you so desired, add ½ teaspoon of vanilla or lemon extract. Bake in loaf or layer pans and ice as desired.)

LEMON PIE

Many California housewives can still pick lemons ripe from the tree. Here is a recipe from a cook who knew how to convert the fruit into a superb pie.

Grate rind and squeeze juice from 2 large lemons. Add yolks of 3 eggs, 1½ cups sugar and 4 tablespoons of corn starch, 2 cups of water and 1 teaspoon of butter. Cook in double boiler about 20 minutes. Cool. Turn into baked crust and add beaten whites of eggs to which 1 tablespoon of powdered sugar has been added. Brown in slow oven (325°).

Crust: 1½ cups flour, 1 tablespoon of lard or butter, 1 teaspoon of baking powder, a pinch of salt and ¼ cup ice water. Bake in moderate oven.

ENGLISH WALNUT PIE

By the last decade of the 19th Century, California was well on its way to topping other states in the production of English walnuts. Cooks from other parts of the country who were accustomed to using pecans found walnuts were more economical, and just as satisfactory, to use for rich pie fillings.

Line deep tin pie plate with pastry, building up a scalloped edge, and set in a cold place while preparing the filling: Beat yolks of 2 eggs with ⅓ cup of sugar. Add 1 teaspoon of flour, ¼ teaspoon of cinnamon, ⅛ teaspoon of cloves, 1 tablespoon of lemon juice and a little grated lemon rind, 1 tablespoon of sweet pickle vinegar and ½ cup of water. When well mixed, add 2 ounces of chopped English walnuts. Prick crust with a fork, brush with white of egg and set in hot oven. Bake until half-done, about 5 minutes. Remove from oven, pour in filling, and finish baking in moderate oven for about 30 or 35 minutes. Cool. Whip whites of 2 eggs until they are frothy, and add gradually 2 rounded tablespoons of sugar and a few drops of vanilla. Spread over pie. Bake in a very slow oven until firm to touch and slightly browned.

APPLE PIE

Pureed apples are used in this California version of a classic French recipe, then meringue tops it off.

8 large ripe, juicy tart apples
3 eggs
Sugar
Vanilla
Lemons
1 9-inch crust

Stew and sweeten apples. Mash smooth and flavor with lemon juice or grated peel. Fill crust and bake till just done. Spread over the apples a thick meringue made by beating to a stiff froth the whites of three eggs to each pie, and three tablespoons of powdered sugar. Flavor with vanilla. Spread over pie and set pie back in oven until meringue is browned lightly. Eat cold.

APRICOT PIE

With California leading the nation in apricot production, it was only natural that the *California Farmer* printed this recipe for apricot pie on its ladies' page.

2 cups dried apricots (cooked)
1 tablespoon butter
1 tablespoon cornstarch
1 tablespoon water
2 eggs
2 tablespoons sugar
1 teaspoon lemon flavoring

Mash apricots and sweeten to taste. Heat in double boiler. Mix water with cornstarch and stir until smooth. Blend into apricots and cook till thick. Add butter and stir until melted. Pour mixture slowly over beaten yolks, beating constantly, and turn into baked pastry shell. Whip whites very stiff, adding sugar gradually and flavoring last. Spread over pie and brown in slow oven.

DATE PUDDING

As locally grown dates came on the market in the late 19th Century, cooks found many ways to make use of them. This rich, delicious steamed pudding found favor among hearty eaters who were not concerned with calories.

3 eggs, well-beaten

½ cup ground suet
1 cup sugar
½ teaspoon salt
½ teaspoon cinnamon
1 cup bread crumbs
1 pound dates, pitted
½ cup sweet milk
1 cup chopped walnuts
1 teaspoon baking powder

Measure and sift baking powder, salt and cinnamon. Combine eggs, suet, sugar, bread crumbs, dates, milk and nuts. Add dry ingredients, and mix thoroughly. Fill well-greased 1-quart pudding mold two-thirds full. Cover tightly. Steam 3 hours. Serve with sweetened, flavored whipped cream.

ENGLISH PLUM PUDDING

A gift to California cookery from England, by way of the Old South, is not made with plums but raisins. Some recipes call for more than the dozen eggs required here. Sometimes it was slowly steamed in a cloth bag, but this recipe is prepared in pudding pans with a cloth cover. It is well-preserved with cognac, and the writer tells us it will keep from year to year.

2 pounds currants, chopped fine and
*   soaked in water*
1 pound Sultanas, chopped fine
1 pound raisins (seeds removed)
1 pound mixed peel, chopped fine
1½ pounds suet chopped fine and
*   sprinkled with flour*
½ pound shelled and blanched almonds
12 eggs, well beaten
½ pint ale
2 wine glasses cognac
2 apples, chopped fine
1½ pounds flour
1 nutmeg, grated
2 teaspoons allspice
1 teaspoon salt
¼ pound sugar

Mix first 10 ingredients in a large pan. Mix flour, spices, sugar and salt in another pan, and add gradually to the fruit-nut-egg combination. Cover bowl with a cloth and let set for a couple weeks, stirring well each day. Add more flour if needed. When ready to steam, divide into 3 parts. Pour into pudding pans, cover with cloth and boil 7 to 10 hours. Will keep from year to year. When ready to serve, reheat for about an hour. Serve with brandy sauce.

Brandy Sauce:
¼ cup butter
1 cup fine confectioners' sugar
2 egg yolks, well beaten
½ cup cream
2 egg whites, beaten stiff
2 tablespoons brandy

Cream butter and sugar. Add egg yolks and cream. Cook over hot water until mixture coats spoon. Pour slowly over egg whites and add brandy. Flame before serving.

GRAHAM BIRDSNEST PUDDING

Baked in the manner of a fruit cobbler, we assume this apple dish was made with graham, or whole wheat flour, although white flour was plentiful by 1861 and was preferred for dessert recipes. The quaint name may have referred to its appearance and could have prompted *California Farmer* to publish it.

Lay in a deep dish, nice quartered apples, and pour over them a thin batter made of flour, one teacup of sour milk, one-half cup of sugar and about one third of a teaspoon of soda. Bake in a moderate oven till the apples are thoroughly cooked.

QUINCE PUDDING

Here is a custard-type pudding with a delightful fruit flavor. It comes from Mrs. Meikle's handwritten cookbook, which was donated to the Anaheim Public Library. After the quince is gently stewed, it is strained, or "sifted" as our cook says, before being added to the custard.

Pare and core six large quinces and cut in quarters. Stew them gently in a little water with lemon peel, until they are tender and then sift them. Sweeten to taste, and add a little cinnamon. Beat four eggs with 1 pint of new milk. Blend into fruit, and cook over low heat for a few minutes, stirring constantly, until thick.

RICE BALLS

A truly American dish with a sweet-tooth flair—these little cooked rice balls are rolled in egg and corn meal, then fried and served with sauce, possibly fruit, or with cream and sugar.

Boil rice until it is soft, and while warm make it into cakes or flat balls. Dip these balls into a beaten egg and then roll them in Indian meal till thoroughly coated. This done, fry them in lard, which is better than butter for this purpose. Serve them with sauce or with butter or cream and sugar.

ROCK CREAM

Creamy rice pudding is made attractive by the addition of meringue heaped on top in mounds to simulate snow.

Wash one cup of the best rice, and boil slowly until quite soft, in milk. Add white sugar to taste, and pile it on a dish. Scatter jelly or thick preserves over it. Beat the whites of five eggs to a stiff froth, and add sugar and flavoring. When well beaten, add a spoonful of rich cream and drop it on the rice imitating the form of a rock of snow.

SPANISH CREAM

Variations of this perennially popular recipe which is made with gelatine, milk and eggs, have appeared in most old California cookbooks.

Soak one-third box of gelatine in one and a half pints of milk for two hours, then set on stove and heat to boiling point, stirring constantly. Beat one cup of sugar with the yolks of three eggs, stir into the hot milk and gelatine, and flavor with 1 teaspoon of vanilla. When taken from the stove, add the egg whites beaten stiff. Let cool a long time.

STRAWBERRY SHORTCAKE

Mrs. Meikle, a resourceful German cook of the mid-1800's, in her hand-written cookbook presented a couple of tricks for making this delectable dessert. The preferred way is with cream, but when not available more leavening can be added to the pastry.

Before making the crust, stir into 3 pints of ripe rich strawberries a coffee cup of granulated sugar. Leave it covered over until the crust is done.

Crust:
Take a coffee cup of cream or sour milk. Beat into it a little salt and a small teaspoon of soda. Before it stops foaming, stir in enough flour to enable it to be rolled out. If cream or milk is not plentiful, use two scant teaspoonsful of baking powder sifted into the flour. Be sure not to get it very stiff. Roll it into three circles; spread ice-cold butter on top of each. Place one on top of the other and bake until well done, then pull apart. Butter one and cover with strawberries, then butter the second. Lay crust downward over the first, pile more strawberries on the second and cover with the third crust. It need not be heaped with berries unless preferred. Set in the oven for a few moments, and serve hot with cream.

GOOSEBERRY FOOL

A recipe for gooseberry custard naturally came from England, where the tart berries grew to perfection. If one does not have time to make the custard, it is suggested that the stewed berries may be served with cream.

Stew gooseberries until soft, add sugar, and press through a colander (an earthen one is best) then make a boiled custard; or sweeten enough rich cream (about one gill to each quart) and stir carefully into the gooseberries just before sending to the table.

PEACH MERINGUE

Not a dish for dieters, this baked casserole of peaches is smothered in a rich custard sauce and topped with a lightly browned egg meringue.

Put on to boil a quart of milk, omitting half a cup with which to moisten two tablespoons of corn starch. When the milk boils, add the moistened corn starch. Stir constantly until thick, then remove from the fire. Add one tablespoon of butter, and allow the mixture to cool; then beat in the yolks of three eggs till the mixture seems light and creamy. Add one-half cup of powdered sugar. Cover the bottom of a well-buttered baking-dish with two or three layers of rich, juicy peaches which have been pared, halved and stoned. Sprinkle them with three tablespoons of powdered sugar, then pour the custard over them. Bake twenty minutes. Remove from oven and spread with the lightly beaten whites, well sweetened, and return to the oven till a light brown. To be eaten with a rich sauce, or cold with sweetened cream.

APPLE DUMPLINGS

These dumplings from an 1854 recipe are wrapped in pie dough and boiled rather than baked, as preferred today.

Make a good paste. Pare some large apples, cut them in quarters. Take out the cores, and in place of them insert a clove and piece of lemon peel cut very thin. Take a piece of crust, enough for one apple, roll it round, put the quarters together, and roll the crust around it with a little flour in your hand. Boil one hour without intermission. When they are done enough, take them up, lay them on a dish, sprinkle fine sugar over them, and send them to the table with fresh melted butter in a boat, and fine beaten sugar in a saucer. Some persons boil apple dumplings without tying them in a cloth, but they are very apt to break and spoil.

FRUIT DUMPLINGS

Such a pretty way to serve up a fruit dessert has a decidedly Russian derivation. A simple dough is wrapped around fruit filling, boiled in water, and presented either with a sprinkle of sugar or a more elaborate fruit sauce.

2 eggs
1 cup water
1 teaspoon salt
Flour
Fresh fruit—sweetened cherries,
*   peach halves or blackberries*

Beat eggs well. Add salt, water and enough flour to make a stiff dough. Roll out thin and cut into circles about 3 inches in diameter. On each circle drop one teaspoonful of filling. Draw edges together and press tightly to make dumpling. Drop into a large saucepan of boiling water. When dumplings rise to the sur-

face, remove with a slotted spoon and drain. Serve with melted butter and sugar. May also be served with a sweet thick sauce made of fresh fruit.

PINEAPPLE SHERBET

Food to be chilled or "set," such as gelatine dishes or one like this sherbet recipe were left overnight in the well or in a "California cooler," a screened opening in the wall where food could be set on shelves and cooled by circulating air. This excellent fruit sherbet has an interesting addition of whipped egg whites.

One pineapple, four lemons, two quarts water, two teacups sugar. Peel pineapple, remove core, and cut into small pieces. Steep in the water for two hours. Strain and add the juice of the lemons and sugar. Whip the whites of five eggs and add to them three tablespoons of sugar, which gives body to the sherbet. Set in icebox or "California cooler" overnight to chill.

ITALIAN SHERBET

Various fruits could be substituted for the peach pulp called for in this recipe.

Make a syrup of 1 pound of sugar and 1 cupful of water. When cool, add ½ cupful of lemon juice, 1 cupful of orange juice and 1 quart of peach pulp (or any other fruit will do). Mix and rub through a sieve. Pour into a tin and pack in ice and salt until frozen—from two to three hours.

RAMONA SANDWICHES

Helen Hunt Jackson's novel entitled *Ramona*, published in 1884, created a wave of romantic interest in Southern California and it became popular to name towns and houses and even sandwiches after the literary figure. This recipe for a sweet molded filling for sandwiches was considered elegant for ladies' teas and luncheons.

Chop fine about equal quantities of figs, dates, raisins, citron, and any candied fruit and a very little candied peel. Place lightly in a square mould and pour over it melted loquat jelly. (Red currant jelly makes a very good substitute). If jelly is not firm, add a little gelatine when melting it. Move a fork gently through the mass to be sure the jelly settles all around the fruit. Set mould on ice till cold and firm, then turn out and cut off jelly in thin slices. Serve on brown bread very lightly buttered, laying a slice of jelly between two slices of bread. These are very delicious sandwiches and will repay all the trouble of making._

MINCEMEAT

Some mid-Western cooks with a strong Fundamentalist background, from an area sometimes referred to as the Bible Belt, eschewed wines and spirits, as the reader will note from this recipe which substitutes strong coffee for the rum or brandy used by more adventurous cooks.

4 cups cooked chopped beef (shoulder)
6 cups apples, chopped
2 cups chopped suet
1 cup citron, chopped
2 cups raisins
2 cups currants
4 cups brown sugar
1½ cups molasses
3 cups sweet cider
1 cup strong coffee
1 cup beef stock
½ cup lemon peel, ground
½ cup orange peel, ground
2 teaspoons nutmeg
2 teaspoons cloves
2 teaspoons allspice
4 teaspoons cinnamon
2 teaspoons salt

Mix well, place in large kettle and cook until done. Seal in jars until ready to use for pies.

TOMATO CATSUP

Savory tomato sauce was made in large quantities in early days. This recipe yields a half-gallon.

Take one gallon skinned tomatoes, four tablespoonsful of black pepper, three tablespoonsful of mustard, ready-made, eight pods

of pepper ground fine with cloves and mace to suit the taste; mix and simmer slowly half an hour, then strain it through a wire sieve. Boil slowly three or four hours in sharp vinegar, and bottle close. Age improves it.

CANTALOUPE PICKLES

An interesting 1861 recipe for pickling cantaloupe, a little less common than our well-known watermelon rind pickles.

Take cantaloupes just when they begin to turn yellow, but while the flesh is still solid, pare and cut up in slices half an inch thick. Dip quickly into hot water, and then pack in jars with spice and cloves. Cover with good pickling vinegar.

SWEET PEPPER RELISH

This is quite a sophisticated recipe for marinating green peppers, to be served as an accompaniment to meat dishes.

8 green peppers
2 teaspoons prepared mustard
2 teaspoons sugar
1 teaspoon salt
2 tablespoons vinegar
½ cup olive oil

Wash peppers well and cut into quarters, discarding seeds and fibers. Place in a deep saucepan, add 2 cups of water and cook for 20 minutes, or until tender. Drain well and cool in refrigerator for at least 1 hour. Mix mustard, sugar, salt, vinegar and oil in a bowl until thoroughly blended. Place peppers in a glass serving dish and pour marinade over them. Chill for at least 2 hours before serving.

ORANGE MARMALADE

The person who recorded this classic English recipe warns that the fruit and peel may burn easily during cooking. Jars of marmalade are welcome Christmas gifts today as they were one hundred years ago.

1 dozen oranges
4 good-sized lemons
1½ pints water to each pound sliced fruit
1 pound 2 ounces sugar to each pound of fruit

Slice oranges and lemons very thin, and

remove seeds. Add water and let stand for 24 hours. Boil till peel is tender (about 1 hour). Let this stand until quite cold, then remove fruit and weigh it. To every pound allow 1 pound 2 ounces of sugar. Mix and boil for one hour, taking great care it does not burn. Stir well with wooden or agate spoon. When done put in glasses and seal while hot. It is best not to boil too long in one pan, as it burns easily.

MEXICAN CHOCOLATE

The title of this recipe appeared as *Chocolate Majicana*, a phonetic approximation of the Spanish pronunciation. Over the years traditional Spanish chocolate, considered bitter by most Americans, evolved into a bland beverage.

Heat 4 small squares of chocolate over the teakettle until soft. Add 1 quart of sweet milk and stir until smooth. Beat yolks and whites of 3 eggs separately. When the chocolate boils, mix a half-cup with the yolks of the eggs. When well mixed, beat rapidly with the remainder of the chocolate. Stir in the beaten egg-whites and serve at once. The eggs must be added whilst the chocolate is hot, but must not be boiled. Serve with this salty, unsweetened wafers.

HOLIDAY CAUDLE

This hot beverage, served in heated mugs, makes a great picker-upper for a chilly California evening, after the big game, or any time.

6 egg yolks
4 cups muscatel or other dessert wine
6 cups strong black tea
1 cup sugar
Grated nutmeg

Beat egg yolks until light and lemon colored. Add wine and tea and beat well with a rotary beater. Stir in sugar and heat in double boiler, continuing to stir until sugar is dissolved. Serve in heated mugs with a dash of nutmeg sprinkled on top.

PUNCH

Anyone who lingered overlong at this punch

bowl may have had some slight difficulty finding his way home; whisky, brandy and champagne are used in good measure, with lemon essence and tea as blending agents.

Boil for 10 minutes peel of 3 lemons, 1 handful of allspice and 1 of cloves, in 1½ pints of water. Strain into a large bowl and add 1 pint of strong black tea, 2 bottles of whisky, 2 bottles of brandy, and sugar to taste. When ready to use, add 1 bottle of good California champagne, maraschino and ice.

COUNTRY SYLLABUB

Bless the cook who brought this recipe to California from Philadelphia, where it first appeared in Miss Leslie's *Complete Cookery*.

Mix half a pound of white sugar with a pint of sweet white wine and grate in nutmeg. Prepare them in a large bowl, just before milking time. Let it be taken to the cow, and have about three pints milked into it. Let it be drunk before the froth subsides.
NOTE: Today's homemaker can produce her version by mixing 1 cup of sugar and ¼ teaspoon of nutmeg with 2 cups of white port or sweet sauterne, then adding 1½ quarts of light cream, and beating until frothy. Additional nutmeg may be sprinkled over the top if desired.

EGGNOG

The secret of a good eggnog "lies entirely in the beating," according to this early California cook. The recipe calls for fine French brandy, but we are almost certain that any lady from Kentucky would have used "whisky" instead.

Separate 12 eggs and beat the yolks 15 minutes, then add 12 scant tablespoons of very fine sugar and beat until the grains are quite dissolved (15 to 20 minutes). Beat in 12 tablespoons fine French brandy and 12 ounces fine old rum. Grate half a nutmeg in 6 cupsful of milk and add very slowly to the mixture. Then add 12 tablespoons of thick cream whipped stiff. Last of all add the whites of the eggs beaten to a froth and give a last hard beating. The art of making good eggnog lies entirely in the beating.

112

Chapter VI

Health and Climate for Sale

Aren't you tired of the doctoring and nursing,
Of the "sickly winters" and the pocket pills —
Tired of sorrowing and burying and cursing,
At Providence and undertaker's bills?
—CHARLOTTE GILMAN

As the reputation of California grew beyond the lure of gold to the attractions of climate and the wonders of agricultural riches, waves of different types of settlers pushed westward from the East and kept coming from other lands.

Fruits and vegetables of Brobdingnagian proportions flourished in the fertile soil. A gigantic pea stalk of a variety called marrow-fat was grown in 1854 on the Keystone Ranch, near the present Amador City. According to the *California Farmer* this seven-foot high plant was a fair example of other stalks in the same garden that year. In a garden at Cache Creek in Yolo County, one F. Moore grew a "very finely formed cauliflower, the head measuring three and one-half feet in circumference." This vegetable was exhibited in Sacramento in 1856. A two-pound, twelve-ounce pear grown in the orchard of a Mr. Beard at the mission at San Jose was exhibited at the State Fair in that city in 1858. The *Los Angeles Star* reported in 1861 on "that tall cabbage" grown by George Lehman:

"It is fifteen feet tall and still growing. The cabbage was planted in 1856. Since that time George has gathered seed from it nine times, made sauerkraut forty times, cole slaw as often, and used it for salad for twenty-five other occasions. It has numerous limbs in the form of a tree, all of which have heads of cabbage, which are from time to time taken off for use. It is in truth a vegetable curiosity, and well worth visiting."

Even chickens cooperated in the California abundance. Mrs. D. B. Bates, who wrote extensively of her experiences in California during the gold fever, described the unusual and welcome contribution of a stray hen. While she was living in a canvas shanty in Marysville in the Sacramento Valley, an old yellow hen entered the room, hopped up on the bed and laid an egg, jumped down and departed, conducting the whole affair in utmost secrecy. Mrs. Bates was grateful for the egg which she sold for 50 cents, and she put out food for the hen. The hen returned every day for twelve days, laying an egg and departing. When the hen indicated she wished to sit on the nest, Mrs. Bates' brother took some eggs to a ranch and exchanged them for fertile ones. The hen set on the eggs and in due course twelve chicks appeared, which were sold for $1 each. The hen laid another clutch of eggs and raised another brood of chicks. Mrs. Bates finally had to board the hen at a ranch, but in all had realized a total of $45.

CALIFORNIA MECCA

The news that the climate was warranted to cure all ills and was particularly favorable for those suffering from tuberculosis and asthma circulated widely in England, and many well-to-do patients came to California in hopes of regaining their health. Thousands of patients from the Eastern United States also joined in the hegira. Happily, many of them did thrive and remained to establish themselves in business or in the professions. Invalids of more moderate means found light outdoor work or turned to fruit farming or honey production.

One enthusiastic amateur apiarist estimated that for $1400 an invalid could buy fifty hives of bees, a honey house, food provisions for fifteen months, a wagon and other supplies needed to establish himself in keeping bees. Needing only time and patience for recovery, the invalid could regain health and live in freedom from the stress of Eastern winters and humdrum labor.

Sufferers from rheumatism benefitted from medicinal springs in Elsinore, Carlsbad, Arrowhead, Warner's Hot Springs and other lesser known spas. Pasadena and Altadena were founded by groups of health-seekers.

Swimming Bath and Sanitarium at Arrowhead Hot Springs

WALLACE W. ELLIOTT & CO., PUBLISHERS, 1883

Hotel del Coronado, Coronado Beach, San Diego County

T. S. VAN DYKE'S *CITY AND COUNTY OF SAN DIEGO*, 1888

In the 1870's the San Gabriel Valley was dubbed the "Great Orange Belt and Sanitarium." Riverside was founded on a slogan of "Citrus and Health." San Diego put in a bid for the invalid population when Elisha Babcock built famed Hotel del Coronado as a winter health resort. Santa Barbara achieved a reputation as a resort for the wealthy and unhealthy.

Sanitariums proliferated, but some were little more than tents or shacks, and the food, a very important aid to recovery, left much to be desired. However, health-seeking physicians helped raise the standard of medical care to a level above what might be expected in the still raw Far West.

One graduate of Harvard Medical College, suffering from asthma, went into the dairy business in Riverside. He circulated cards bearing a message to prospective customers which introduced himself as M. B. Johnson, M.D. (which means Milk Distributor). Cookbooks of the period included advice to those preparing food for the sick. The following is taken from *Buckeye Cookery and Practical Housekeeping*:

"It is of the utmost importance that food served to the sick be delicately and carefully administered and this should never be left to servants. It should be made as attractive as possible, served in the choicest ware, with the cleanest napkins and the brightest of silver.

"If tea is served, it should be freshly drawn, in a dainty cup, with a block of white sugar and a few drops of sweet cream. Toast should be thin, symmetrical, well yellowed, free from crust, and just from the fire. Steak should be a cut of the best tenderloin, delicately broiled, and served with the nicest of roasted potatoes. The attention given to these simple matters is, in many cases, worth more than the physician's prescriptions."

In 1885 a group of philanthropic women in Los Angeles organized the Festival of Flowers in order to provide funds for building a home for invalid women and destitute widows. The annual event developed into an

The Tournament of Roses in Pasadena

important municipal affair which was held each April. The parade of *caballeros,* who wore colorful Spanish costumes of the rancho period, and great two-hundred foot Chinese dragons delighted the crowds lining the sidewalks. *La Fiesta de las Flores,* or the Feast of the Flowers, was the first of similar festivals which were held in other Southern California communities for the benefit of the ill who thronged the area in search of health.

LAND OF PROMISE

The flow of emigrants from the East was expanded with thousands of Europeans who learned about the new promised land in the distant West and came to the shores of America seeking a better life. The influx of tillers of the land was welcome news to the *California Farmer,* which dedicated its efforts to the increasing agricultural development of the state.

California owes a debt of gratitude to Armenian settlers who came to the San Joaquin Valley in the mid-1800's. Recognizing the suitability of the area for raisin production, long a part of their cultural heritage, they experimented with several varieties of grapes, particularly the muscat and Thompson seedless, until with a little luck, they found a successful raisin grape. As production increased, they tried to sell them with little success as "dried grapes." Good marketing potential was discovered only when they were simply labeled "raisins." The Raisin Growers Association, a cooperative group organized in 1896, controlled the bulk of the crop.

The slogan "Had your iron today?" focused the nation's attention on the nutritional value of raisins. Though the slogan was banned later by the Food and Drug Administration, the sale of raisins as a snack item continues today. California produces about ninety percent of the nation's raisins.

Besides spurring raisin production, the Armenians' lamb and stuffed vegetable dishes, their pastries and distinctive flat cakes of unleavened bread have added materially to the diversity of the California cuisine.

For centuries the raising of sheep had been the primary industry in the Basque country between Spain and France, so it was not strange that as the sheep population in California increased, Basque sheepherders began to arrive, hoping to find new and more prosperous lives for themselves. They settled in the meadows and mountains throughout California. The loneliness of the sheepherder's life was not the hardship for them as it seemed to be for the more gregarious Americans. Loyal sweethearts in the home country waited patiently for their young men to earn enough money for passage to the land of promise. Basque families were good citizens and have added their bit to the flavoring of California's potpourri. Lamb of course held first place in their choice of meat for the diner's delight and was served up in many variations of roasts and stews. Sheepherder's Stew served today is credited to Basque cooks.

By 1882 California's Italian colony, then in the general vicinity of San Francisco, was "pretty numerous." In later years Italians spread out into the fertile Sacramento River Valley, and not surprisingly their chief occupations were those related to food. They were grocers, butchers, restaurateurs, farmers, fruit growers and gardeners. They also were excellent musicians.

In 1869 John Stillwell Morgan, a New Yorker who had tried his luck in the gold mines, planted oysters along Mission Creek south of San Francisco. The highly prized bivalves were ensconced in a cluster of little oyster houses, surrounded by partially submerged wickets to insure safety in their salty beds. His company did not come up to his expectations and he sold out. However, his efforts were not in vain and a few of these oyster houses are still in existence around Morro Bay and Moss Landing.

Far-sighted agriculturists increased their efforts to experiment with new and different vegetables and fruits. Machinery which was constantly being improved helped to spur production of rich field crops. Transcontinental railroad service enabled growers to ship grain, fresh produce and meat safely and speedily to the expanding eastern markets. Improved water supplies helped expand production of field crops.

EVOLUTION OF WINE MAKING

The story of California's enormously successful wine industry, and the elegant wine cookery which evolved among the good eaters in the state, had not been written in final form at the close of the 19th century, for the prestige of imported wines was still largely unchallenged.

Due in large part to the efforts of Agoston Haraszthy, the findings of the mission padres were confirmed—the virgin soil and temperate climate of Southern California assured larger grape crops than in other parts of the world.

Haraszthy was born in Hungary in 1812 of a noble family. He was banished because of his activities in the revolution and immigrated to Wisconsin where he pioneered in farming and in a steamboat line. He was a vineyardist and a wine lover, which led to his departure on Christmas Day in 1848 for San Diego, traveling via the Santa Fe Trail. In the spring of 1850 he set out his first vineyard in Mission Valley near San Diego, and ordered some grape cuttings from his native Hungary, including the Zinfandel. He was elected to the State Legislature in 1851 and as his vines in San Diego had failed to prosper, in 1857 he transferred his grape cul-

ture efforts to northern California where he established the Buena Vista Winery near General Vallejo's rancho.

In 1861 Haraszthy was appointed by Governor John G. Downey to observe and report on wine culture in Europe. Haraszthy purchased 100,000 vines of 1400 different varieties in Europe, primarily in Germany and France. California's fine wines of the present day are the product of descendants of these vines which he so wisely and carefully selected. Haraszthy had unbounded faith in the future of the wine industry, and after introducing new varieties of grapes to Southern California from Europe, he planted more than 85,000 vines of one hundred and sixty-five varieties in Sonoma County.

In 1831 Louis Vignes had come to Los Angeles from Bordeaux, France, and finding the climate ideal for viniculture, he sent back to his homeland for vine species. The cuttings were delivered to Boston and shipped around the Horn to Los Angeles. His wine business progressed so favorably that he sent for his nephew, Pierre Sansevain, and later Pierre's brother, Jean Louis. By 1842 Vignes, probably California's first permanent French resident and a Los Angeles pioneer, was producing wine and brandy which he sold in northern California and in the coastal trade. A Los Angeles street is named in his honor.

William Wolfskill, Kentucky-born trader, trapper, and a pioneer citrus and fruit grower, also added grapes to his orchards. In 1859 a barrel of wine from his vineyard was presented to President Buchanan, along with oranges, lemons, citrons, almonds, walnuts and grapes. The sale of wine and brandy contributed materially to his financial success.

From the vines of these pioneers, and other less well-known growers, almost 2,000,000 gallons of wine were produced by 1870, one-fourth of which consisted of sweet wines from Los Angeles County, while Sonoma, where

Oak Dale Vineyard and Ranch in San Diego County

Haraszthy resided, produced one-sixth of this total output in dry wines. A destructive disease to grape vines checked wine production for several years, but the industry was firmly established by 1900, when 19,000,000 gallons were produced—more than eighty percent of the national output. Napa Valley wines soon came to be recognized as the choicest in the state, and in years to come they successfully challenged France's claim to superiority.

One of the factors contributing to Wolfskill's success was his open-minded attitude toward new methods of production, which he quickly incorporated in his wine-making. Though many tradition-minded people clung to the idea that the "barefoot" method produced superior wine—a belief which persisted until the late 1880's—most

forward-thinking Californians were convinced that this was an antiquated practice. Wolfskill developed an assembly-line system from field to vat, using a Yankee-invented machine that enabled two men to do the work of ten "foot treaders."

In 1880, during Anaheim's ascendancy as a wine-making center, a gentleman from that community sent a keg of Angelica, a keg of port and a keg of vinegar to his son-in-law in San Francisco. The shipment arrived in due time at the consignee's house and the keg marked "Angelica" was tapped without delay. It gave forth sparkling water. The port had also been tampered with, but the vinegar had not been molested. A newspaper reported the incident and stated that this was not the first time such a thing had occurred, but there seemed to be no way of obtaining

The Camel in California

redress. In 1857 the *Los Angeles Star* commented:

"Angelica is a popular ladies' wine, or sweet liquor, admirably designed to please the palate, but producing the largest sized headache on those who indulge in it too liberally. It is made by adding one gallon of grape brandy to three gallons of unfermented grape juice, allowing a slight fermentation to take place. If bottled it becomes somewhat sparkling."

Dr. Nicholas Culpeper wrote in his book on herbs that the herb angelica was so named because of its "angelical virtues." He described it as "an herb of the sun in Leo, to be gathered when he is there, the Moon applying to his good aspect, in his hour or in the hour of Jupiter; let Sol be angular." The good doctor attributed many healing powers to this herb. Angelica was used in California in soups, confections and cake decorating, in addition to its being a much-liked sweet liquor.

SUCCESS WITH OLIVES AND DATES

In the burgeoning agricultural expansion of California the olive, a treasured fruit of mission and rancho days, came into important commercial recognition. Thousands of trees were planted, most of the fruit at first being used for making oil. When it was fully realized that olives could be completely tree ripened, the industry flourished. Today, California leads the world in ripe olive production.

Olives are an important addition to many meat and vegetable dishes in California cookery, and of course no cocktail party is complete without a bowl of ice-cold, juicy and eye-appealing olives. Both the ripe black olives and the green ones have their devotees.

Even desert country was put to good use. Dates, one of the oldest fruits cultivated by man, have been served as delicacies since written history began. The wandering nomads of the Arabian desert lived on a diet of dates, milk and honey. We do not know how successful the missions were in producing dates but Edith Buckland Webb in her book on Indian life mentions the venerable date palms which stood near the missions at San Buenaventura and Santa Clara in the 1930's. In addition to whatever date crops were harvested from mission plantings, we assume the padres also received shipments of this fruit from their native Spain via the trading ships.

Agriculturists on the lookout for food-producing plants to be grown in California imported date shoots to the Coachella Valley in the late 1800's. The "harem" of forty-eight female palms and one male palm thrived. Since then, more than a hundred varieties have been planted in the desert country around Indio. All dates produced in the United States are grown in California.

A favorite sweetmeat of the late 1800's was stuffed dates. The pits were removed and walnut meats inserted in the cavity, the edges of the fruit pressed tightly together and rolled in granulated sugar.

Visitors to the annual Date Festival in Indio are reminded of another link between interior California and the Arabian Desert. In an effort to solve the overland freight problem before railroads were completed, the Camel Corps was organized by Jefferson Davis while he was Secretary of War. Several trips were made between Albuquerque, New Mexico, and Fort Tejon, the mountain outpost north of Los Angeles. American drivers really did not have the knack of handling the fractious beasts, and camel drivers imported from Arabia were resented by Californians. The Dromedary Express was a dismal failure, and the camels were set adrift when the Civil War erupted and Jefferson Davis left Washington to become president of the Confederate Republic.

CITRUS—GOLD OF THE SUN

Horace Greeley, the editor who had advised young men to "go west," also predicted that "fruit is destined to be the ultimate glory of California." During the 1850's orange, lime and lemon plantings, which had been neglected after secularization of the missions, were regenerated by seeds and seedlings from Hawaii and Central America. Agoston Haraszthy, best remembered for his contributions to California viniculture, proved beyond the shadow of a doubt that most of the fruits and vegetables of temperate and semi-tropical climates would thrive in California.

It remained for William Wolfskill to demonstrate the profitable nature of fruit growing. Starting with orange and lemon cuttings from San Gabriel Mission, by 1849 he had thriving groves. Wolfskill's orchards also included apricots, pears, apples, peaches, olives and figs. In 1852 Mrs. Emily C. Hayes, wife of Judge Benjamin Hayes, pioneer lawyer and traveling judge who had come to California over the Southern Trail, bought two dozen oranges from Mrs. Wolfskill for

$1. In 1853 Wolfskill shipped peaches, pears and apples to San Francisco. He introduced the delectable Japanese persimmon and was one of the first to grow eucalyptus trees in the state. His nephew John is credited with introducing large-scale lima bean culture into Los Angeles County.

In the late 1850's a scurvy epidemic broke out in Mexico, in the territory of Sonora. Wolfskill shipped his thick-skinned lemons to the area, as they had a longer shipping life than oranges. In doing so he was competing with John Sutter, Jr. who was growing limes and lemons in Acapulco for shipment to California. He also cut into the monopoly of Queen Pomari of Papeete, Tahiti.

Before railroads opened up new markets to the East, the wealth of California fruit presented some minor disadvantages. In 1861 the *California Farmer* complained of fruit-skin litterbugs:

"Would it not be well if all persons would refrain from throwing peach or plum-pits or fruit-skins on the sidewalks? How often do we notice persons slip and fall by treading on them, and often times the injury is serious. We wish the Press in general would notice this subject. Limbs have been broken by falls caused by these things, and a little care would prevent it."

By the 1870's there were more than 45,000 citrus bearing trees in California, almost two-thirds of them in Wolfskill orchards. His orchards suffered from frost and the scale, as others did, but survived without ruinous damage. In 1877 Wolfskill's son shipped the first trainload of oranges to eastern markets via the Southern Pacific Railroad. The oranges were wrapped in paper and iced for refrigeration. The shipment arrived in St.

Orange Grove and Home in Riverside

WALLACE W. ELLIOTT & CO., PUBLISHERS, 1883

Days of Steam–Halt for a Leisurely Lunch

Louis a month later in good condition, the ice being replaced eleven times en route.

The navel orange, brought from Brazil, was introduced in Riverside. It proved so successful that these large seedless oranges of excellent color and flavor took all prizes at the New Orleans Exposition in 1884. One of the parent trees survives to this day.

In 1886 the Wolfskill orchards introduced the Valencia, a summer orange which would be found to thrive best in California. Valencia oranges were originally known in California as the Rivers Late Oranges. They were imported early in the 1870's in unlabeled packages from the Thomas Rivers Nursery of Sawbridgeworth in Hertfordshire, England. The names were left off of the trees and the nursery sent no clue as to where they originated. As they were beginning to prosper in California, an orange grower from Spain visiting one of the groves remarked, "that is the late orange of Valencia." News-

papers predicted that this new orange would become "a great favorite with growers."

Increasing production of citrus fruit during the latter years of the century presented a marketing problem which was happily solved by the introduction of refrigerator cars, improved grading, packing and shipping methods. These improvements, coupled with heavy advertising promotion by The California Fruit Growers' Exchange, a cooperative, by 1900 pushed annual shipments of the golden globes (oranges and lemons) to 24,000 cars and made the name "Sunkist" synonymous with California oranges and lemons.

AN EMBARRASSMENT OF RICHES

California's glorious promise of future agricultural greatness was dramatized at the Columbian Exposition in Chicago in 1893. A life-sized elephant built entirely of California walnuts, and flanked with boxes and baskets of oranges and lemons, drew attention

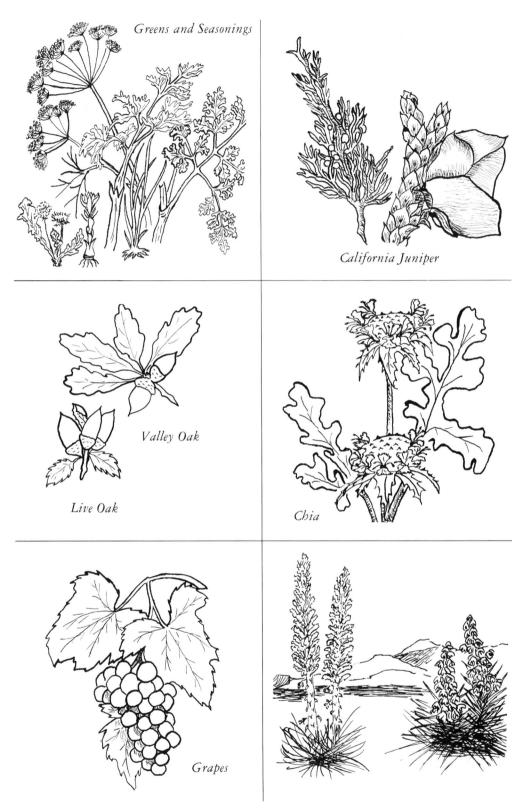

Greens and Seasonings

California Juniper

Valley Oak

Live Oak

Chia

Grapes

Characteristic Food Plants of California

SKETCHES BY DORIS LOEWNAU

to the California Building.

Approximately one million acres of California land were under irrigation by 1890. In the years to follow the state would lead the nation in growing many foodstuffs, including almonds, apricots, artichokes, asparagus, avocados, lima beans, spinach, broccoli, brussels sprouts, carrots, cauliflower, celery, lettuce, olives, chili peppers, tomatoes, walnuts, sweet cherries, figs, cantaloupes and honey dew melons, lemons, nectarines, peaches, pears, persimmons, plums, prunes, strawberries, rice, seed clover, sugar beets, and dates. It would lead other states in production of farm chickens and eggs, and rank near the top in beef cattle, sheep, turkeys and dairy products.

This embarrassment of riches naturally produced a state of better than average eaters, large in size and with the glow of sun-tanned health. The exuberant self-assurance of many a Californian stood out—and still stands out —from the crowd in Eastern cities. While it is doubtful that many could foresee with accuracy that in a new century the Golden State would eventually lead in population, technological and scientific research, education, and in entertainment and tourist industries, there seemed no question that agriculture and the wine industry would provide income and bountiful living in a measure to stagger the imagination.

Recipes

HERBS AND SPICES

Cooks from other parts of the country as well as those coming in from many nations of the globe, found their favorite herbs and spices could be grown in California. An 1860 issue of the *California Farmer* gave the following directions for preserving herbs:

Dried Herbs:

All kinds of herbs should be gathered on a dry day, just before or while in blossom. Tie them in bundles, and suspend them in a dry, airy place, with the blossoms downward. When perfectly dry, wrap the medicinal ones in paper and keep them from the air. Pick off the leaves of those which are to be used for cooking, pound and sift them fine and keep the powder in bottles, corked up tight.

Commonly used Herbs and Spices:
Aniseed: *seed for flavoring, used in candy and cookies.*
Basil, sweet: *leaves dried and ground, used in sauces, gravies, stews, sausage and tomato dishes.*
Bay Leaf: *usable fresh, but more commonly dried and used in soups, gravies, meat dishes and spaghetti sauce.*
Coriander: *seeds used for flavoring cheese, bread, chili, hot tamales, egg dishes, and sauerkraut.*
Cumin: *used either whole or ground in meat loaf, hamburgers, chili con carne, tamales, wild game, eggs, soup, stews and vegetable dishes.*
Dill: *mainly used in pickling, but can be added fresh to soups, sauces and salads.*
Fennel: *tender leaves used as a fish garnish; fennel seed is good in dark breads.*
Marjoram: *wild, used widely for tomato dishes; also good in pork or beef dishes and in omelets.*
Mint: *many varieties—spearmint, peppermint and other—tender young leaves used in juleps, iced tea and other cooling drinks.*
Parsley: *generally used fresh as a garnish for salads and meat dishes, or dry for soups.*
Rosemary: *used fresh or dried, in stews, sweet sauces, soups, meat dishes, or as a garnish.*
Saffron: *an essential ingredient in certain Spanish and Mexican dishes; but also may be used in yeast breads, soups, cakes, sauces and sea food dishes.*
Sage: *used fresh or in dry form in poultry dressings, sausage making, green beans, stewed tomatoes and many cheese dishes.*
Thyme: *used in fresh or dry form; particularly valued for adding zest to left-overs.*

FOOD FOR THE SICK

Tempting the appetite of invalids was a challenge for doctors and nurses during the influx of ill and suffering people in the last decades of the century. These easily digested and palatable suggestions are as sound now as they were then.

Crust Coffee:
Toast bread very brown, pour on boiling water, strain and add cream and sugar. Nutmeg may be sprinkled over the top if desired.

Cream Soup:
1 pint boiling water
½ teacup cream
Add broken pieces of toasted bread and a little salt.

Baked Milk:
Bake 2 quarts of milk for 8 or 9 hours in a moderate oven, in a jar covered with writing paper, tied down. It will then be as thick as cream, and may be used by weak persons.

Chicken Broth:
Take the first and second joints of a chicken, boil in 1 quart of water till very tender, and season with a very little salt and pepper.

Beef Tea:
Cut a pound of best lean steak in small pieces, place in glass fruit jar (a perfect one), cover tightly and set in a pot of cold water. Heat gradually to a boil, and continue this steadily three or four hours, until the meat is like white rags and the juice thoroughly extracted. Season with very little salt, and strain through a wire strainer. Serve either warm or cold. To make beef tea more palatable for some patients, freeze it.

Vegetable Soup:
Peel 2 tomatoes, 2 potatoes and 2 onions, slice and place in deep saucepan with 1 tablespoon of rice. Boil in 1 quart of water for an hour. Season with salt. Dip dry toast in this till quite soft and eat. This may be used when animal food is not allowed.

Oatmeal Gruel:
Put 2 heaping tablespoons of oatmeal in one quart of cold water, place on stove and stir till it commences to boil. Cook one hour, stirring occasionally. Do not let it scorch. Season with salt, sugar, and any spice desired. For infants and very sick patients it must be strained and not salted.

Egg Gruel:
Beat the yolk of an egg with a tablespoon of sugar, beating the white separately. Add a tea cup of boiling water to the yolk, then stir in the white and add any seasoning desired. Good for a cold.

Uncooked Egg:
This is quite palatable and very strengthening, and may be prepared in a variety of ways. Break an egg into a goblet and beat thoroughly. Add a teaspoon of sugar, and after beating a moment longer, add a teaspoon or two of brandy or port wine. Beat well and add as much rich milk or part cream and milk, as there is of the mixture. Or, omit brandy and flavor with any kind of spice; or, milk need not be added; or, the egg may be beaten separately, stirring in lightly the well-whipped whites at the last.

Parched Rice:
Cook in custard-kettle a half-cup of parched rice in 1 pint of boiling salted water. When done, serve with cream and sugar.

Broiled Beefsteak:
Many times a small piece of tenderloin or porterhouse is more wholesome for an invalid than broths and teas, and with this may be served a potato, roasted in the ashes, dressed with sweet cream or a little butter and salt, or nicely cooked tomatoes. Have the steak from half an inch to an inch thick, broil carefully for two or three minutes over hot coals, turning often with a knife and fork, so as not to pierce it. When done, put on a small dish, season slightly with salt and pepper, and a small piece of butter, garnish with the potato and serve hot.

Raw Beef:
Chop fresh, lean beef (the best steak or roast) very fine, sprinkle with salt and pepper, and put between thin slices of graham or white buttered toast. This is a very nutritious diet.

BAKING POWDER

When a recipe called for baking powder it often meant the homemade variety.

8 ounces flour

8 ounces English bicarbonate of soda
7 ounces tartaric acid

Mix thoroughly by passing through a sieve several times.

RUBBING HAMS

An 1870 hand-written German cookbook gave these directions for preparing ham.

*3 ounces salt peter
4 ounces brown sugar
1 pint fine salt*

Rub ham all over and lay on a board for 24 hours, and then pack down, adding 2 quarts of fine salt. Ham should remain packed 15 days.

PICKLED WALNUTS

Perhaps this very old recipe was first printed in the United States in Mrs. Beecher's *Domestic Receipt Book* in the early 1800's. It is included in early California cookbooks, and Doris Loewnau remembers that her father brought a similar recipe to California from England in the 1890's.

Walnuts should be picked about midsummer, before the shells have formed and while they are still in the green stage. Pierce each nut in several places with a pin or larding needle. Place nuts in a large crock and cover with a brine made of salt and water, using ½ cup of salt to each quart of water. Allow nuts to stand in this brine for 1 week. Remove nuts and drain thoroughly. Place them in a large kettle and cover with fresh brine made in the same proportion. Simmer gently for 30 minutes. Remove from brine and place in a sieve to drain. When dry, arrange on a flat surface and leave them there until they turn black, which will take several days. Fill sterilized jars about two-thirds full of walnuts and cover with pickle sauce made as follows: For every quart of cider vinegar, add 2 tablespoons of black pepper, 1 tablespoon of ginger, 1 tablespoon of salt, 1½ teaspoons of allspice and ¼ teaspoon of cayenne pepper. Bring to a boil and cook for 10 minutes. Seal jars at once.

ORANGE FLOWER SYRUP

As the name implies, this syrup is made from the blossoms of the orange tree. The almost lyrical writer says it has the scent of an orange grove in spring and suggests the syrup makes an intriguing ingredient for numerous kitchen masterpieces.

*1 pint fresh white orange petals
1 quart rich syrup made of granulated
   sugar and water*

Select and wash without bruising the white petals of the orange flowers. While petals drain on a cloth, prepare a rich syrup of granulated sugar and water, allowing 1 quart for each pint of blossoms. After skimming syrup carefully, drop in the petals and simmer 2 minutes. Stir gently, strain and bottle. Seal while hot. It will be a delicate sea green color, retaining all the fragrance of the flower and reminding one when opened of an orange grove in spring. A teaspoonful added to a glass of water makes a most delicious drink. Also an agreeable flavoring for custard, icing or pudding sauce.

FLAVORING EXTRACTS

Making extracts of vanilla, lemon or orange flavoring was a commonplace necessity in early days. The chore usually required time, patience, and quite a bit of alcohol.

Vanilla: *Take 1 ounce of fresh vanilla beans, cut fine, and rub thoroughly with 2 ounces granulated sugar. Put in a pint bottle and pour over it 4 ounces of pure water and 10 ounces of 95% deodorized (pure grain) alcohol. Set in a warm place and shake occasionally for 14 days.*

Lemon: *Cut the rinds of 2 lemons in small pieces, put in a 4-ounce bottle and fill with deodorized strong alcohol. Set in a warm place for a week; then put 2 drachms fresh oil of lemon, 4 ounces of deodorized (pure grain) strong alcohol, and the juice of half a lemon, in a bottle of sufficient size to hold all; then strain in the tincture of lemon peel. To make orange extract, use the rind and oil of orange, as directed for lemon.*

OLD FASHIONED ROSE JAR

The rose jar was kept in the parlor, and when guests were expected the lid was removed, permitting the pleasant fragrance to permeate the room. A friend has a pair of handsome Meissen vases with perforated lids, designed for use as rose jars, which were brought from England to California by her mother in the 1890's. Orris root called for in this recipe comes from a European iris.

4 quarts dried rose petals
¾ cup salt
2 ounces cloves
2 ounces mace
8 ounces powdered orris root
1 ounce whole cinnamon
1 ounce rose or jasmine oil
A little dried lavender

Pick rose petals in the morning while still heavy with dew. Lay out on paper in a dark, cool place to dry. When dry, place layer in stone crock and cover lightly with salt. Continue till jar is filled. Crush spices slightly with rolling pin and pour oil over them. Let dry a little so oil does not make top leaves soggy. Mix spice mixture and dried lavender into petals. Let stand covered for one week, stirring once a day. Place in decorative jars with lids. Lasts for years.

LAVENDER SACHET

Another nostalgic item that has retained its appeal is the sachet, made from carefully dried lavender blossoms. The blossoms are lightly crushed and placed in small envelopes of China silk or other very thin material, trimmed with lacy edges, and used in lingerie drawers and linen closets.

ROSE WATER

Distilled water from rose petals has a delicate fragrance; it was used by itself or added to cologne mixtures.

When the roses are in full blossom, pick the petals off carefully, and to every quart of water add a peck of them. Put them in a cold still over a slow fire, and distill very gradually; then bottle the water, let it stand in the bottle three days, and cork it close.

COLOGNE

The bergamot called for in this recipe comes from an oil extracted from the rind of a variety of pear-shaped orange-colored fruit.

One and a half pints of alcohol, one and a half drachms bergamot, one drachm of lemon, one-half drachm of rosemary, one and a half drachms of garden lavender, musk and rosewater as you like.

HINTS FOR HOUSEWIVES

Today's cooks will be interested in this collection of wise hints gleaned mostly from mid-century issues of the good *California Farmer*.

Baking potatoes:

When baking potatoes, first let them stand in boiling water for 15 minutes. They will bake in one half the usual time. Or, if time is very short, try boiling them till nearly done, and finish them in the oven. Pierce them with a fork before baking them and they will not burst open in the oven.

Fried Potatoes:

Sprinkle a little flour on potatoes before frying to make them an attractive, appealing golden brown.

Cabbage Odors:

To prevent odor when cooking cabbage, cut the cabbage in halves or quarters, and with a sharp knife, remove the little curl or center of the cabbage. Most of the strength is in the bud, and if it is removed most of the unpleasant odor will disappear.

Tenderizing Meat:

To make tough meat tender, rub baking soda into it. Let stand several hours and wash thoroughly before cooking.

Cooking Rice:

When cooking rice, add a teaspoon of lemon juice to each quart of water, to help keep the grains separate and make them white.

Meat and Fowl Stuffings:

Farces or stuffing should be made so the bread comprises one-third, and the other two-thirds meat. Add butter or suet, season with pepper and salt; if too hard, soften with cream or milk.

Extra Stuffing:

When extra dressing is to be baked, cut off one thick slice of a dry loaf of bread and scoop out the inside, leaving only a thick crust. Fill with dressing, pin on the end slice and bake. It will be as delicious as if baked in the fowl. The scooped-out bread may be used in the dressing.

Varieties of Sugars:

Buy sugars for various purposes as follows: For baked custard, mince pie, squash pie, fruit cake, gingerbread, most Indian puddings, use brown sugar. For all light-colored cakes, icing, floating island, blancmange, meringues, whips, use powdered sugar. For pudding sauce, use powdered or brown sugar. For sweetmeats, jelly and raspberry vinegar, use granulated sugar.

Baking Cakes with Fruit:

To prevent currants, raisins or citron from sinking to bottom of cake, warm them well in oven before adding them to the batter, then stir in lightly the last thing.

How to Eat Strawberries:

Place as many berries as will form one layer at the bottom of a dish and sift some fine loaf sugar over them, then place another layer and sift again. When there are five or six layers, cut a fresh lemon and squeeze all over them. Before serving, let them be gently disturbed that they may have the benefit of the lemon juice and sugar.

How to Eat Grapes:

When in health, the pulp only shall be swallowed. When the bowels are costive, swallow the seeds with the pulp, ejecting the skins. When the bowels are in a too relaxed state, swallow the pulp and skin, and reject the seeds. Thus the grape may be used as a medicine, while at the same time it serves as a luxury unsurpassed by any other fruit. There is but little danger of over-eating grapes, if the above rules are followed; particularly if taken with and as a part of the regular meal. We should advise eating them before rather than after other courses.

Preserving Suet:

Suet keeps good all the year round, if chopped and packed down in a stone jar, covered with molasses. Mince pie meat may be equally well preserved if boiled, chopped and similarly packed.

Preparing Green Corn for Winter:

When green or in good boiling condition, husk and put in the oven after the baked bread is removed. Allow it to remain until the sun shines next day. Expose to the sun a few days, carefully protecting it at night, and when dry, put in bags for winter use. To prepare for the table, remove the grains from the cob (it is easily shelled) soak for an hour, boil soft, and serve up with butter and salt to your taste.

Preserving Dead Game:
(See cautionary remarks in Foreword)

Take out the intestines and fill inside with unground wheat, and place the fowl in a heap or cask of the same grain in such a manner as to insure its being completely covered. In this way, fowls may be preserved perfectly sweet for months. The feathers should be removed.

WEIGHTS AND MEASURES

In the days before Fannie Farmer devised a standard system of weights and measures, published in the 1890's, cooks learned to judge for themselves. Some of the approximate measurements in use are listed here.

Dash (of salt) ....1/16 *teaspoon*
Small pinch ....1/16 *teaspoon*
Large pinch ....⅛ *teaspoon*
3 teaspoons ....1 *tablespoon*
1 dessertspoon ....2 *teaspoons*
1 wineglass ....¼ *cup*
4 tablespoons ....¼ *cup*
1 gill ....½ *cup*
1 small coffee cup ....¾ *cup*
1 large teacup ....1 *cup*
Lump ....*if teaspoon doesn't work, double it*
Butter size of walnut .1 *rounded tablespoon*
Butter size of pigeon's egg ....2 *tablespoons*
Butter size of hen's egg ....4 *tablespoons*
1 pint ....2 *cups*
1 pound white granulated sugar .....2 *cups*
1 pound powdered sugar, sifted ....3⅓ *cups*
1 pound brown sugar packed firm ..2¼ *cups*
1 pound wheat flour ....4 *cups*
1 pound fresh shredded coconut ......5 *cups*
9 raw egg whites ....*about 1 cup*

Acknowledgments

Research for this book has led down many interesting paths; along the way new friends have been made, doors have been opened, and helping hands have been extended. I am grateful for this opportunity to acknowledge these kindnesses and to make those concerned aware of my deep gratitude for their assistance and encouragement.

To begin, my sister Lyla Graul, who pointed the way; Margaret Key of the Bowers Museum in Santa Ana, who grasped immediately what I was trying to do and has continued to send along helpful material; Marion Gore, bookseller, of San Gabriel; Marion Abrecht and other staff members of the Anaheim Public Library; also staff members of the libraries in Santa Ana, Fullerton, Long Beach Bixby Branch, Los Angeles, Pasadena and Westminster; Kent Grothjan of the El Dorado County Library in Placerville, for cooperation in supplying specific data, including one of the recipes for Hangtown Fry; Ronald Mahoney, Special Collections Librarian of Fresno State College, who steered me to rare old volumes on wines, wine cookery and enology, filling my cup to overflowing, as it were; he has also sent along helpful information from time to time.

Dr. Tad Lonergan of Tustin is due very special thanks, for his encouragement and for putting me in touch with others who have helped: Mrs. Ed Ainsworth, who introduced Doris and me to Genevieve Golsh of Pala, creator of beautiful Indian ceramics and an expert in Indian lore; her husband Marcus Golsh, equally respected in the history of his people; Carey Bliss of the Huntington Library, Mary Isabel Fry and other staff members of that marvelous storehouse of history; Don Meadows, historian and learned gentleman, of Santa Ana, who gave us valuable help in several areas. For reading parts of the manuscript for historical accuracy, I am indebted to Richard Dillon of Sutro Library in Sacramento, the late W. E. Robinson, historian and book reviewer of Los Angeles; and Abraham Nasatir of California State University, San Diego

Food companies replied to my requests with valuable historical information as well as tested recipes: California Avocado Advisory Board; California Date Administrative Committee; Dried Fig Advisory Board; Apricot Producers of California; California Raisin Advisory Board; California Meat Council; California Wine Advisory Board. The Sheraton-Palace shared some of their world-famed recipes, along with their historical background.

Long-time friends Maxine Kelley Lutz and Dot Farnsworth responded nobly to my questions with practical ideas and suggestions. Husband Bob patiently sampled the various new dishes which I set before him. He liked some of them. The disasters were buried.

Doris Loewnau and her sister Rosemary Curtis are native Californians and have set me straight on numerous points when varying accounts in source books seemed contradictory. Rosemary read several drafts of this book and her comments and suggestions have been gratefully received and acted on. Doris' delightful illustrations grace the book and I am honored to include her name on the title page.

Last but by no means least, this is an humble memorial to my mom and dad who taught me to appreciate history as well as cookery.

Bibliography

Tracing California's development from the Acorn Culture of the Indians to the sophisticated blend of European-American food cultures of corn, rice and wheat has led down many paths. Personal diaries of individuals who arrived in California from various countries and the eastern United States often deal in some detail with foods, food products and agriculture, as well as social manners. Other authors provide background for the fascinating growth of the nation's most charismatic state. Recipe history, from the handwritten type to other publications is listed separately.

Social History

AMERICAN HERITAGE, *The California Gold Rush,* New York, 1961.

ATHERTON, Faxon Dean, *California Diary, 1836-1839.* California Historical Society, San Francisco, 1964.

ATHERTON, Gertrude, *California; An Intimate History.* Boni & Liveright, New York, 1927.

BAER, Kurt, *Architecture of The California Missions.* University of California Press, Berkeley, 1956.

———, *The Treasures of Mission Santa Ines; a History and Catalog of the Paintings, Sculpture, and Craft Works.* Academy of California Church History, Fresno, 1956.

BAILEY, L. H. *The Standard Cyclopedia of Horticulture.* 3v. Macmillan, New York, 1914.

BANCROFT, Hubert Howe, *California Pastoral–1769-1848.* Vol. XXXIV of Bancroft's Works. The History Co., San Francisco, 1888.

BANNING, William, and BANNING, George Hugh, *Six Horses.* Century, New York, 1930.

BARTLETT, Lanier, *Los Angeles In 7 Days.* R. M. McBride, New York, 1932.

BARY, Helen Valeska, comp., *The Course of Empire: First Hand Accounts of California In The Days Of The Gold Rush of '49.* Coward-McCann, 1931.

BATES, Mrs. D. B., *Incidents On Land and Water; Or, Four Years On The Pacific Coast,* Boston, 1857.

BAUER, Helen, *California Indian Days.* Doubleday, New York, 1963.

BAUR, John E., *The Health Seekers of Southern California, 1870-1900.* Huntington Library, San Marino, 1959.

BEAN, Walton, *California; an Interpretive History.* McGraw-Hill, New York, 1968.

BEEBE, Lucius, and CLEGG, Charles, *San Francisco's Golden Era; A Picture Story of San Francisco Before the Fire.* Howell-North, Berkeley, 1960.

BEEBE, Lucius. *The Overland Limited.* Howell-North, San Francisco, 1963.

BELL, Horace, *On the Old West Coast; Being Further Reminiscences of a Ranger.* Morrow, New York, 1930.

BENSON, Ivan, *Mark Twain's Western Years, Together with Hitherto Unreprinted Clemens Western Items.* Russell & Russell, New York, 1966.

BERGER, John Anton, *The Franciscan Missions of California.* Doubleday, New York, 1948.

BIDWELL, John, *Echoes of the Past About California.* Citadel Press, New York, 1962.

BIDWELL, John, BANCROFT, Hubert Howe, and LONGMIRE, James, *First Three Wagon Trains: To California, 1841; To Oregon, 1842, To Washington, 1853.* Binfords & Mort, Portland, Ore., n.d.

BISHOP, Mrs. Isabella Lucy, *A Lady's Life In The Rocky Mountains.* Putnam, New York, 1879-80.

BISHOP, William Henry, *Old Mexico And Her Lost Provinces–A Journey In Mexico, Southern California, and Arizona By Way of Cuba.* Harper, New York, 1883.

BLACKMAR, Frank W., *Spanish Institutions of the Southwest.* Johns Hopkins Press, New York, 1891.

BLEGEN, Theodore Christian, ed., *Land of Their Choice; The Immigrants Write Home.* University of Minnesota Press, Minneapolis, 1955.

BLOK, T., *The Russian Colonies in California. A Russian Version Translated From T. Blok's Brief Geographical Statistical Description of California,* St. Petersburg, 1850. In California Historical Quarterly, Vol. XII, no. 3, September, 1933, p. 189.

BOLTON, Herbert Eugene, and ADAMS, E. D., *California's Story.* Allyn & Bacon, New York, 1922.

BOLTON, Herbert Eugene, ed., *Historical Memoirs of New California,* by Fray Francisco Palou. Translated into English from the manuscript in the Archives of Mexico. 4 vols. University of California Press, Berkeley, 1926.

BORTHWICK, J. D., *3 Years in California (1851-54) Or, The Gold Hunters.* W. Blackwood & Sons, London, 1857.

BOSCANA, Geronimo, *Chinig-chinich.* A revised and annotated version of Alfred Robinson's translation of Fr. Geronimo Boscana's Historical Account of the Belief, Usages, Customs and Extravagances of the Indians of this Mission of San Juan Capistrano Called the Acighohemem Tribe. Fine Arts Press, 1933.

BOWLES, Samuel, *Across the Continent; A Summer's Journey.* San Francisco, 1875.

BREWER, William H., *Up and Down California, In 1860-1864.* Yale University Press, New York, 1930.

BROWN, D. Mackenzie, *China Trade Days in California; Selected Letters From the Thompson Papers, 1832-1863.* University of California Press, Berkeley, 1947.

BROWN, Karl, *California Missions.* 2d ed. Nourse Pub. Co., San Carlos, Calif., 1954.

BROWN, Vinson, and ANDREWS, Douglas. *The Pomo Indians of California And Their Neighbors.* Naturegraph Publishers, Healdsburg, Calif., 1969.

BRUFF, J. Goldsborough, *Gold Rush; The Journals, Drawings, and Other Papers of J. Goldsborough Bruff, Captain Washington City And California Mining Association, April 2, 1849-July 20, 1851.* Columbia University Press, New York, 1949.

BRYANT, Edwin, *What I Saw in California; The Complete Original Narrative And Appendix From the 1849 Appleton Edition in True Facsimile.* Lewis Osborne, Palo Alto, 1967.

BUCKBEE, Edna Bryan, *Pioneer Days of Angels Camp.* Angels Camp, Calif., 1932.

BUEHR, Walter. *Home Sweet Home in the 19th Century.* Crowell, New York, 1965.

CALIFORNIA HISTORICAL SOCIETY, *The Plate of Brass; Evidence of the Visit of Francis Drake to California In The Year 1579.* San Francisco, 1953. *California Information Almanac.* Rev. and Ed. by Adolf Stone et al. Lakewood, Calif., 1960.

CAUGHEY, John Walton, *California.* 2d ed. Prentice-Hall, New York, 1953.

CHALFONT, W. A., *Gold, Guns & Ghost Towns.* Stanford University Press, San Francisco, 1947.

CHAPMAN, Charles Edward, *The Founding of Spanish California, The Northwestward Expansion of New Spain, 1687-1783.* Macmillan, New York, 1916.

CHAPMAN, John L., *Incredible Los Angeles.* Harper & Row, New York, 1967.

CHEVIGNY, Hector, *Russian America: The Great Alaskan Venture, 1741-1867.* Viking Press, New York, 1965.

CHIANG, Yee, *The Silent Traveller in San Francisco.* Norton, New York, 1964.

CHIU, Ping, *Chinese Labor in California, 1850-1880.* State Historical Society of Wisconsin, Madison, 1963.

CHRISTMAN, Enos, *One Man's Gold: The Letters and Journal of a Forty-niner.* Whittlesey House, New York, 1930.

CLAPPE, Louise Amelia Knapp Smith (Dame Shirley) *California in 1851; The Letters of Dame Shirley.* Grabhorn Press, Los Angeles, 1933.

CLARK, Sydney Aylmer, *Golden Tapestry of California.* R. M. McBride, New York, 1937.

CLELAND, Robert Glass, *California Pageant; The Story of Four Centuries.* Knopf, New York, 1946.

————, *From Wilderness to Empire; A History of California.* A Combined and Revised Ed. of From Wilderness to Empire (1542-1900) and California In Our Time (1900-1914) Knopf, New York, 1967.

————, *A History of California; The American Period.* Macmillan, New York, 1922.

CLELAND, Robert Glass, and HARDY, Osgood, *March of Industry.* Powell Pub. Co., Los Angeles, 1929.

CLEMENTS, Edith, S., *Flowers of Coast and Sierra.* H. W. Wilson, New York, 1928.

COLTON, Walter, *Three Years in California.* A. S. Barnes, New York, 1850.

CONNER, Palmer, *The Romance of the Ranchos.* Los Angeles, 1941.

CORLE, Edwin, *John Studebaker, An American Dream.* Dutton, New York, 1948.

COSSLEY-BATT, Jill L., *The Last of the California Rangers.* Funk & Wagnalls, New York, 1928.

COWAN, Robert Granniss, *Ranchos of California: A List of Spanish Concessions and Mexican Grants.* Fresno, Calif., 1956.

COY, Owen Cochran, *Gold Days.* Powell Pub. Co., Los Angeles, 1929.

CRONISE, Titus Fey, *The Natural Wealth of California.* H. H. Bancroft, San Francisco, 1868.

CROSS, Ralph Herbert, *Early Inns of California, 1844-1869.* San Francisco, 1954.

CURTIN, L. S. M. *Some Plants Used By The Yuki Indians of Round Valley, Northern California.* Southwest Museum, Los Angeles, 1957.

DAKIN, S. B., *Scotch Paisano.* University of California Press, Berkeley, 1939.

DANA, Julian, *Sutter of California; A Biography.* The Press of the Pioneers, New York, N.Y., 1934.

DANA, Richard Henry, *Two Years Before The Mast; A Personal Narrative.* Houghton Mifflin Co., Boston, 1884.

DAVIS, William Heath, *Seventy-five Years in California.* J. Howell Books, San Francisco, 1967.

————, *Sixty Years in California.* A. J. Leary, San Francisco, 1859.

DAWSON, Grace S., *California, the Story of Our Southwest Corner.* Macmillan, New York, 1962.

DEMOREST'S MONTHLY MAGAZINE, Nov. 1882-1883. W. Jennings Demorest, New York, N.Y., 1883.

DENIS, Alberta Johnston, *Spanish Alta California.* Macmillan, New York, 1927.

DICKSON, Samuel, *San Francisco Kaleidoscope.* Stanford University Press, San Francisco, 1949.

————, *Streets of San Francisco.* Stanford University Press, San Francisco, 1955.

————, *San Francisco Is Your Home.* Stanford University Press, San Francisco, 1955.

DILLON, Richard H., *Humbugs and Heroes: A Gallery of California Pioneers.* Doubleday, New York, 1970.

DOBIE, Charles Caldwell, *San Francisco; a Pageant.* Appleton Century, New York, 1943.

————, *San Francisco's Chinatown.* Appleton Century, New York, 1936.

DUMKE, Glenn S., *The Boom of the Eighties in Southern California.* Huntington Library, San Marino, 1944.

DUTTON, Davis, *A California Portfolio. . . .* Auto. Club of So. Calif., 1970.

ELDER, Paul, *The Old Spanish Missions of California.* Paul Elder & Co., San Francisco, 1913.

ELWOOD, Louis Butler, *Queen Calafia's Land; An Historical Sketch of California.* Grabhorn Press, Los Angeles, 1940.

ENGELHARDT, Zephyrin, *The Franciscans in California.* Holy Childhood Indian School, Harbor Springs, Mich., 1897.

———, *The Missions and Missionaries of California.* 4 vols. James H. Barry, San Francisco, 1908-15.

ESSIG, E. O., *The Russian Settlement at Ross.* In California Historical Quarterly, Vol. XII, no. 3, September, 1933, p. 191-209.

EVANS, George W. B., *Mexican Gold Trail: The Journal Of A Forty-Niner.* Huntington Library, San Marino, 1945.

EVANS, Howard E. and EBERHARD, Mary Jane West. *The Wasps.* U. of Michigan Press, Ann Arbor, 1970.

FAIRCHILD, Lucius, *California Letters.* State Historical Society of Wisconsin, Madison, 1931.

FARNHAM, Eliza W., *California Indoors and Out.* Dix-Edwards, New York, 1856.

FARNSWORTH, Harriett, *Remnants of The Old West.* Naylor, San Antonio, Tex., 1965.

FAVOUR, Alpheus, H., *Old Bill Williams, Mountain Man.* University of Oklahoma Press, Norman, 1962.

FEDERAL WRITERS' PROJECT, *California; A Guide To The Golden State.* Hastings House, New Yok, 1954.

———, *Death Valley; A Guide.* Houghton Mifflin, Boston, 1939.

FISH, Frank L., *Buried Treasure and Lost Mines.* Amador, 1956.

FISHER, Walter Mulrea, *The Californians.* Macmillan, London, 1876.

FORBES, Mrs. A. S. C., *Mission Tales In The Days Of The Dons.* A. C. McClurg, New York, 1909.

FORBES, Alexander, *California; A History of Upper and Lower California From Their First Discovery to the Present Time, Comprising An Account of the Climate, Soil, Natural Production, Agriculture, Commerce, &c; A Full View of the Missionary Establishments And Conditions of the Free and Domesticated Indians.* Smith, Elder & Co., London, 1839.

GARNER, Bess. *Windows In An Old Adobe.* Pomona, Calif., Printed by Progress Bulletin in collaboration with Saunders Press, Claremont, Calif., 1939.

GARNER, William Robert. *Letters From California, 1846-1847.* U. of California Press, San Francisco, 1970.

GARRISON, Myrtle, *Romance and History of California Ranchos.* Harr Wagner Pub. Co., San Francisco, 1935.

GIFFEN, Helen Smith, *Casas and Courtyards; Historic Adobe Houses of California.* Biobooks, Oakland, 1955.

GILES, Dorothy, *Singing Valleys; The Story of Corn.* Random House, New York, 1940.

GILLINGHAM, Robert Cameron. *The Rancho San Pedro; the Story of a Famous Ranch in Los Angeles County And Of Its Owners, The Dominguez Family.* Cole-Holmquist Press, Los Angeles, 1961.

GILMORE, N. Ray, and GILMORE, Gladys, *Readings in California History.* Crowell, New York, 1966.

GOSS, Helen Rocca, *When East Was East In The Old West.* In Southern California Historical Quarterly, Vol. 36, Dec. 1954, p. 301.

GREELEY, Horace, *An Overland Journey.* H. H. Bancroft Co., San Francisco, 1860.

GUDDE, Erwin Gustav, *German Pioneers In Early California.* Concord Society, Hoboken, N. J., 1927.

———, *100 California Place Names; Their Origin and Meaning.* University of California Press, Berkeley, 1965.

GUINN, James Miller, *Historical And Biographical Record of Southern California..* Chapman Pub. Co., 1902.

HANNA, Phil. Townsend. *Dictionary of California Land Names.* Auto. Club of So. Calif., Los Angeles, 1946.

HARLAN, Jacob Wright, *California, '46 to '88.* Oakland, 1896.

HARTE, Bret, *Bret Harte in Prose and Poetry, Now First Collected.* Chatto & Windus, London, 1872.

HAYES, Benjamin Ignatius, *Pioneer Notes From the Diaries–1849-1875.* Los Angeles, 1929.

HEIZER, R. F., and WHIPPLE, M. C., eds., *The California Indians; a Source Book.* University of California Press, Berkeley, 1962.

HERRICK, Elizabeth Webb, *Curious California Customs.* Pacific Carbon & Print Co., Los Angeles, 1935.

HIJAR, Carlos. *Recollections of California in 1834.* MS in Bancroft Collection.

HINE, Robert V., *California's Utopian Colonies.* Huntington Library, San Marino, 1953.

HITTELL, Theodore Henry, *History of California.* 4 vols. N. J. Stone, San Francisco, 1897.

HODGE, Frederick Webb, ed., *Handbook of American Indians North of Mexico* (in 2 parts) Smithsonian Institution, Bureau of American Ethnology, Bulletin 30, Government Printing Office, Washington, 1912.

HOLMES, Maurice G., *From New Spain By Sea To The Californias, 1519-1668.* Arthur H. Clark, Glendale, Calif., 1963.

HOOVER, Mildred Brooke, *Historic Spots in California; Counties of the Coast Range.* Stanford University Press, San Francisco, 1937.

HOWARD, Robert West, *Flag of the Dreadful Bear; The Story of the Republic of California.* Putnam, New York, 1966.

HUNT, Rockwell D., *California In The Making; Essays and Papers in California History.* Caxton Printers, Ltd., Caldwell, Idaho, 1953.

HUNTLEY, Henry V., *California: Its Gold and Its Inhabitants.* London, 1856.

HUTCHINGS, James Mason, *Commandments to California Wives,* 1855.

———, *The Miners' Ten Commandments. In* Quarterly

of Society of California Pioneers, Vol. I, no. 79, pg. 1006, 1853.

———, *In The Heart of the Sierras.* Pacific Press Pub. House, San Francisco, 1886.

HUTCHINGS' CALIFORNIA MAGAZINE, Vol. I, no. 6, December 1856. (Pack mules)

———, Vol. V, no. 4, October 1860 (Chinese costumes)

———, Vol. V, no. 5, November 1860, p. 209 (Bear flag)

———, Vol. V, no. 6, December 1860, pp. 276-280.

HUTCHINGS' ILLUSTRATED CALIFORNIA MAGAZINE; Scenes of Wonder & Curiosity. Howell-North, Berkeley, 1962.

JACKSON, Helen Hunt, *Father Junipero and the Mission Indians of California.* Little Brown, Boston, 1902.

———, *Glimpses of California And Its Missions.* Little Brown, Boston, 1902.

JACKSON, Joseph Henry, *Anybody's Gold; The Story of California's Mining Towns.* Appleton-Century, New York, 1941.

JAEGER, Edmund C., and SMITH, Arthur C., *Introduction To The Natural History of Southern California.* U. of California Press, Berkeley, 1966.

JAMES, George Wharton, *In and Out of the Old Missions of California; An Historical and Pictorial Account of the Franciscan Missions.* Little Brown, Boston, 1905.

JEPSON, Willis Linn. *A Manual of the Flowering Plants of California.* U. of California Press, San Francisco, 1925.

JOHNSON, Paul C., *Pictorial History of California.* Doubleday, New York, 1970.

JOHNSTON, Bernice Eastman, *California's Gabrielino Indians.* Southwest Museum, Los Angeles, 1962.

KAHN, Edgar M., *Cable Car Days in San Francisco.* Stanford University Press, San Francisco, 1944.

KAINEN, Ruth Cole, *America's Christmas Heritage.* Funk & Wagnalls, New York, 1969.

KIRSCH, Robert R., *West of the West; Witnesses to the California Experience, 1542-1906. The Story of California From the Conquistadores To The Great Earthquake . . . .* Dutton, New York, 1967.

KNOWLAND, Joseph R., *California; A Landmark History, Story of The Preservation and Marking of Early Day Shrines.* Tribune Press, 1941.

KROEBER, Theodora, *Ishi In Two Worlds; A Biography of the Last Wild Indian in North America.* U. of California Press, Berkeley, 1961.

KRYTHE, Maymie R., *Daily Life in Early Los Angeles. In* Southern California Historical Quarterly, Vol. 36, June 1954, pps. 123, 327.

———, *Pico House: The Finest Hotel South of San Francisco. In* Southern California Historical Quarterly, Vol. 37, June 1955, pp. 139-160.

LEWIS, Oscar, *Bay Window Bohemia, An Account of the Brilliant Artistic World of Gaslit San Francisco.* Doubleday, New York, 1956.

———, *California Heritage.* Crowell, New York, 1949.

———, *San Francisco: Mission to Metropolis.* Howell-North Books, San Francisco, 1966.

———, and HALL, Carroll D., *Bonanza Inn, America's First Luxury Hotel.* Knopf, New York, 1940.

LOS ANGELES STAR (newspaper) Microfilm copies of various issues, 1860.

LUMMIS, Charles Fletcher, *The Spanish Pioneers and the California Missions.* New and enl. ed. A. C. McClurg, 1929.

MACARTHUR, Mildred Yorba, *Anaheim "The Mother Colony."* Ward Ritchie Press, Los Angeles, 1959.

MARRYATT, Francis Samuel, *Mountains and Molehills; Or, Recollections Of A Burnt Journal.* Harper, New York, 1855.

MARSHALL, James Wilson. *California–Marshall's Own Account Of The Gold Discovery,* as Related to Charles B. Gillespie. Century Magazine, 1891.

MASSEY, Ernest de, *A Frenchman In The Gold Rush; the Journal of Ernest de Massey, Argonaut of 1849,* translated by Marguerite Eyer Wilber. California Historical Society, San Francisco, 1927.

McFIE, Maynard, *The Gay Nineties.* Sunset Club, Los Angeles, 1945.

McGLASHAN, Charles F., *History of the Donner Party.* Truckee, Crowley and McGlashan, San Francisco(?) 1879.

McGROARTY, John Steven, *California; Its History and Romance.* Grafton Pub. Co., Los Angeles, 1911.

McPHEE, John. *Oranges.* Farrar, Straus and Giroux, New York, 1967.

MIGHELS, Ella Sterling, *Life And Letters of a Forty-niner's Daughter.* By Aurora Esmeralda (pseud.) Harr Wagner, San Francisco, 1929.

MONAGHAN, Jay, *Australians And The Gold Rush; California and Down Under, 1849-1854.* U. of California Press, Berkeley, 1966.

MOODY, Ralph, *Stagecoach West.* Crowell, New York, 1967.

MUIR, John, *The Mountains of California.* Century Co., New Yok, 1903.

MUNZ, Philip A. and KECK, David D. *California Flora.* U. of California Press, San Francisco, 1959.

NADEAU, Remi. *Ghost Towns And Mining Camps of California.* Ward-Ritchie Press, Los Angeles, 1965.

NASATIR, Abraham P., *French Activities in California; An Archival Calendar-guide.* Stanford University Press, Berkeley, 1945.

———, *A French Journalist In The California Gold Rush; The Letters of Etienne Derbec.* Ed. by Abraham P. Nasatir. Talisman Press, Georgetown, Calif., 1964.

NELSON, Edna Deu Pree, *The California Dons.* Appleton-Century-Crofts, New York, 1962.

NEWMARK, Harris, *Sixty Years in Southern California 1853-1913.* 2d Ed. Rev. and Augmented. Ed. by Maurice H. Newmark and Marco R. Newmark. Knickerbocker Press, 1926.

NEWMARK, Marco, *Pioneer Merchants of Los Angeles. In* Historical Quarterly of Southern California, Part I, Vol. 24, September 1942, pp. 77-97.

NORDHOFF, Charles, *California: For Health, Pleasure and Residence; A Book for Travellers and Settlers.* Harper, New York, 1872.

O'SULLIVAN, St. John, *Little Chapters About San Juan Capistrano.* 8th ed. 1912.

PACKMAN, Ana Begue, *Leather Dollars; Short Stories of Pueblo Los Angeles.* Times Mirror Press, Los Angeles, 1932.

PARSONS, Marion Randall, *Old California Houses, Portraits and Stories.* U. of California Press, Berkeley, 1952.

PAUL, Rodman W., *The California Gold Discovery; Sources, Documents, Accounts and Memoirs Relating to the Discovery of Gold at Sutter's Mill.* Talisman Press, Georgetown, Calif., 1967.

PEATTIE, Roderick, ed., *The Pacific Coast Ranges.* Vanguard Press, New York, 1946.

PERKINS, Elisha Douglass. *Gold Rush Diary; Being the Journal of Elisha Douglass Perkins on the Overland Trail In The Spring and Summer of 1849.* U. of Kentucky Press, Louisville, 1967.

PETERSON, P. Victor. *Native Trees of Southern California.* U. of California Press, San Francisco, 1966.

PHILLIPS, Catherine, *Through the Golden Gate. San Francisco, 1769-1937.* Sutton House, Los Angeles, 1938.

PITT, Leonard, *The Decline of the Californios; A Social History Of The Spanish-speaking Californians-1846-1890.* U. of California Press, Berkeley, 1966.

POURADE, Richard F., *The Silver Dons.* Union-Tribune Pub. Co., San Diego, 1963.

———, *Time of the Bells.* Union-Tribune Pub. Co., San Diego, 1961.

PRIESTLY, Herbert Ingram. *Franciscan Explorations in California.* Ed. by Lillian Estelle Fisher. Arthur H. Clark, Los Angeles, 1946.

QUAIFE, Milo Milton, ed. *Pictures of Gold Rush California.* Citadel Press, New York, 1967.

RAND, Christopher, *Los Angeles, The Ultimate City.* Oxford University Press, London, 1967.

RAUP, Hallock F., *The German Colonization of Anaheim, California. In* Publications in Geography, University of California, Berkeley, 1932.

RICHMAN, Irving Berdine, *California Under Spain and Mexico, 1535-1847* . . . .Cooper Square, New York, 18--.

ROBINSON, Alfred, *Life in California: During a Residence of Several Years in That Territory* . . . .Private Press of T. C. Russell, San Francisco, 1925.

———, *Life in California; A Historical Account of the Origin, Customs and Traditions of the Indians of Alta-California.* Biobooks, Oakland, Calif., 18--.

———, *The Key to Los Angeles.* Lippincott, New York, 1963.

ROBINSON, W. W., *Los Angeles From The Days of the Pueblo, Together With A Guide To The Historic Old Plaza Area, Including The Pueblo de Los Angeles, State Historical Monument.* California Historical Society, San Francisco, 1959.

———, *Old Spanish & Mexican Ranchos of Orange County.* Title Insurance and Trust Co., Los Angeles, 1964.

———, *Panorama; A Picture History of Southern California.* Title Insurance and Trust Co., Los Angeles, 1953.

ROLLE, Andrew F., *California, A History.* 2d ed. Crowell, New York, 1969.

ROYCE, Josiah, *California; From The Conquest in 1846 to the Second Vigilance Committee in San Francisco; A Study of American Character.* Knopf, New York, N.Y., 1948.

ROYCE, Sarah Eleanor, *A Frontier Lady; Recollections of the Gold Rush And Early California.* Yale University Press, New York, 1932.

RUSH, Philip Scott, *A History of the Californians.* 2d ed. (San Diego, 1964).

SALVATOR, Ludwig Louis, *Los Angeles In The Sunny Seventies; A Flower From the Golden Land.* Bruce McCallister, 1929.

SANCHEZ, Nellie, *Spanish Arcadia.* Powell Pub. Co., Los Angeles, 1929.

SAUM, Lewis O. *The Fur Trader and the Indian.* U. of Washington Press, Seattle, 1965.

SAUNDERS, Charles Francis, *Under the Sky in California.* C. F. & E. H. Saunders, New York, 1913.

SHIELDS DATE GARDENS, *Coachella Valley Desert Trails: The Salton Sea Saga, and The Romance and Sex Life of the Date.* 4th ed. Indio, Calif., 1957.

SHIPPEY, Lee, *It's An Old California Custom.* Vanguard Press, New York, 1948.

SMITH, Sarah Bixby, *Adobe Days.* The Torch Press, New York, 1925.

SPEARS, John R., *Illustrated Sketches of Death Valley.* Rand McNally, New York, 1892.

SPIER, Robert F. G., *Food Habits of Nineteenth Century California Chinese. In* California Historical Society Quarterly, Vol. 37, March-June, 1958, p. 79.

SPINDEN, Herbert J., *Fine Art and the First American.* The Exposition of Indian Tribal Arts, Inc., New York, 1931.

SPLITTER, Henry Winfred, *Los Angeles Recreation 1846-1900. In* Southern California Historical Quarterly, Vol. 43, March 1961, pp. 35-68.

STELLMAN, Louis J., *Mother Lode; The Story of California's Gold Rush.* Harr Wagner, San Francisco, 1934.

STEPHENSON, Terry Elmo, *Don Bernardo Yorba.* Dawson Bros., Los Angeles, 1963.

SUNKIST GROWERS, *The Story of California Oranges and Lemons.* California Fruit Growers Exchange, n.d.

SYMONDS, George W. D., *The Tree Identification Book; A New Method For The Practical Identification and Recognition of Trees.* Morrow, N. Y., 1958.

TAYLOR, Bayard, *Eldorado, Or, Adventures In The Path of Empire; Comprising A Voyage to California Via Panama; Life in San Francisco and Monterey; Pictures Of The Gold Region, And Experiences of Mexican Travel.* 2 vols. Putnam, New York, 1850.

TAYLOR, R. R. *Seeing The Elephant; Letters of R. R. Taylor, Forty-Niner.* Ward-Ritchie Press, Los Angeles, 1951.

THOMPSON, Robert A., *Russians in California; Fort Ross, Founded 1812, Abandoned 1841. Why the Russians Came and Why They Left.* Bio-books, Oakland, 1951.

TINKHAM, George Henry, *California Men and Events, Time 1769-1890.* California Record Publishing Co., Stockton, 1915.

TOMPKINS, Walker A., *Santa Barbara's Royal Rancho; The Fabulous History of Los Dos Pueblos.* Howell-North, San Francisco, 1960.

TRUMAN, Benjamin Cummings, *Semi-tropical California.* A. L. Bancroft, San Francisco, 1874.

TWAIN, Mark, *Roughing it.* 2 v. in 1. Harper, New York, 1913.

UNDERHILL, Ruth, *Indians of Southern California.* Sherman Pamphlets, Department of Interior, n.d.

VALLEJO, Guadalupe. *Ranch and Mission Days in California.* Century Magazine, Dec., 1890.

WALKER, Edwin F., *Indians of Southern California.* Southwest Museum, Los Angeles, n.d.

_____, *World Crops Derived From the Indians.* 4th ed. Southwest Museum, Los Angeles, 1967.

WARE, Joseph E., *The Emigrants' Guide to California.* Ed. by John Caughey from edition of 1849. Princeton University Press, New York, 1932.

WEBB, Edith Buckland, *Indian Life At The Old Missions.* Warren E. Lewis, Los Angeles, 1962.

WEST, Henry Josiah, comp. *The Chinese Invasion; Revealing the Habits, Manner, and Customs of the Chinese Political, Social and Religious, of the Pacific Coast . . . . Containing Careful Selections From the San Francisco Press.* Bacon, 1873.

WESTON, Otheto. *Mother Lode Album.* Stanford U. Press, San Francisco, 1948.

WILSON, Iris Higbie, *William Wolfskill, 1798-1866; Frontier Trapper To California Ranchero.* Arthur H. Clark Co., Glendale, Calif., 1965.

WINTHER, Oscar Osburn, *Express And Stagecoach Days in California, From The Gold Rush To The Civil War.* Stanford U. Press, 1936.

_____, *Via Western Express & Stagecoach.* Stanford U. Press, 1945.

WISE, Winifred E., *Fray Junipero Serra and The California Conquest.* Scribner's, New York, 1967.

WRIGHT, Ralph C., ed., *California Missions.* California Mission Trails Assn., Ltd., Printed by Sterling Press, Los Angeles, 1950.

WYLLYS, Rufus Kay, *French in Sonora (1850-1854); The Story of French Adventurers From California into Mexico.* University of California Press, Berkeley, 1932.

WYMAN, Donald. *Wyman's Gardening Encyclopedia.* Macmillan, New York, 1971.

YOCUM, Charles, and DUSMANN, Ray. *The Pacific Coastal Wildlife Region; Its Common Wild Animals and Plants.* Rev. Ed. Naturegraph Co., Healdsburg, Calif., 1966.

Recipe History

AARON, Jan, and SALOM, Georgine Sachs, *The Art of Mexican Cooking.* Doubleday, New York, 1965.

AINSWORTH, Edward Maddis, *Bill Magee's Western Barbeque Cookbook.* Murray & Gee, Culver City, Calif., 1949.

_____, *Early California Cooking Treasures.* Desert Printers, Palm Desert, Calif., 1965.

AMERICAN HERITAGE *Cookbook and Illustrated History of American Eating and Drinking.* New York, 1964.

ANGIER, Bradford, *Wilderness Cookery.* Stackpole Co., Harrisburg, Pa., 1961.

APRICOT PRODUCERS OF CALIFORNIA. *Apricots.* Berkeley, Calif., 1970.

ARESTY, Esther B., *The Delectable Past; the Joys of the Table—From Rome to the Renaissance, from Queen Elizabeth I to Mrs. Beeton, the Menus, the Manners—and the Most Delectable Recipes of the Past, Masterfully Recreated for Cooking and Enjoying Today.* Simon and Schuster, New York, 1964.

BALL, Edward K., *Early Uses of California Plants.* University of California Press, Berkeley, 1962.

BALZER, Robert Lawrence. *The Pleasures of Wine.* Bobbs-Merrill, New York, 1964.

BEETON, Isabelle, *The Book of Household Management* ..., S. O. Beeton, London. Reproduced in facsimile in U.S. by Farrar, Straus and Giroux, New York, 1969.

_____, *Mrs. Beeton's All About Cookery.* S. O. Beeton, London, 1861. Reprinted by Ward, Lock & Co., London, 1961.

BELLE, Frances P., *California Cookbook; an Unusual Collection of Spanish Dishes and Typical California Foods for Luncheons and Dinners Which May be Quickly and Easily Prepared.* Regan Pub. Corp., Chicago, 1925.

BONI, Ada, *Talisman Italian Cookbook.* Translated and Augmented by Matilda La Rose. Crown Publishers, New York, 1950.

BOOK CLUB OF CALIFORNIA, *Authentic Menus of the Past.* Ed. by Joseph Henry Jackson. Anderson & Ritchie, Los Angeles, 1950.

_____, *The Vine in California.* San Francisco, 1955.

BOOTH, George C., *The Food and Drink of Mexico.* Ward Ritchie Press, Los Angeles, 1964.

BROWN, Alice Cooke, *Early American Herb Recipes.* Tuttle Pub. Co., Rutland, Vt., 1966.

BROWN, Mrs. Cora Lovisa. *The South American Cookbook; Including Central America, Mexico and the West Indies.* Doubleday, New York, 1939.

BROWN, Dale, and the Editors of Time-Life Books. *American Cooking.* New York, 1970.

BROWN, Marion. *Marion Brown's Southern Cookbook.* New ed. University of North Carolina Press, Chapel Hill, 1957.

BUCKEYE COOKERY AND PRACTICAL HOUSEKEEPING. Buckeye Publishing Co., Minneapolis, 1880.

BUEHR, Walter, *Home Sweet Home in the 19th Century.* Crowell, 1965.

BURT, Elinor, *Olla Podrida; Piquant Spanish Dishes From the Old Clay Pot.* Caxton Printers, Caldwell, Idaho, 1938.

CALIFORNIA AVOCADO ADVISORY BOARD. *The Avocado Bravo.* Newport Beach, Calif., 1970. (Excerpted from February 1967 Gourmet Magazine issue).

CALIFORNIA BEEF COUNCIL, *Beef.* Redwood City, 1970.

CALIFORNIA DATE ADMINISTRATIVE COMMITTEE, *Dates From Antiquity to Contemporary; Fresh Date Recipes.* Indio, 1970.

CALIFORNIA DRIED FIG ADVISORY BOARD, *The Story of California Figs.* Fresno, 1970.

CALIFORNIA RAISIN ADVISORY BOARD, *The Raisin in the United States.* Fresno, 1970.

THE CALIFORNIA FARMER, Vols. I-IV, 1854-1855; VI, 1856-1857, VII, 1857, Jan. 16-June 28; X, 1859;XII,1860;XIII-XVI,1863-1864.Sacramento, Calif.

THE CALIFORNIA PRACTICAL COOKBOOK, Pacific Press Pub. Co., Oakland, 1882.

CALIFORNIA. WINE ADVISORY BOARD, *Favorite Recipes of California Winemakers.* San Francisco, 1963.

CALLAHAN, Genevieve, *The New California Cook Book; For Casual Living All Over the World.* M. Barrows Co., New York, 1955.

CAROSSE, Vincent P., *The California Wine Industry; a Study of the Formative Years, 1830-1895.* University of California Press, Berkeley, 1951.

CATHOLIC WOMAN'S CLUB OF LOS ANGELES, *Gathered Crumbs; a Collection of Choice and Tested Recipes For the Women of Our Homes.* Los Angeles, n.d.

CHILD, Mrs., *The American Frugal Housewife, Dedicated to Those Who Are Not Ashamed Of Economy.* 22d ed., enlarged and corrected by the author. Samuel S. & William Wood, New York, 1838.

CLEVELAND, Bess A., *California Mission Recipes.* Charles E. Tuttle Co., Rutland, Vt., 1965.

COFFIN, Mrs. M. G., *Our Girls in the Kitchen, Being the Fifth Edition of the Original California Recipe Book.* Pacific Press, San Francisco, 1883.

COLUMBIA, CALIFORNIA CHURCH OF THE 49ERS., *The 49ers Own Cookin' Book,* 1962.

CONSOLIDATED OLIVE GROWERS, *Lindsay Ripe Olive Recipes.* Lindsay, Calif., 1969.

_____, *History of Olives.* Lindsay, Calif., 1969.

_____, *The Romantic History of California Olives.* Lindsay, Calif., 1969.

CORNELIA COOKS. Cornelia Club, Los Angeles, 1949.

CRUESS, William V., *A Half-Century in Food and Wine Technology.* University of California Bancroft Library Regional Oral History Office, San Francisco, 1967.

CULPEPER, Nicholas, *Culpeper's Complete Herbal.* W. Foulsham & Co., London, n.d.

CUPID'S BOOK. Kissling Pub. Co., Oakland, Calif., 1939

DE BEERS, Helen Bell. *Food From the Stars.* Los Angeles, 1950.

DELINEATOR (Periodical) *Ramona lunch.* New York, October, 1896.

DOYLE, Harrison, *Chia. In* Desert Magazine, October, 1963, pp. 18p19-33.

EASTLAKE, Martha Simpson, *Rattlesnake Under Glass; a Roundup of Authentic Western Recipes.* Simon and Schuster, New York, 1965.

EBELL SOCIETY OF THE SANTA ANA VALLEY COOK BOOK. A. G. Flagg, Los Angeles, 1926.

FERGUSON, Erna, *Mexican Cookbook.* University of New Mexico Press, Albuquerque, 1945.

FISHER, M. F. K., *The Story of Wine in California.* University of California Press, Berkeley, 1962.

FITZGIBBON, Theodora, *The Art of British Cooking.* Doubleday, New York, 1965.

FOOD AND DRINK THROUGH THE AGES 2500 B.C. to 1937 A.D. A Catalogue of Antiquities, Manuscripts, Books, and Engravings Treating Of Cookery, Eating and Drinking, Including Books From the Library and With the Bookplate of Robert Viel, the Famous Restaurateur. Maggs Bros.,Ltd.,London,1937.

FOWLER'S BLUE BOOK of Selected Household Helps and Guide to Household Economuy. A. L. Fowler, 1925.

GINGER, Bertha Haffner. *California Mexico-Spanish Cookbook; Selected Mexican and Spanish Recipes.* 1927.

THE GROCER'S COMPANION AND MERCHANTS HANDBOOK. New England Grocer Office, Boston, 1883.

HALE, William Harlan., *The Horizon Cookbook and Illustrated History of Eating and Drinking Through the Ages,* by William Harlan Hale and the Editors of Horizon magazine. American Heritage Publishing Co., New York, 1968.

HAWAIIAN CUISINE; a Collection of Recipes From Members of the Society Featuring Hawaiian, Chinese, Japanese, Korean, Filipino, Portuguese and Cosmopolitan Dishes. Published for the Hawaii State Society of Washington, D.C. by Charles E. Tuttle Co., Rutland, Vt. 1963.

HAYES, Elizabeth S., *Spices and Herbs Around the World.* Doubleday, N. Y., 1961.

HEATON, Nell, and Andre Simon. *A Calendar of Food and Wine.* Cresta Books, London, n.d.

HENDERSON, Mrs. Mary F., *Practical Cooking and Dinner Giving.* Harper, New York, 1876.

HOGROGIAN, Rachel., *The Armenian Cookbook.* Atheneum, New York, 1971.

JAEGER, Edmund C., *Desert Wild Flowers.* Stanford University Press, San Francisco, 1940.

JEPSON, Willis Linn, *A Manual of Flowering Plants of California.* University of California Press, Berkeley, 1953.

JOHNSTON, Mary Alice, *Spanish Cooking.* Los Angeles, 1895.

KIMBALL, Yeffe, and ANDERSON, Jean., *The Art of American Indian Cooking.* Doubleday, New York, 1965.

LADIES' SOCIAL CIRCLE, SIMPSON M.E. CHURCH, LOS ANGELES, CALIF. *How We Cook in Los Angeles; A Practical Cookbook Containing Six Hundred Or More Recipes Selected and Tested by Over Two Hundred Well Known Hostesses, Including a French, German and Spanish Department With Menus . . . .* Commercial Printing House, Los Angeles, 1894.

LEGGETT, Herbert B., *Early History of Wine Production in California.* 1941.

LEHNER, Joseph Charles, *The World's Fair Menu & Recipe Book; A Collection of the Most Famous Menus Exhibited at the Panama-Pacific International Exposition.* Lehner Sefert Pub. Co., San Francisco, 1915.

LODE OF VITTLES, From the Gold Discovery Site, Coloma, Calif. 2d ed., 1965.

LOS ANGELES TIMES, *The Times Cookbook, No. 2, 1905; No. 3.* n.d.

MacARTHUR, Mildred Yorba, *Recipes of the Ranchos.* Comp. for Saddleback Inn, Santa Ana, Calif., 1969.

MACKENZIE, *Five Thousand Recipes in All The Useful and Domestic Arts: Constituting A Complete Practical Library.* Philadelphia, James Kay, Jun. and Brother, 1829.

McLAREN, Linie Loyall, comp., *High Living. Recipes From Southern Climes.* Published for the benefit of the Telegraph Hill Neighborhood Assn., Elder, San Francisco, 1904.

————, *Pan-Pacific Cookbook: Savory Bits from the World's Fair.* Blair-Murdock, San Francisco, 1915.

MICKLE, Anna M., *Handwritten Cookbook,* MSS *In* Anaheim Public Library.

MORROW, Kay, ed. *Culinary Arts Western Cookery.* Culinary Arts Press, Reading, Pa., 1936.

MUENSCHER, Walter Conrad, and RICE, Myron Arthur, *Garden Spice and Wild Pot Herbs.* Comstock Pub. Associates, a div. of Cornell U. Press, New York, 1955.

NEW HOME COMPENDIUM, New Home Selling Service, San Francisco, 1914.

PACKMAN, Ana Begue, *Early California Hospitality; the Cookery Customs of Spanish California, With Authentic Recipes and Menus of The Period.* Arthur H. Clark Co., Glendale, Calif., 1938.

PARLOA, Maria, *Miss Parloa's New Cook Book; A Guide to Marketing And Cooking.* H. B. Nims Co., Troy, N. Y., 1880.

PARSONS, Mary Elizabeth, *Wild Flowers of California.* H. S. Crocker, San Francisco, 1906.

PETROVSKAYE, Kyra, *Kyra's Secrets of Russian Cooking.* Prentice-Hall, New York, 1961.

PFAU, C. F., *A Book of Cooking and Pastry; A Collection of Original Receipts Gathered During A Life Time And Especially Arranged.* Cadogan & Hatcher, Quincy, Ill., 1887.

REEVE, Thomas V., *El Camino Real; Special Occasion Recipes.* El Camino Bank, Anaheim, 1971.
RINGLAND, Eleanor, and WINSTON, Lucy Ringland. *Fiestas Mexicanas; Menus and Recipes.* Naylor, 1965.
ROGERS, Ann, *A Basque Story Cook Book.* Scribner, New York, 1968.

SHERATON-PALACE HOTEL. *Recipes.* San Francisco, 1970.
SIMON, Andre L. and HOWE, Robin. *Dictionary of Gastronomy.* McGraw-Hill, New York, 1970.
SOUTHERN CALIFORNIA GAS COMPANY, comp., *Fiesta Foods: California Dishes in the Mexican Tradition.* Compiled from recipes submitted to the Mexican Recipe Fiesta. Los Angeles, 1971.
STANDARD LIGHTING COMPANY, *Cooking Made Easy By Using The Wonderful New Process.* Cleveland, Ohio, 1894.

TIME-LIFE BOOKS, *Recipes: The Cooking of Spain and Portugal.* New York, 1969.

TYREE, Marion Cabell. *Housekeeping in Old Virginia.* Reprinted 1965 by Favorite Recipes Press, Louisville, Ky., from original 1879 ed.

VAUGHAN, Beatrice, *The Old Cook's Almanac.* Stephen Greene Press, Brattleboro, Vt., 1961.
VERRILL, A. Hyatt, *Foods America Gave The World.* L. C. Page, New York, N.Y., 1937.

WEBSTER, Helen Noyes, *Herbs; How to Grow Them And How To Use them, With A Chapter on Biblical Herbs.* Rev. ed. Charles T. Branford Co., Newton Centre, Mass., 1942.
WICKSON, Edward J., *The California Fruits And How To Grow Them.* 7th ed. fully rev. Pacific Rural Press, San Francisco, 1914.

YEP, Madame Chiang. *Madame Chiang's Chinese Cookbook.* Frederick H. Girnau Creations, Minneapolis, Minn., 1946.

ZELAYETA, E., *Elena's Favorite Foods, California Style.* Prentice-Hall, New York, 1967.

Index

Social History

Recipes

PANCAKES: flapjacks, 69; German, 94; no matters, 94.

PICKLES: cantaloupe, 111; oyster, 71; walnut, 127.

PIES: apple, 107; apricot, 107; English walnut, 107; lemon, 107; soda cracker, 75.

PINEAPPLE: sherbet, 110; with spareribs, 102.

PORK: Hongkong roast, 72; pork stew, 21; sausage, 46; spareribs Hawaiian style, 102.

PUDDINGS: apple (graham birdsnest), 108; caramel, 75; date steamed, 107; fruit, 75; Indian, 25; plum, 108; quince, 108; rice, 76; rice rock cream, 109.

RABBIT: fricassee, 22; stew, 9, 72.

RAMONA SANDWICHES: 110.

RENNET: making of, 50.

RICE: cooking of, 128; dessert balls, 109; in beef casserole, 100; in paella, 23; parched, 126; pilaf, 104; pudding baked, 76; rock cream, 109; Spanish, 74.

ROSE PREPARATIONS: rose jar and water, 128.

SALADS: cole slaw, 105; chicken, 99; cooked wild greens, 50; hot potato, 103; oyster, 98; tongue, 48; watercress, 51.

SALMON: baked, 71; steaks broiled, 8.

SAUCES: caper, 101; chili pulp, 24; chili sauce for basting turkey, 45; hot chili, 25; jellied white sauce, 99; mole, 45; sweet pepper relish, 111; tomato catsup, 111; velouté, 99.

SAUCES AND SYRUPS FOR DESSERTS: brandy, 25; orange flower, 127; sugar syrup with aniseed, 51.

SAUERKRAUT: making of, 74; borscht, 96; soup, 96.

SEAFOOD: abalone fried, 70; bouillabaise, 95; clams roasted, 9; crab deviled, 97; crab fried, 97; frog legs fried, 97; mussels, 9; in paella, 23. *See* oysters.

SEEDS: aniseed cooky, 51; in mole sauce, 45; piñole, 8; used as spices, 125.

SHERBETS: Italian, 110; pineapple, 110.

SOUPS: almond cream, 104; borscht, 96; bouillabaisse, 95; chicken-ham, 94; chicken ball, 70; Italian onion, 95; meat ball, 21; mock turtle, 95; mushroom, 8; oyster stew, 70; piñon nut, 8; sauerkraut, 96; vegetable, 126.

STEWS: beef, 22; boiled dinner, 47; fish, 96; jack rabbit, 72; Mexican with wine, 47; oyster, 70; pigeon, 98; pork, 21; sheepherder, 101.

STUFFINGS: extra, 129; for turkey, 128.

SUET: preserving of, 129.

SUGARS: use of, 129.

TAMALES: with beef filling, 48; green corn, 49, swee twith fruit filling, 51.

TONGUE, bear, 23; salad, 48, smoked, 22; spiced Chinese style, 72.

TORTILLAS: making of, 21; sweet bunuelos fried, 51.

TRIPE: 46.

TURKEY: baked Spanish style, 44; with mole sauce, 45.

VEAL: boiled dinner, 47; mock turtle soup, 95; roulette of, 102.

VEGETABLES: artichokes fried, 104; beans baked, 73; beans and wheat gruel, 23; boiled dinner, 47; cabbage odors, 128; cactus cubes, 49; celery stewed, 104; colache, 104; corn prepared for winter, 129; corn pudding, 24; corn roasted, 49; eggplant, 104; frijoles, 49; garbanzo beans, 24; green string beans, 49; green corn tamales, 49; greens and eggs, 50; hot potato salad, 103; Indian potatoes, 10; onions boiled, 24; onions in milk, 103; potatoes a la Cannes, 103; potatoes baked, 128; potatoes fried, 128; potato muffins, 94; potato-onion casserole, 73; pumpkin candied, 52; string beans, 49; sweet potatoes, 103.

VINEGAR: chili, 24.

WALNUTS: English walnut pie, 107; pickled, 127; cookies, 75.

WEIGHTS AND MEASURES: 129.

YEAST: home made, 68; sourdough starter, 68.